Leaving
a Doll's House

A MEMOIR

CLAIRE BLOOM

LITTLE, BROWN AND COMPANY
BOSTON   NEW YORK   TORONTO   LONDON

Originally published in hardcover by Little, Brown and Company, 1996
First Back Bay paperback edition, 1998

Library of Congress Cataloging-in-Publication Data
Bloom, Claire.
Leaving a doll's house : a memoir / Claire Bloom. — 1st ed.
p. cm.
ISBN 0-316-09980-5 (hc)
0-316-09383-1 (pb)
1. Bloom, Claire. 2. Actors—Great Britain—Biography.
I. Title.
PN2598.B639A3 1996
792'.028'092—dc20
[B]   96-8831

10 9 8 7 6 5 4 3 2 1

MV-NY

Published simultaneously in Canada
by Little, Brown & Company (Canada) Limited

Printed in the United States of America

For my family: Anna, Sheila, and John.

And for my friends: Rachael and Rafael, Francine and Cleve.

Contents

Preface

I AM AN ACTRESS. I have been a professionally independent woman since the age of fifteen. My career has been adventurous, sometimes mercurial, frequently precarious, always exciting.

I am no longer the fervent and impressionable young girl who appeared in Chaplin's film *Limelight;* I am a woman whose life experience has been unusual and diverse. I have been daughter and wife; I am a mother, a friend, a performer. Some years ago I wrote a modest account of my professional life, *Limelight and After,* in which I attempted to reveal only what was relevant to my career while carefully and self-protectively concealing my full identity as a woman. Now all the factors have altered, and I am free to tell my story in full.

I have been fortunate in many ways. Success came to me early — perhaps too early for my emotional development — nevertheless I have managed, by a kind of inborn tenacity, to sustain its course for most of my adult years.

My marriage to the writer Philip Roth ended in 1995. It was the most important relationship of my life. This forced me on a path which I am only now beginning to appreciate. I am aware that, to a majority of women, I must seem more privileged, better equipped to embark on a new future than they — perhaps so. But moving on has required taking stock, addressing the past in order to come to terms with and better understand what happened, how it happened, and — the most difficult part — to accept all of it.

Preface

I now have the freedom to do whatever I want with my life. This is a hard-won dividend. I have the support of my family and my friends. My career still flourishes. But loneliness is a hard outgrowth of loss, and independence is daunting for someone who never sought it. My future is now truly my own.

By tracing the path of my childhood, my early career, my formative years, my relationships and subsequent marriages, my experiences in the different arenas of theater and film, of England and America, I have tried to shed light on an unfinished journey. It has been a trip worth taking. And understanding does away with every regret.

Acknowledgments

THIS BOOK would not be complete without an acknowledgment of the men and women whose efforts have been instrumental in its shaping. My gratitude to William Phillips and Philippa Harrison of Little, Brown, for their faith and encouragement during its conception and their infinite care during the editing process; to Lynn Nesbit for her early support of my story; to Tom Cole for his patience in transcribing my occasionally confused typewritten pages onto the computer screen; and above all, to Rafael Garcia Navarro for his perfect pitch and clarity of vision. I have always been lucky with my friends. Some of their names appear during the course of the book; others do not. Without their unstoppable affection and generosity of spirit during these difficult three years, I would not have emerged unbroken. To my friends and allies I offer my deepest appreciation: Linda and Aaron Asher; Rosemary and Joss Ackland; Ann and Al Alvarez; Julian Beinart; Janet Malcolm and Gardner Botsford; Robert Brustein; Helen Cannell; Virginia Cooper; Jeremy Conway; Barbara Epstein; Norma Fortuin; Jan and Jeremy Geidt; Susan and Denys Lasdun; Klaus Kolmar; Bab and C. H. Huvelle; Gore Vidal and Howard Austen; Lalla Ward and Richard Dawkins; Honor Moore; Sidney Liebowitz; Vita and Arthur Muir; Bryan Robertson; Heather Previn; Helen Jaeger Roth; Ron Protas; Marion Rosenberg; Gaia Servadio; Joyce Tinlin; David Plante and Nikos Stangos; Margot and Nicholas Snowman; Lia Schorr; Phyllis Cohen; Paolo Segunti, Nick Coster, and Martha Byrne; Brian Zeger and Eugenia Zuckerman. And in memory of Shelley List and Greta Herman.

Leaving
a Doll's House

CHAPTER ONE

Where I Came From

I WAS BORN in the North London suburb of Finchley on February 15, 1931, the eldest of two children born to Edward Blume (originally Blumenthal) and his wife, Elizabeth (née Grew). My parents were both born in England — my mother in London, within the sound of Bow Bells, making her an official Cockney, and my father from farther north, in Liverpool — although neither my maternal nor paternal grandparents were of English origin.

My father's family were from the cradle of European Jewry: my grandmother Caroline from Riga in Latvia, my grandfather from somewhere in greater Russia. And my mother's family went back to an ancient Jewish community on the banks of the Vistula, some miles northwest of Warsaw.

My maternal grandmother, Paula, and her husband came to England at the start of this century, as did my father's parents. My grandmother Paula's marriage was an arranged one, something not uncommon in young Jewish couples of that time and place. My maternal grandfather, Henry Griewski, his surname later to metamorphose into Grew, is described on my mother's birth certificate as a cabinetmaker. Some knowledge of timber my grandfather must certainly have brought with him from Russia, where his family were overseers of large and wooded estates belonging to the Russian gentry. He started a modest workshop in the East End of London, turning out small "fancy goods," wooden boxes and picture frames, and went on to manufacture furniture and wooden moldings. This led to some improvement of my grandparents' financial position, and by the time my mother was a small child, they had moved from the East End to the more comfortable suburb of Cricklewood, in North London.

In those days, the tyrannical behavior of the husband, the timid subservience of the wife, the adoration of male children, and the use made of daughters as domestic help were accepted in most lower-income families. Although in a Jewish household only recently arrived in Western Europe the male prerogative may have been even stronger, I doubt if Paula and Henry's household differed enormously from those of their more assimilated neighbors, but the dominant male authority that my grandfather exerted had an indelible effect on the character of my mother and her sister, Mary, and possibly, in a more distanced way, on my own.

My mother's name was Elizabeth, though she was known as Alice by everyone except her mother, who always called her Alishce. Born in 1903, she was the second daughter and third child born to my grandparents. Her elder sister, Mary, had arrived three years earlier.

My mother and aunt dealt with this problem of their female identity in completely different ways. Mary saw in her upbringing a challenge, and she fought with strength and determination to escape her family and make a successful career as an actress. After an early and ill-starred romance, Mother set about leading the most conventional of lives, and continued to do so until her middle age, when she opened an antique shop in London and ran it with great success. She determined to marry and have a large family. Mary, a "bluestocking" as well as a recluse, would have none of that.

From her earliest memories, Mary's answer to any family commotion was to retreat into her room and read. She read voraciously and passionately; her greatest happiness was to read and reread the great English poets, and, above all, to immerse herself completely in the works of Shakespeare.

Her love of literature, plus a longing to escape the restrictive atmosphere of my grandparents' house, fed Mary's determination to become an actress.

Mary entered a beauty contest, knowing no other way to penetrate this unknown world. The scheme was devised by my mother. Looking back on it, there is more than a little irony pondering the fact that this actress, described in a London *Times* obituary some forty years later as a leading player in the intellectual theater of the twenties and thirties, should have entered her profession in this way. Mary won first place; her photograph appeared in the newspapers.

Having wasted no time telling the press of her ambition to go onstage, Mary received several offers in theater and film as a result. Among these came a surprising one, from Mary's future husband, Victor Sheridan, who had been one of the judges.

Victor was taken with Mary's dark-eyed looks, even if he was somewhat wary of her intellectual predilections. Although associated with the stage as owner of several "variety theaters" around the country, he was more businessman than artist, and therefore a far cry from Mary's ideal of the man to share her life with.

With an alacrity that must have astonished even Mary, she and Victor became engaged. After their marriage, Mary Grew Sheridan, formerly of Hoxton and more recently of Cricklewood, moved to an elegant flat in Mayfair, with a staff of servants waiting upon her. She was dressed by the House of Worth, and dined out with her husband nearly every night at the Savoy Grill or the Ritz. But her opulent lifestyle wasn't enough to quench Mary's overpowering thirst to express herself artistically.

With Victor's financial assistance, Mary was able to take lessons from the famous teacher Elsie Fogarty, vocal coach to the young Laurence Olivier and Peggy Ashcroft. After a year as Miss Fogarty's pupil, Mary played the role of Mme. Moskowski in Israel Zangwill's play *We Moderns.* Produced in 1925 at London's Fortune Theater — whose manager was her husband, Victor — she scored a modest, though distinct, success.

Shortly afterward, she found herself pregnant with her only child. This unexpected interruption to her career came as an extreme blow. When my cousin Norma was born, in keeping with the practice of the day among people of means, she was swiftly passed on to a nurse. Then, just as swiftly, Mary returned to her beloved profession.

Mary was to have a brutally brief career. Her greatest moment on the stage — and also her harshest trial — came when she played "The Young Woman" in *The Life Machine* — called *Machinal* in the United States — a play by the American Sophie Treadwell, an early defender of women's rights. Treadwell wrote a stunningly honest play about a woman who is convicted for murdering her brutal husband, and condemned to die in the electric chair. This harrowing story was an extraordinarily exhausting role for an actress, both physically and psychologically; the play takes her to the very moment she is led to her execution. Mary appeared in every scene; the play was given not only for the usual six evening performances per week, but in addition there were matinees on Monday, Wednesday, and Saturday.

Mary suffered a physical and mental breakdown, and was forced to leave the play altogether — and, indeed, the stage, for some time. This pause of over a year was enough to damage her fragile career; thereafter, Mary's brief period as a star was over. Her run had lasted barely a decade. By the time I came to know my aunt Mary, the pursuit of a role worth playing had become a fruitless burden and only a source of sorrow and frustration.

Until I found my own path, somewhere in my mid-twenties, Mary played a role almost equal to my mother's in the forming of my artistic life.

The strongest memories I have of my earliest years consist of following my mother everywhere, of clinging to her skirt, of wanting to be one with her. Also of the constant trembling of her hands, a genetic weakness inherited from her father. My own father doesn't seem to exist in my mind, perhaps because he was away so often; possibly because although only a small child, I already sensed my mother's deep disappointment in her marriage and rejected my ineffectual father in favor of my protective and adored mother.

Alice remembered the difficult years before her father's business began to flourish, the Saturday dinners where one chicken was divided among nine hungry children. Coming somewhere near the center of the age group in my grandparents' large family, Alice became chief helpmate to her mother in running the household, particularly in caring for the younger children.

When she was in her early twenties, my mother had taken a job with an American firm of film distributors; she worked as a secretary to Bobbie Brenner, a married man about fifteen years older than she. His marriage, so he claimed, was unsatisfactory; his wife had remained behind in the States while he worked in London. Alice and he very soon became lovers, and remained so for the time that Brenner worked in England. However, after about eighteen months of happiness — at least for my mother — he was posted back to New York, and he implored my mother to follow him. She must have agreed to do so with a great deal of trepidation, but agree she did. For a middle-class Jewish girl to take such a step in the 1920s was a serious flouting of morality. How she squared all this with her parents I have no idea; I think the probability was that she told them nothing of the truth, but let them believe that she was going to America to take up a job as a secretary in New York.

Her loneliness in New York, as she described it to me, was extreme; she even welcomed a mouse who came for the leftover bread crumbs; it was a relief from the isolation of the hours, or even days, when she waited for her married lover to visit her. For Mr. Brenner, in the good old tradition of married men, turned out to have no serious intention of leaving his wife. He just wanted my mother as well. After enduring two years of misery — tempered by the fact that even under these melancholy circumstances, Alice found New York to be both thrilling and vibrant — she decided to go back to London.

She very soon met and married my father. My mother and

father, Edward Blume, met at a dance at my grandparents' house. Alice was now twenty-seven, Eddie was twenty-three. He spoke with the nasal Liverpool accent that he never completely lost. He was of a light build, with dark curly hair and dark eyes. I doubt he was ever good-looking. His charm lay more in the swiftness of his repartee than in the handsomeness of his features. Mother was captivated by his quick wit and taken with his dry Liverpudlian humor, though that didn't stop her from noticing the weakness of his mouth, or being more than a little concerned that he had no noticeable profession. Scarred by her unhappy first love affair, Alice settled for the attainable: she married Eddie in the hope that she could "make something of him." They were married in a synagogue, my mother dressed in silver lace, her bridesmaids in pale apple green. They settled in the north of London. There I was born, one year later. My father's profession, on my birth certificate, is described as traveling salesman.

When I once asked Mother why she married Eddie, she replied that they enjoyed a cup of tea together, a cigarette, and a good laugh. If there was more to it than that, and I hope there might have been, she never told me.

The year was 1935 or 1936. I distinctly remember climbing a staircase behind my mother, above a darkened shop. Upstairs, men, including my father, sat around a table playing cards. There followed an angry exchange between my parents, and Mother left in tears, dragging me, also weeping inconsolably, behind her. In my child's mind I sensed that the quarrel had been about money, and saw Mother upset terribly. I am certain now that my father was playing away our household funds; the fact that he was a hopeless gambler only came to be clear to me many years later.

I cannot say how many times my father lost his job — or even what jobs he held — but from the number of times we changed homes and I changed schools, he must have lost them regularly. Each time we shifted homes we moved up or down the socioeconomic scale; at one point we lived in a small bungalow in Hampshire, at another in a substantial middle-class house in Bristol, and so it went. At the start of the Second World War, we moved for some months to a primitive cottage in Cornwall. None of these changes troubled me too much, although they must have caused Mother considerable anxiety.

In spite of these dark periods in her life, she seemed to find fulfillment in our close bond. As my greatest joy was to be with her, I think hers was to be with me, and as long as we could remain at the center of each other's lives, where we lived made little difference.

What I remember most from those early days is the sound of Mother's voice as she read to me from Hans Christian Andersen's *The Little Mermaid* and *The Snow Queen*. These emotionally wrenching tales, to which I raptly listened and to which I was powerfully drawn, instilled in me a longing to be overwhelmed by romantic passion and led me in my teens and early twenties to attempt to emulate these self-sacrificing heroines, at least on the stage.

The sound of Mother's voice and the radiance of those long summer afternoons are fused in my childhood memory, creating a pleasurable sensation of warmth and comfort and safety.

I lived very much in a world of fantasy. I remember no childhood playmates. I invented a phantom friend, someone I conducted long discussions with, who was my constant playmate, whose hand I held regularly, and whose ghostly company appeared to be quite sufficient. I attended so many different schools, due partly to my father's uncertain employment, and later to the war, that I never settled long enough in one place to have time to make friends with other girls.

My real friend and true companion from the beginning was my mother. We were much closer than would seem normal for a mother and daughter, almost like beleaguered inmates of a walled city. I never wanted her to feel lonely, so I would remain at home and keep her company even when I might have been outside playing. Even then I sensed I was becoming a painfully "intense" young person. All I remember of my years at school was the feeling of desolation when Mother dropped me off, and the feeling of relief when she picked me up again.

Because of our rootless and nomadic life, Mother also seemed to have few close friendships. She must have had some social life: I can recall how, during one of our family's few brief affluent periods, she came to kiss me goodnight, wearing a black chiffon dress and a white gardenia in her hair. This image of my young and lovely mother remains with me after so many others have faded with time.

In spite of my love of reading, I was never cut out to be an academic; I distinguished myself only in English and history classes at school. I hardly excelled at sports, which are such a vital part of the school curriculum of English boys and girls. Hockey was always a mystery to me, and a source of some misgiving; I never fathomed what could motivate a group of girls to thunder about a field smacking one another with long wooden sticks. I might have enjoyed netball, the English version of basketball, had I been chosen for the team, which I wasn't. Only at rounders, an earlier incarnation of American baseball, did I experience any success, and that by sole virtue of being very fast on my feet.

There is a photograph from the same period that records my incursion into theatrical life — and plainly shows that I took myself with extreme seriousness: Dressed as Juliet in a satin dress made by her mother, the young actress, aged about eight, is seated on the floor. A Juliet cap perches on her straight, rather lank brown hair, and she humorlessly surveys the camera while the surrounding children, dressed as Little Bo-Peep and Little Red Riding-Hood, cheerfully smile into the lens.

I can remember, in clear and specific detail, the long satin dress onto which my mother and I had painstakingly sewn tiny iridescent stones, and the feel of the silk skirt against my legs. I had recently been taken to see the film of *Romeo and Juliet* starring Leslie Howard and Norma Shearer. I went home and learned the verse to perform the balcony scene over and over; I memorized the soliloquies, rejoicing in the sound of Shakespeare's language. While other children might be satisfied with being Little Miss Muffett and Mary with her little lamb, I said to myself that I was destined for "higher things."

Higher things began very modestly.

During our somewhat more prosperous days — prosperity being a qualitative concept in our family — we lived in Bristol, an important city in West England, and I attended an expensive girls' school, Badminton. In previous years we had resided in Cardiff, the capital of Wales, and before that in Ruislip, a quiet and dull suburb near London, where my brother, John, was born. Apart from his birth, which immediately filled me with fierce jealousy — alongside a secret desire to have him quietly disappear — I remember little of that early period before moving to Bristol.

The year was 1938 and I was seven years of age. In Bristol we were able to afford a "mother's help," a young woman named Kathleen Jones, who was from a small town in South Wales. Kathleen was no more than eighteen or nineteen at the time; though she was older by ten years, she became a proper friend to me and became my first acting partner.

She also shared the same girlish delight in games of "let's pretend," and had a talent, which she attempted to pass on to me, in the design and sewing of costumes. We gave nightly performances in the spare bedroom — always, we averred, to full houses — creating our space by hanging a bath towel across the entrance. Kathleen and I had no written text, but improvised our words as we went along. The stories we played were either taken from fairy stories or were potted versions of Shakespeare plays. I always played the lead. My chosen heroines were rarely, if ever, heroic; instead, they were tormented by hateful stepparents, imprisoned by wicked witches. Always at the end, and most delightful of all to me, was the certainty that I would be rescued by a handsome and daring young prince.

Then, to my great joy, I was cast in the school play as the maiden who spins straw into gold in *Rumpelstiltskin*. A strange and wonderful thing happened: I found in this disguise an unknown freedom and independence. It was an immediate, startling discovery; I could be at one with myself, while playing someone else.

Prior to that performance of *Rumpelstiltskin* I had gone unnoticed. Suddenly I became, for a brief moment, the Badminton School celebrity. Although I had never expected to be the center of attraction in the guise of someone else, I found the notice taken of me exhilarating, and my self-confidence began to soar. I had my requisite fifteen minutes of fame.

The second year of our stay in Bristol, we went on holiday to Cornwall, where my mother had rented a cottage for the summer. I don't recall my father visiting us, although he may have done. I recollect only my mother, my brother, John, and myself as a complete and closed unit. My brother was nearly three years old; I was eight. The cottage was close to a village near Treyarnon Bay. The beach, when the tide went out and revealed pools of sparkling seawater, was magically alive with algae of every kind, covered with stranded starfish and scuttling sea crabs, which John and I attempted, usually without success, to catch and take home for supper. My brother and I spent all day at the beach, and went back home in the early evening to our cottage. It had an outdoor privy and an iron stove for cooking. Paraffin lamps lit the small rooms. I can almost smell the stews my patient mother simmered slowly on the primitive stove. There were a series of books commonly read by children before the war, *The Spartan Twins* and *The Greek Twins,* that enchanted me. I imagined that our life in Cornwall was a re-creation of the classical, bygone world opened to me in these stories. Many years later, I would buy a cottage in Connemara in the west of

Ireland, and later another house of some antiquity in Corsica, and try in earnest to re-create this simple and beautiful life.

During the final week of our stay, we went to a café we frequented every afternoon for our tea. Perched high above the beach and overlooking Bedruthan Steps, the café served Cornish clotted cream, strawberry jam, and scones; the radio was playing, and John and I peacefully ate our scones. The other customers were quiet, listening intently — as was Mother. John and I went on enjoying our tea. Although we were full of the joys of summer and glowing from the sun and fresh air, the spirit of holiday relaxation had completely left the room. I remember looking around and not understanding how grownups could look so sad on such a beautiful afternoon. The radio music was interrupted by an announcer, pronouncing his words very formally and deliberately. The prime minister, Neville Chamberlain, was about to speak. Chamberlain's voice came over the radio, and he sounded feeble and exhausted: "His Majesty's Government has received no such communication or assurance. I must therefore tell you that a state of war has been declared between . . ."

I had seen the newsreels of the bombing of children during the Sino-Japanese War, which was still raging as Chamberlain spoke. I heard we were at war, and thought I understood a little of what that could mean. Someone near us started to cry. I cried, too, with my mouth full of scones, cream, and jam. My little brother kept asking me what was wrong. We left the café and were making our way back to our cottage, which seemed so safe from war and its troubles, when the siren sounded — apparently all over the country.

We didn't know what we were supposed to do, whether to run for home or hide by the edge of the road. We crouched in a ditch. The all clear sounded fairly soon afterward, one long, drawn-out note, as opposed to the undulating sound of the air-raid alarm we would come to know so well in the years that lay ahead.

Notwithstanding the relative safety of Cornwall, my mother felt we should return to Bristol. I was sad to leave our cottage and tranquil country life. John and I had Mother all to ourselves, and while in Cornwall she was more carefree than we had ever seen her, upon our return to Bristol the old worries and tensions came swiftly back. The crisis she found waiting for her had little to do with world events and everything to do with my father's finances. My father had lost yet another job.

The bombing of Bristol began. Badminton School, like most of the other schools in Bristol, was evacuated to the country; and as the fees had become too much for my father to pay, I was left at home to read my books in peace.

At first the air raids were almost exciting. I would be awakened in the night and taken from my own bed to a mattress in the hallway, away from the flying glass of the windows; there I would share midnight tea and sandwiches with my parents. So much did a world war mean to a child of eight. But, as the bombing got more serious, and half our roof was blown off, my understandably alarmed parents decided to sell our house at any price they could get and move out of the city. The obvious course was to return to Cornwall. Our former cottage had been rented, but another was found, slightly more weather-beaten and definitely less picturesque. I was entered in the village school, while John, not yet of school age, remained at home in our cottage with Mother.

A few years ago, while working nearby on location for a film, I retraced my morning walks to this school. I recognized the country lanes where I had strolled, the beach where my brother and I had played at being fishermen. The cottage either I couldn't find or it had disappeared — swallowed up in the rash of semidetached villas that had sprouted since that unspoiled time. The village school remained intact.

Even when I attended this school it had hardly altered since the nineteenth century. One large room held all the classes, with boys and girls aged six to fourteen. A sizable metal stove stood in the center of the room, and the Cornish pasties the local children had brought for their lunch — pies of chopped meat, onion, vegetables, and black pepper — warmed on it, filling the classroom with mouth-watering smells. The lessons themselves were rudimentary and made no lasting impression on me, but I can clearly remember the shrill squeals of boys being beaten for misdemeanors that would seem petty today.

Winter was coming on, and I recall the comfortable glow from the iron range, which was fueled by coal, and on which Mother cooked her stews. It was one of our few modern comforts. I can summon as if it were yesterday the freezing cold in our cottage and the frosty bite of sitting hunched up in a large metal tub Mother habitually used for laundry, while she poured a jug of hot water over my shivering body.

Although this period is filled with nostalgia, for Mother this isolated life was undoubtedly trying, particularly in light of the Spartan conditions and the fact that her only company consisted of two children. There were limits to how many stews she could prepare while waiting for me to come home from school; there also was some limit to her patience. She contacted Eddie and asked him to find accommodation for us in New Milton, the small Hampshire town he had moved to after leaving Bristol to be near his brother, Isadore, Isadore's wife, Dolly, and my two cousins Erica and Michael.

The so-called bungalow my father was able to rent was a disheartening sight when we first arrived. The rain had been pouring down for days and made running streams up the pathway through to the drab, colorless house. The front had a "rock garden," started, but not completed, by the former owners, and the water coursing downward formed a series of miniature mud slides. Even to my young eyes, this disaster was scarcely what my mother had been led to expect of our new home. When the rain finally cleared, the house was still an eyesore, and the town dreary and dull. Yet another count against poor Eddie.

War eventually caught up even with New Milton. The

bombing began, quite regularly, at around three in the morning. Lying on our mattresses in the hallway, we listened as the explosions got closer. The sense of excitement I had initially experienced in Bristol turned into dread. I learned how to tell the difference between the sounds made by different plane engines: the German planes emitted a short, rhythmically repetitive buzz, while ours sounded a long, drawn-out hum.

The bombings became so intense that there was little chance of sleep. We got most of the bombs the Luftwaffe hadn't had time to drop on London. Why waste them on the English Channel when they could be hurled at the welcoming little community of New Milton? Twice the Germans machine-gunned our high street. Fern Hill Manor, the private girls' school where I was next enrolled, was evacuated deeper into the country, and my cousin Erica went with them. Why I wasn't sent away as well remains a mystery; perhaps I just downright refused to go. My aunt Dolly and uncle Isadore went away for a few days' rest at a safer location, and invited the four of us to use their house, which had an air-raid shelter located at the bottom of the garden, to get some sleep.

Our first night there we went to sleep in our bunks in the shelter, hoping that, at long last, we could look forward to an undisturbed night.

Sometime around midnight, the entire shelter rose up off the ground. We were thrown from our bunks and lay petrified on the floor, finding somewhat to our own surprise that we were still alive. About an hour later the air-raid warden came by to check on us, and reported that several land mines had been dropped in a complete circle around the house we were staying in.

When dawn broke, my father and I went to see the craters formed by these huge missiles when an explosion, not too far off, and more ear-splitting than anything we had heard until then, sent us scurrying home again. As we arrived back in stunned silence, we were met by the local police, who ordered us to leave the area immediately, because these bombs, timed to explode long after they had been dropped from the air, were all around us, and there was no way of knowing when the next one would go off.

We went back to our house in New Milton. A few days later the church bells rang, a signal to be sent only in case of an actual invasion. The bells had not been heard since the declaration of war. It was now 1940 and France had already fallen. The entire country was acutely aware that England was to be next.

Mother went silently upstairs and put on her fur coat. We sat in the living room, waiting for the Germans to arrive. We waited until the police came round some hours later, knocking on every door in the neighborhood to say that the bells had been rung by mistake. My parents entertained no illusions regarding Hitler's designs for the Jews.

Years later, when I reminded her of this incident, she said that although she remembered putting on her coat, she had absolutely no idea what had motivated her.

Mother felt that we could be no worse off in London at my grandparents' house. It would only be a matter of time before we were bombed out of our house in New Milton; blitz or no blitz, it was decided, and off to London we went. At this point, we had nowhere else to go.

Under My Grandmother's Kitchen Table

My grandparents' house was in a state of utmost confusion; every room that could be used was filled with cots. My grandfather was gravely ill with tuberculosis; my grandmother was valiantly trying to cope with an impossible situation. Mother, John, and I slept in one bed, while Eddie slept on the floor on a spare mattress. After our recent experience of near burial in the country, the air-raid shelter had become a place of danger to me and my mother. I spent a great deal of time under the kitchen table, as safe a haven as any from the war.

My father, whose eyesight was too weak to allow him to be taken into the army, became an air-raid warden. I can't remember where he was posted, I only know he had to leave us. Thereafter, we were supported by my grandparents.

I recollect aspects of those war years with a clarity I have retained about no other period in my life, for each moment was heightened by the sense of shared danger. The secretive nature of the English mentality, even the class differences that have had such an overwhelming and detrimental effect on the English character, seemed to evaporate. The forced camaraderie of the shelters, the strong allegiances created by the tension of the war, vanished after V.E. Day. Soon afterward, all the old class barriers would be hoisted up once more, and the ancient islanders' distrust of one another would resume.

I can only try to imagine the strain of these tumultuous times on Mother, mostly alone and responsible for two small children, with no other means of support than her parents, and with no home of her own. That is the only way I can explain her decision to leave England.

In the early months of 1941, a letter arrived from the United States, asking us, in the most affectionate terms, to come to Florida for the duration of the war. This invitation came from my father's brother David, and his wife, Estelle. The British government had asked anyone who could find a sponsor in a nonaligned country — the United States was months away from Pearl Harbor and entry into the war — to take their children and leave. The threat of invasion was still a distinct possibility, and we couldn't impose on my grandparents forever. But I believe these dangers played a very small part in Mother's calculations. She simply had reached the end of the line; this seemed the only way she could see to solve her immediate problems. The invitation was accepted and we were booked to leave for America.

Mother's decision was momentous. She knew almost nothing of the relatives on whom we were to be totally dependent

— my father hadn't seen his brother since David had emigrated to the United States fifteen years before and had never met his sister-in-law Estelle — and Mother must have known that, once there, it would be almost impossible to return home. My grandfather was in failing health; my grandmother was getting older. I'm sure it was agony for this dutiful daughter to leave her parents, not knowing whether she would ever see them again. The perils of taking her children across the Atlantic during the war were also glaringly obvious to her. But just as the selling of our house in Bristol, and our move to Cornwall, was governed as much by our precarious financial position as by wartime worries, so too did her infinitely graver choice to move to America find its roots in her continuing financial distress.

Until the moment of departure, my imagination was filled with visions of waving palms and flamingos. But the reality of the adventure we were really to undertake I couldn't even begin to imagine.

We had no house to close up, no friends to whom to say good-bye. My father was granted leave to escort us to Glasgow in Scotland, which was the port of exit from which his wife and two children were to sail to America.

After we were led to our cabin, we sat in gloomy silence, waiting nervously for the signal notifying us that Eddie would have to disembark. He went up on deck to buy us a packet of biscuits, and when he came back, he was weeping bitterly. I had never seen a man cry before, and I started to sob as well. All of a sudden, this undeniably self-centered little girl realized something terrible was about to happen, and that the entire fabric of the life she had hitherto known was about to be torn apart.

Although my father may appear from time to time in these recollections as a shadowy and irresolute figure, my feelings for him must have been much stronger than I allowed myself to recognize. To be wrenched apart in this manner gave me much more anguish than could have been possible if, however deeply hidden even from myself, I had not loved him. I felt guilty and miserable; I know that I had always sided with my mother, and denied my feelings for this other needy parent. He had been affectionate and loving, and yet, to a great degree, absent. Partly due to financial pressures, but also to some lack of center within himself. Even as a child, I had felt more pity for him than confidence or respect. Seeing him weep in this way was overwhelming. I had not experienced desolation and abandonment of this magnitude. I was certain I would never see him again, and that we were moving inexorably toward a terrifying, unknown territory.

CHAPTER TWO

Abroad

In order to avoid the dreaded U-boats, our ship was forced to take a swerving, indirect course across the Atlantic, making the voyage longer than the usual six days. We slept fully clothed in our bunks, expecting at any second to hear the warning bells ring and to have to rush up on deck; throughout the crossing, my mother never really slept at all.

The crossing was tedious and frightening. The entire ship stank of engine oil, and the food tasted as though it had been deep-fried in it. Once or twice a game for the children was organized, although usually we were left to our own devices.

However, on our last evening at sea, a dance was held in the main salon, and I was allowed to wear my one and only precious rose pink party frock.

There was excitement and apprehension among the passengers. Encouraged by the British government to take their children out of the country, each family had been permitted to carry only the minimum amount of money with which to begin a new life abroad. As most of us had never met the families who had invited us, we were to be entirely dependent on their generosity and goodwill. A willful and high-strung little girl, an anxious and insecure mother, and a vulnerable little boy would hardly be the easiest guests to take into a household. And, more to the point, we were a family who might have to stay on for many years.

The immigration authorities came on board and we were

interviewed in the ship's main dining room. To go through the passenger list took nearly all day. Every family had to be questioned about their political views — we ourselves didn't have any — and then about their finances, ours none too promising. However, toward evening we were granted our visas and made our way down the gangplank to begin our American sojourn.

The trip from Newark to Fort Lauderdale by Greyhound bus took three days and three nights. I can date this trip exactly. It fell on John's fifth birthday, September 12, 1941.

Dave and Estelle greeted us warmly enough. Everything in Florida looked white and shining to our eyes, accustomed as we were to London gray. The sun blindingly bright, and the palm trees, as expected, swaying in the breeze. My two cousins, Richard and Shirley, struck me as very American and offhand. We must have seemed to them overly polite and "British." Uncle Dave resembled Eddie minus the charm, and Estelle was a Fort Lauderdale battle-ax. She had lots of cronies like herself, and they would spend hours playing mah-jongg. Click! Click! Down went the ivory counters. Richard talked of baseball and Shirley talked of boys. Mother, John, and I tried to settle down to a normal life of some kind. Mother missed England and her family — perhaps she missed her husband, although I don't remember her saying so. I was too excited by the strangeness of everything around me to reflect on what I might or might not miss. John was only five, my mother was unhappy, and I felt I had to be strong and protective. I liked the new feeling of responsibility. I started to inhabit my new role, one I was to play for many years.

John, who was not of school age as yet, stayed at home with the maid. I went to the local public school, and Mother went to work in Estelle's dress shop.

Apart from John's loneliness at home, and Estelle's open dissatisfaction with my mother as a saleslady — too well-mannered, not nearly pushy enough to perform a hard-sell job on Estelle's Fort Lauderdale clientele — at first all went relatively well.

At school, I was the center of attraction for a while as the first refugee child to arrive in Florida. Once again, I found I enjoyed the attention that was paid me. One day I heard an announcement on the radio inviting children of my age to take part in a "talent competition"; fueled by my successes in *Rumpelstiltskin* at school, I begged Mother to let me compete.

I sang a Scottish folk song and won the contest. My award was the fantastic sum of five dollars. The program was heard by Betty Boxer and her husband, Irving Plumber, who ran the local dancing school. They telephoned the radio station to offer me a free place, an invitation that completely changed my life in Florida and provided the escape route I needed from the pressures that were intensifying on a daily basis between our two ill-matched families at home.

My mother, always highly nervous, and with a constant tremor in her hands, drove businesslike Estelle into a fury. I was rather pleased with myself, and thought I was a tiny star. This, understandably, upset Richard, a definite nonachiever. Even my little brother came under criticism for not being "aggressive" enough. I think the David Blooms very much regretted inviting these London cuckoos into their hygienic Floridian nest.

The British War Relief Organization approached the Plumbers for help in raising money to send back to England. They chose me as the perfect child to stir the hearts and open the pockets of well-to-do Floridians, and Irving Plumber wrote a song for me to perform in various hotels and clubs throughout the South Florida area.

The verse went as follows:

> *I'm a little English girl*
> *Knocking at your door.*
> *Driven from my home*
> *By the Gods of war.*
> *Asking but the right*
> *To live and share the sun.*
> *Praying for the night*
> *When peace once more will come.*

There were at least two more verses on the same theme; I can carry the tune to this day.

Mother would wake me up and dress me in my finery; then we would be driven to Palm Beach, Miami, or wherever it was that I was scheduled to perform. I remember in detail the signs outside the entrances of many fashionable hotels, which informed potential guests that the management welcomed "restricted" patrons only. I instinctively sensed who would and wouldn't be honored; had I not been the performer, this would certainly have included my mother, myself, and, more than likely, the Plumbers as well.

The presence of racial hatred played a great part in my desire to succeed professionally in later years, to feel myself on such a firm footing that nothing could ever wound me or my family. My mother was a product of first-generation Jews transplanted to England. Much was expected of my generation, although such pressures were usually applied to the sons rather than the daughters. Jewish sons were intended to use their good Jewish brains to climb rapidly into the worlds of commerce, the groves of academe, and even the mysterious world of the arts; the daughters were expected to be content with marriage to these good sons and aid them on their path toward success. I feel profoundly Jewish ethnically and historically, but religion itself holds absolutely no attraction for me, nor can I imagine deriving any consolation from it. Unlike many Jewish actresses of my generation, I never made any attempt to hide my origins or to change my name. Later, the perspicacious British press, who misunderstand or misrepresent practically everything, would insist on calling me "The English Rose." My family would comment at home, in strong Yiddish accents, on my English rosiness, and we always found it a great source of amusement and wonder.

The difficult family stress between our two households continued for the time that we remained in Florida. Mother was deeply unhappy in Fort Lauderdale and began to make inquiries regarding some other way to survive the war years. Lily, my mother's cousin, found a room for us in Forest Hills, New York, that was available to rent for a nominal sum. She was sure, she wrote, that Mother could easily earn some extra money as a baby-sitter. My mother believed that our moving would be as great a relief to Dave and Estelle as to us, and gathered the courage to ask Uncle Dave to give us fifty dollars a month in order to survive the rest of the war on our own. Although I was sad to leave the Plumbers, and had enjoyed my lessons at their first-rate dancing school, I was extremely happy to be leaving my uncle and aunt. The atmosphere between the two families was becoming more and more strained, the tension unbearable.

On one occasion, the Blooms being out of the house, I accidentally tripped over an electric wire and broke their precious toaster. Carrying it with us, my mother and I, with John in tow, dashed from shop to shop to find an identical model. We managed to get it back in place only minutes before Estelle and Dave returned home. Another crisis had been averted.

My little brother came in for some of Dave's punitive criticism. In his boredom and loneliness, John had tried to trade a watch the Blooms had given him for some tin soldiers belonging to a neighboring boy in order to gain his friendship. Dave, upon hearing of this, berated my brother. Mother attempted to intercede and Dave lifted his hand, as if to strike her. I started to scream and tried to pull him away, at which point he hit me hard on both sides of the face. No one had ever hit me before, and the shock was enormous. I became hysterical and tried to attack him. The entire family joined in and all pretense of civility — let alone family kinship — came to an abrupt end. Dave and Estelle openly let loose their hatred, screaming that they couldn't wait to see our backs out the door, that we should take their fifty dollars a month and get out. This episode was the last act of our Florida sojourn. There was no turning back. Plainly and simply, we couldn't stay — so we left.

I cannot remember the return journey to New York; sitting

up all night had lost its previous charm. I was sharing my mother's uneasiness with being uprooted and cut adrift yet again in a strange country. My next memory is our arrival in Forest Hills.

The room Cousin Lily had found for us was in an apartment belonging to Alma Jorgenson, a young widow who was renting out one of her bedrooms to make ends meet. Mrs. Jorgenson was a good-looking woman in her late thirties, as was my mother. All of us were to use one bathroom, and my mother and Mrs. Jorgenson would share the kitchen. Our room contained one double bed, which Mother and I slept in, a small bed for John, and an armchair minus most of its stuffing. In this setting we settled down to await the end of World War II.

Alma Jorgenson had two children, roughly the same ages as John and me: Ronnie, and Virginia, who was to become my lifelong friend. Virginia and I both adored games of make-believe and dressing up. As the life we were living in the borough of Queens was light-years away from the life we imagined for ourselves, we simply decided to invent another in its place.

I must have been enrolled at a school and had some homework to do while attending, but I remember nothing of it. All I remember is the excitement of choosing a new girl's adventure book — I was riveted by a series dealing with a character called Sue Barton — *Sue Barton, District Nurse; Sue Barton, Hospital Nurse.* This wholesome fare was interspersed with borrowings of adult novels, from the Brontës to A. J. Cronin, and others dealing with sexual matters, which I withdrew from the local library with my mother's card, saying they were for her. I read Hardy's *Jude the Obscure,* sensing that the passion that drove Jude to his death was of an altogether different order from that which drove Walter Pidgeon toward Greer Garson at the local cinema, but understanding little else. The thrill when we saved enough money to go to the movies was immense: my affections were unreservedly given to tall, dark, handsome Tyrone Power; every article of the movie magazines of the period, *Screen Romances* and *Movie Life,* Virginia and I scanned for fresh news of Power and his glamorous French wife, Annabella. *The Black Swan,* a pirate film in which Power plays a swashbuckler who captures and damn near violates the copper-haired heroine, Maureen O'Hara, was our particular favorite. When the money was found we would rush to the movie house on Continental Avenue to see evocative, sensual South Sea island films with ardent Jon Hall and sarong-encircled Dorothy Lamour — *Volcano, Tornado, Hurricane.* Hibiscus flowers and mountains of lava. Blue grottoes and mysterious idols. Total escape.

I loved the suspense of waiting for my favorite radio programs, notably the Jack Benny and Burns and Allen shows; we waited eagerly for *Allen's Alley,* a series of ethnic vignettes full of deliciously politically incorrect characters, among whom we singled out for our delight Mrs. Nussbaum, who answered each summons of Fred Allen with a questioning "Nuuuuu?" in her best Borscht Belt vernacular.

One memorable day, a letter arrived from a bank on Wall Street. My mother was asked to come to the office as soon as possible, so we all went to the city. When she came out of the meeting my mother said, in an uncertain voice, "Eddie has been allowed to send us an allowance each month. Let's go and buy you some clothes." After a windfall of such enormous proportions, we imagined this to be a sign that the war would soon come to an end, and we would go back to our life in England.

But another four years were to go by before the war in Europe was over. The following spring found us still at the Jorgensons', and Mother was feeling unwell. She went to see a specialist. On her return she took me out alone for a walk.

Though I didn't understand her fully, I grasped easily enough what lay under the information she passed on to me. As carefully and tenderly as she could, Mother was trying to break serious news. She said she had to go into hospital for an operation, and would need to stay there for several weeks. A provisional plan had to be devised to care for us in her absence. Although I was just eleven years of age, I would have to be a grown-up and responsible girl, and take care of my younger brother. I started to cry, and it took us both a long time before we were able to deal with the first order of business: pretending to John, only six years of age, that everything was normal.

The British War Relief, the same organization for which I had sung my little song in Florida some months before, once again came to our rescue. A place was found for us at Sharilawn, a summer camp in Massachusetts, whose generous owners had been told of our difficult position and had offered to take us in for nothing.

The week before we left was excruciatingly painful. The last few months had been a seemingly endless succession of traumas, separations, and losses. I had come to mistrust the present and dread the future. First my home. Then my father. Now my mother. Galvanized by fears and insecurities, I was certain I would never see her again. When we said good-bye at the train station, I experienced the same overwhelming despair I had when we set sail for the United States — a sense of spinning in space, of losing my grip, with no assurance of finding a firm footing anywhere again.

The first weeks at camp were overshadowed by worries over my mother's illness. I missed her terribly. To make matters worse, John and I were separated. He was placed in the boys' camp quite far away, and I only saw him on rare occasions. After we received news that Mother's operation was successful, I began to relax. Then and only then did the beauties of New England's countryside reveal themselves to me. I also took on a small creative project: I made a copper ashtray for Mother, whose illness made no dent in her love of tobacco. But my main interest and objective was to gain a role in one of the productions to be given that summer at Sharilawn.

I auditioned for Gilbert and Sullivan's operetta *Patience*. The larger roles were cast with older girls; I got the part of one of Patience's companions, with a little solo of my own to sing. That was all I concentrated on for the rest of the summer.

When performance time came around, I never tired of looking at myself in the mirror, at my spangled tulle dress and the multilayered makeup covering my face, applied by me with enough enthusiasm to embellish the complexions of twelve mature actresses. My only sorrow was that Mother was not yet strong enough to travel to Massachusetts to see me.

My singing was a little wobbly and my acting was probably very stiff. Nevertheless, it confirmed my absolute conviction that here was the life I wanted when I grew up. I felt secure and totally in command of myself when on the stage.

At the end of the summer I left Sharilawn with the same degree of reluctance as I had entered it three months before. We were met by Mother at the bus terminal; she looked so frail that it was difficult for John or me to pretend everything was fine. She had been staying in our room in Forest Hills, barely able to take care of herself during that brutally hot New York summer — this was before air-conditioning — while my brother and I had been swimming in cool Massachusetts lakes and feasting happily on the camp's nourishing meals. I had been rehearsing and performing a play, which I discovered was the thing I loved most in the world, while she had been ill, alone, too weak even to buy herself food.

I wanted to make this cruel difference up to her somehow, and hoped that my future triumphs in my new vocation, the theater, would do just that.

For my twelfth birthday present, Mother purchased tickets for both of us to attend a performance of a play on Broadway, entitled *Junior Miss*. It left me longing for more. On one never-to-be-forgotten matinee day, we went to see Chekhov's *The Three Sisters*. The leading players were Katharine Cornell, Ruth Gordon, Gertrude Musgrove, and Judith Anderson.

I recognized for the first time, as part of my barely formed sexual identity, the sisters' compulsion to replace their lost father with another masculine figure: a need so fundamental that Masha is drawn to an unattainable married man, Olga marries a pedantic schoolmaster many years her senior and light-years away from her delicate sensibilities, and Irina is induced to become engaged to someone she doesn't love. All the more heartbreaking is that, at the close and despite their choices, there they are, still deriving some pleasure from the sound of the regimental band and still clinging to expectations of a better life.

From that moment on, my single desire was to act in a play by a great master. *Junior Miss* may have been fun, but *The Three Sisters* was the genuine article.

I begged my mother for another chance to go to the theater, but there was no money. Mother adored the theater as much as I did, and promised me that when we returned home to England and things got better, we could go as often as we wished.

At about this time, I started to listen to a children's show on the radio: Robert Emory's *Rainbow Hour,* a program of plays for children performed by child actors. An announcement was made inviting children wanting to take part in one of the broadcasts to write in, explaining why they wanted to act. With Mother's help, I composed a letter which I sent eagerly and immediately; soon after, I received the reply, inviting me to an audition a few weeks later. Mother and I set off for the studio. Led into a brightly lit room, I was invited by a remote voice emanating from another studio to tell them about myself.

Mysteriously, the shy girl vanished and the confident performer took over. I went into every detail of my young life at extreme length until, in midlecture, I was suddenly interrupted and asked to read from a script. With almost superhuman self-assurance, I read the role of England's Queen Elizabeth I. I read the part in a blustery, rather bullying tone that I thought suitable to convey the character of a great queen. I was told to wait in the adjoining room while my attributes were discussed in private. After about half an hour, during which my entire future was seemingly suspended in midair, I met Mr. Emory himself, and was offered the role of Elizabeth I.

John had come with us to the audition, and the three of us went to celebrate the birth of my brilliant career as a "real actress" at the Automat on West 57th Street across from Steinway Hall.

To anyone who missed the wonders of the Horn and Hardart Automat, I can bear witness to its peculiar enchantment. The walls of the vast eating area were lined with metal containers bearing glass windows, in which rested every imaginable food available: delicious and delectable pies, both sweet and savory, Salisbury steak with gravy, macaroni and cheese, Boston "pork and beans" baked in their own earthenware crock, frothy lemon meringue pies, and glistening, iced angel food or coconut layer cakes. Single portions could be freed from their glass prisons by inserting nickels into the slots; the windows would fly open, leaving the hungry customer — in this instance, me — to simply remove her chosen plate of food, ready to plunge in. The Automat was fast food with an element of fantasy, and, as a means of dining out, it was enchanting to a child — indeed, to many adults as well: it became the weekly treat for our family during our time in New York, a never-failing source of pleasure.

I arrived at the radio station the following week for the broadcast and made no major mistakes. Convinced that the entire world was listening to my radio debut, I was soon disabused. Apart from the Jorgensons and Cousin Lily, nobody's life appeared to have been changed in any way by my voice on the air.

The summer of 1943 came, and although still expecting a summons that might take us home, John and I were again invited to Sharilawn. This time we both looked forward to a return; for John, now seven, it was the opportunity to be with boys his own age, out of the constant vigilance of his mother and sister. For me, aged twelve, there was the hope that this time I would be cast in a more important role at the theater. There was no cloud of illness hanging over Mother and no reason not to look forward to a long, healthy summer out of the infernal heat of the city.

That year I was cast as Gretel in Englebert Humperdinck's opera *Hansel and Gretel*. I had reached my full height and was a foot taller than the poor youth who sang Hansel. Although I was not then — nor was ever to become, alas — a good singer, I enjoyed every moment onstage, and was quite capable of carrying a tune. This time Mother was able to come and I had the thrill of showing her how much I had learned in my two years at Sharilawn.

Mother arrived with important news — news that both John and I were waiting to hear: we were booked to leave for Lisbon on a neutral Portuguese ship that would embark for Europe in the fall. Eddie had arranged for our passage, and appeared to have enough money to pay for the expensive fares. Once in Portugal, we were to stay in a hotel with other returning British subjects, until room was found for us on a flight back to England.

We began to organize our few possessions, and get all the necessary papers in order. No longer a child, I was now a young girl who had been through some very grueling experiences; I was also much clearer about the possible dangers of this sea voyage.

Like Spain, Portugal had maintained its neutrality since the beginning of the world conflict, making our vessel supposedly safe from enemy attack. Our ship was crammed with women and children who were making this journey across an ocean teeming with enemy submarines in order to return to a country still at war.

Shortly after we set sail, a fierce hurricane began to blow, and some days later the news spread among the cabins that the Germans were questioning the neutrality of Portugal as a consequence of the Portuguese allowing Allied ships to refuel in the Azores. So, in the end, our second transatlantic journey was almost as frightening as the first; seasick from the rough seas, besieged by foul food, we wondered whether being torpedoed and sunk by U-boats was easier than holding out for Lisbon.

However, we arrived after ten days, very much alive and deliriously relieved to be ashore. I remember the luminous colors of late autumn, still the most ravishing time to be in the south of Europe. We were booked into what, sometime prior to the war, must have been a grand hotel in the resort town of Estoril, but now was filled to capacity with women and children; except for the waiters, there was not a man in sight. Most of the guests were returning home because of family illness or death. We were returning because we just wanted to go home. Each evening everyone assembled in the main salon to hear a list of those scheduled to return to England that night. I made a number of friends among the children. As the names were read out every evening, I saw them vanish one by one, starting out on the same perilous homecoming we were soon to undertake. It was an extraordinarily transient period, a state of uninterrupted anxiety and excitement.

We waited three months. Then, one night, our names were read, and I remember the shock of hearing the announcement, and also the fear that suddenly came over me. We didn't need much time to pack; we had never really unpacked. Driven to the airport after midnight, we found our plane waiting for us, heavily camouflaged and ominous. We were hustled off the bus and into the belly of the plane, where all the seats had been removed and the windows blacked out. We took our seats on the floor. I remember two nuns onboard; one of them was chewing gum. The mechanical movement of her jaws was the single sound I fixed upon, even above the roar of propellers, for the next tension-filled five hours. No one spoke. Finally, one of the crew put his head round the door. "Hold tight," he announced. "We are about to land."

The doors opened, and with the rush of fresh air, we saw that we had landed on water. None of us even knew that we had flown on a seaplane. We were home.

CHAPTER THREE

Home

WARTIME SECRECY had made it impossible for Eddie to meet us when we landed. He was telephoned and told to make his way to Waterloo Station at a designated time.

The familiar, smoky smell, the gray, gloomy light of London, that known and well-loved sense of being home, greeted us. There was the image of Eddie, peering nervously into each passing carriage, hoping to catch his first glimpse of us, his family that had been away so long as to seem almost an abstraction. The reunion was touching and emotionally difficult for us all.

The train drew up, and I rushed impulsively toward my father. He threw his arms around me; Mother hesitated, unsure as to how she should greet this man standing on the platform, her husband; John also hung back, extremely nervous. He wasn't certain how to behave toward a father he could only faintly remember.

As we stood there, people pushing all around us, there was an awkward silence. Then Eddie picked John up with one arm, and with the other embraced my mother. We were trying to find some words that could express the intensity of our feelings; suddenly the air-raid alarm rang. In the weeks before our arrival, there had been a pause in the bombing — the siren had hardly sounded. As luck would have it, on the very day of our return, the second blitz on London began. After two years in America, it all felt unreal to me, not even remotely frightening, as though I was stuck in a wartime film that never moved beyond the opening credits. We were hurried by Eddie through the complete and unfamiliar darkness of a blackout to a taxi, and to our new home.

Which wasn't a home at all, or not the home we had longed for during our wandering in America. It was a bachelor flat in which Eddie had been living for the past year. However, his fortunes must have improved, for it was possible for him to live in the heart of London's fashionable Mayfair district.

Eddie's flat was situated on Curzon Street above the Mirabelle, an elegant and prohibitively expensive restaurant. Although barely appropriate for a newlywed couple, the flat was hopeless for a family of four. I disliked it on sight, and was never to feel differently for the next ten years we were to make it our home.

What followed was a period of confusion, of air raids, schools attended by John and me, schools bombed out. Above all, the interminable wait for the war to end.

For our small family, as for every family in Britain during the war years, it was a time of transition. John was sent to a boarding school a short distance from London, but presumably safer from the air raids. He felt abandoned, and Mother and I took the train to visit him every weekend. I refused to be "evacuated" again, and I refused to leave Mother in London. Eddie came and went; as I recall, he was now part owner of a factory in Nottingham.

I was entered in the Cone School, a school for professional children near Berkeley Square, where ballet, tap, and acting classes were seriously conducted, with rudimentary formal schooling in the afternoon. This latter part of our education was never taken too seriously. I loved the school, the dance classes, the slightly frivolous atmosphere.

The closeness that had at first seemed possible for my parents to achieve after such a long separation soon disintegrated. My father proved himself as feckless as ever, my mother was as disappointed. I was once again torn between my pity for my indecisive father and my total loyalty to my mother. The Cone School was a cheerful antidote to the pressures at home. Apart from the rockets and pilotless missiles that descended on London during the final months of the war, I recall this period as a delicious pause between childhood and adolescence. This light-hearted education, however, was brought to a stop by my aunt Mary, who sensed I was not studying earnestly enough to be an actress.

Aunt Mary was becoming a major influence in my life. As my path toward the life of an actress became more defined, I turned more and more to Mary for advice. Perhaps without enough consideration, for I didn't stop to think that my bond with Mary might have been hurtful to my mother. Still, Mother was unflinching in her certainty that I had a brilliant future, and never gave so much as a hint that she may have felt herself supplanted in my affections.

CHAPTER FOUR

My Profession

It was 1945. The war was over. Like everyone else in Britain, we had passed the last two years in waiting; waiting for life to become normal again. Together with other Londoners, we stood in front of Buckingham Palace to applaud the king, the queen, and the two young princesses as they waved to the crowd from the balcony. We were there until late in the night, cheering, dancing, singing — letting go.

I was now fourteen, and at Mary's suggestion, I entered the Central School of Speech Training and Dramatic Art. It certainly wasn't as much fun as the Cone School. In fact, I never enjoyed my time there. But I knew better than to question my aunt Mary. I was the youngest in my group; in order to be accepted into school, I had made myself out to be two years older than I was. As England's young men had not yet been released from the army, the classes were composed mainly of girls. Food rationing was a wartime reality that would take many years to eradicate, heat was scarce to nonexistent, and the school code resembled that of the armed forces — the girls along with the few young men were called by their surnames. To be addressed as "Bloom" seemed a little unglamorous to a hopeful actress. But sexlessness and utilitarianism were givens of the Central School. Many students entered hoping to teach drama, not lead professional actors' lives. As I hadn't achieved my "school leaving certificate," the equivalent of a high school diploma, I was considered too unqualified to be allowed into lectures on the history of the theater and others, such as Greek drama, that I would have enjoyed. Instead, I was handed a course in Greek dancing, mime, improvisation, and in acting short scenes from the classics. I found it disappointing, and a trifle silly. But it was better than nothing.

In the first-year students' performance of scenes from *School for Scandal* I was told by the principal that my "performance was acceptable although my appearance deplorable." As I had to change in a few brief seconds from the ingenue to the maid, then back from the maid to the ingenue again, and then make a brief appearance as an aged crone — I was still six months short of fifteen — I felt this note to be a bit unjust. My way of escape was clear when an important theatrical agent, Olive Harding, came to this performance. Although coming to see another student, she discovered me instead, and offered to represent me. Olive Harding sent me to the BBC to give an audition and I was offered the role of Anne of Oxford Street in a radio dramatization of Thomas de Quincey's story *Confessions of an English Opium-Eater*.

The Central School insisted that I choose — either I stay with them for another two years and finish the course, or leave and do my first professional job for the BBC. The choice was not hard to make.

Anne of Oxford Street is a young streetwalker. My only experience of such women came from having seen prostitutes in Shepherd's Market, a small but legendary red-light district less than five minutes from our apartment. I once witnessed a fight between two of them that was as brutal as any between two men; perhaps even more terrifying in its hysterical violence. The way these women lurked amidst shadowy doorways and lifted their skirts to show off their legs was seedily compelling; I envied the tarty clothes they wore. What they actually did when they reeled in their customers I hadn't the faintest idea — and no one seemed in a great rush to enlighten me.

Of course I longed to know, as I was a perfectly normal

young girl with perfectly healthy curiosities and appetites. Hard as it is to understand in this very different age, young girls at that time were still kept in almost Victorian ignorance about the "facts of life," and I was no exception. That I was involved in theater made this even more complicated, for to become an actress as young as I did was to enter into a cloister of my own making; I believed my dedication to this strange profession required the exclusion of nearly everything else. Consequently, there were no boyfriends, no necking, I attended no parties, and there was hardly any of the otherwise commonplace sexual experimentation. Woefully, painfully ignorant of the most basic facts of life, I was always ill at ease in the company of men. The sexual feelings that I undoubtedly had were repressed in me. I was able to act out these hidden desires only in crushes on my leading men, which, in the charmed atmosphere of our work together, were almost as real to me as the real thing. I felt absolutely complete, and considered myself to be the luckiest of young women to lead such an enchanted life.

An outsider is something I have always known myself to be. In the theater we are all outsiders of one kind or another. I doubt if many actors have gone into that particular profession because they are in tune with the climate of their times. Acting can be a refuge for those who are sexually, psychologically, or socially wounded. I have found the escape I sought in the theater, in a strange occupation that allows me to change my being for the brief time that I am performing; to do something few other so-called sane people are permitted freely to do: to pretend, and sometimes for a brief period even to believe, that I am someone other than myself.

I never gave a thought to the fact that there might be other possibilities open to me: alternative ways for an attractive young girl in her teens to conduct her life; that it might have been possible to use these delightful years in freedom and sexual exploration instead of in pursuit of the perfect role and the purely imaginary lover.

I auditioned for the Oxford Playhouse, and was contracted to appear as the "Juvenile Lead" in three plays of that season. I remained with the company for the agreed-upon three months, and had my first lessons in what it would be like to be alone, performing at night, trying to fill the meaningless days as best I could. Although my mother visited me nearly every weekend, I was brutally lonely. Despite the excitement I felt at being "A Professional," I was not nearly ready to be out there on my own at such a young age. As I put another coin in the meter of the gas fire in my room, over which I sat huddled from the cold, all I wanted was to be at home with Mother.

My baptism over, I returned gratefully to home and London. Olive Harding sent me to audition for a walk-on and understudy role in London's West End, and I was given the job. This newly formed theater was headed by the actor/dancer Robert Helpmann, and all the wonderful opportunities I was soon to be given in the world of theater were in great part due to his belief in me. Although only a walk-on, this was an auspicious beginning; I was starting, in however modest a way, by working and learning from fine actors and performing in first-class theater.

Helpmann had been the partner to the prima ballerina of the Royal Ballet, Margot Fonteyn; although never a great dancer, he was a great mime, and quite definitely, a great *homme de théâtre.*

Helpmann's speaking voice was high, lacking resonance. Onstage, his face was mercurial; at one moment malevolent, at others marvelously comic. His heavily made-up eyes were hugely prominent and extremely hypnotic. As Oberon, as Flamineo in *The White Devil,* and the Clown in Andreyev's *He Who Gets Slapped,* he was a fine and accomplished actor.

Helpmann must have seen something in me of the actress he thought I could become, and with great kindness arranged for me to take ballet class at the studio of Vera Volkova, where he himself still studied. Volkova, who had taught all the great English dancers of the time, including Fonteyn herself, was a tiny, extremely expressive dancer, trained in the classical Russian tradition. Through her artistry I saw that the more rigid form of ballet, in which I had been trained, could, in the hands of this master, be transmuted very simply into the most beautiful and passionate of movements. How a mere turn of the shoulder could transform a stiff and inexpressive line of the body into an instrument of romance and sculptural beauty. Many years later, after I had achieved some fame in my early career, I encountered Madame, as in those days we always addressed our teachers. She recognized me, and gave me one of the most precious compliments I was ever to receive. "Claire," she said, "I always knew you were an artist; *not* a dancer, but an artist."

I was still living at home, still protected by my mother's presence. John was at boarding school, and my small salary must have been, in large part, supporting our family.

In 1947, some time before I had left the Central School, Eddie had decided to go join his sister Freida, in South Africa, to seek his fortune. Nothing that he had tried his hand at in England had succeeded. I remember a time when our flat was crammed with linen and silver, china and fine glassware, all initialed "L.H." Eddie had bought the contents of the Langham Hotel, and we were the recipients of some of its finery. Then as suddenly as this had appeared, it vanished. I must presume the "deal," whatever it may have been, had not gone through as planned. There must have been many such incidents. Eddie told my mother that he was going to leave England, he and Mother would divorce, and he would then marry some rich woman in South Africa; that would enable him to send money home to support us. This was indeed an eccentric plan. I don't know what effect this irrational decision had on Mother, but I know that *I* was filled with terror. The fear of such sensations of emptiness and desolation as I then experienced was to mark me for the rest of my life. My fear of abandonment began at that moment; it has never left me.

As good as his word, Eddie left some weeks later. I remember him kissing my mother and me, then walking down the long corridor of our apartment building as we watched. I am sure he didn't want to go through with this plan of his, so irrationally conceived. But he continued to walk down the corridor, and disappeared around the corner without looking back. Perhaps he was weeping. I recollect hugging the radiator for warmth, yet feeling cold through and through with fear; I remember my mother shutting herself in the bedroom. John came home from school, and we made some strong tea and waited for her to come out.

Some months later — it is hard for me at this distance to say exactly when — I was tested for the role of Ophelia in Laurence Olivier's film of *Hamlet*.

I had seen Laurence Olivier in his roles of Heathcliff, Maxim de Winter, and Lord Nelson. His overwhelming presence as a stage actor, his remarkable masculine beauty and glamour on the screen had bewitched every young and romantically inclined young girl of my age. I was certainly no exception.

In the late years of the war, when I was still a young adolescent, my mother and I used to go every Saturday night to queue for tickets at the New Theatre, the headquarters of London's Old Vic Theatre. There Laurence Olivier and Ralph Richardson were appearing in a repertory of classic plays. One week you could watch as Olivier performed *Richard III*, with Richardson playing a small supporting role, and the next see Richardson as Peer Gynt with Olivier in the minor role of the Button Moulder. Olivier as Oedipus, Richardson as Falstaff, Olivier as Harry Hotspur, and Richardson as Uncle Vanya; these magnificent performances are indelibly seared in my memory. When I am asked where I studied acting, my reply is that I was lucky enough to see the greatest actors of my time, and I watched them again and again. John Gielgud as Hamlet, Edith Evans as Katharine of Aragon — I consider myself incredibly fortunate to have lived in London during my formative years and to have been able to watch these great teachers perform. With all these actors, so towering and unapproachable to me then, I was later to have the opportunity to work.

To my great disappointment, I lost the role of Ophelia to Jean Simmons. I was certain that my life was over, and spent days moping around the house, weeping and complaining about my fate. I felt that everyone must know that I had been tried and found wanting, although the truth of the matter was that Olivier had always wanted Jean Simmons, and it was only when he thought she would be unavailable that he tested other young actresses.

The immense attraction that this older actor had exercised over the romantic imagination of my sixteen-year-old self, and the near idolatry in which I held him, made me almost inconsolable. I had been very close to getting the role; Olivier had encouraged me, reading Hamlet's lines offscreen for me to respond to. I had been costumed under his supervision in a pale blue dress. He had declared how impressed he was with me, and that we would have time to rehearse together for our scenes. Of course I thought I had been the chosen one. But I waited for a long, long weekend, and then read in the evening paper that Jean Simmons was to play Ophelia. It would take several more years in the theatrical profession to begin to understand that you believed no one. Youth having the capacity for regeneration, however, life moved on, and the sense of pain and failure went away.

The Helpmann season closed, and I first tasted the misery that is a major part of the life of any actor: being out of work; waiting for the telephone to ring; calling your agent and asking for news, although, of course, if there had been anything of interest to report, she would have called herself. The infantilizing effect that this passive waiting can have on adults is terrifying; that it was a part of my life as a teenager now seems to me a sad and wasteful use of my precious young years. I hung around the telephone — it was, of course, long before the invention of the answering machine — fearful of going out in case I missed that important call. The call finally came in the form of a summons from Robert Helpmann and the director Michael Benthall, asking me to audition for a place in the company they were forming for the 1948 season at the Shakespeare Theatre in Stratford-upon-Avon; there were two young girls' roles they had in mind for me. They didn't tell me which roles they were.

I had been asked to prepare the "nunnery scene" from *Hamlet,* the scene that I performed when I tested for the role of Ophelia in Olivier's film some months earlier. I arrived, on a very hot summer's day, shaking with excitement and with the desire to excel. I performed the scene with Helpmann, and was asked to wait while my performance was discussed. I went next door to one of London's dingier cafés, and drank a cup of strong tea to calm my nerves; then I went back to the theater. Benthall told me that I was to join the company, and play Ophelia opposite the alternating Hamlets of Helpmann and Paul Scofield. I was just seventeen years of age. I went running all the way home to tell my mother. I couldn't even wait for a bus. The three of us, John, Mother, and I, danced round the living room from sheer joy.

The brilliant British actor Joss Ackland has been a friend of mine since our early days in the theater. He loved to tell the story of a "little girl," whom he had last met as a student in drama school, approaching him on the street and asking him whether he knew any good "digs" at Stratford-upon-Avon. Assuming her to be an extra at the festival, he inquired in which play she would be walking-on. "I am playing Ophelia," gravely replied the child.

I was the next to youngest actor in the company; apart from the young boy who played Prince Arthur, I was the only member still to have a child's ration book. This entitled me to one banana and one extra egg per week, and was also the cause of much teasing from older members of the company. This time I was really away from home, although the atmosphere at Stratford was extremely familial and protective. Many of the actors stayed in a country house owned by the theater, and Mother thought it the perfect place for me. I adored going back to supper after the show and hearing all the theatrical gossip: who was sleeping with whom, who was going to be asked back next season. As the finest young actor in England, Paul Scofield was the subject of much speculation. Extremely reclusive, a countryman from Sussex, his onstage glamour and offstage reticence were a source of great frustration to the young and pretty actresses in the company. Since Scofield was happily married and had a young son, no one wanted seriously to interfere with his marriage; only perhaps to be flirted with and taken some notice of. But Scofield never so much as glanced at any of them. I could never make up my mind which of my two Hamlets I found the more devastating: the openly homosexual, charismatic Helpmann, or the charming, shy young man from Sussex.

As neither was remotely interested in me, it didn't much matter. I was treated as a child by the other members of the company, although, at seventeen, I felt I was a young woman. There was something undeveloped in my nature that must have made itself felt. I still appeared a protected and nurtured young girl. I felt that, as an attractive young woman, I was not being taken seriously enough, although as an actress I received some attention.

I had a success as Ophelia, and desperately hoped that I would be invited to remain with the company for another year; Helpmann and Benthall, however, were not invited to return, and neither was I. I went home to await further events.

On my return to London, life seemed dismal and dull. I had enjoyed the freedom of being on my own among spirited actors talking "shop," and of acting opposite not one but two fascinating leading men. I longed for something else to come into my life; I longed to be a grown actor; although never labeled as a "child actress," what I really had been up to now was a child who acted. Now I was eighteen, and I hoped that a little more might happen to me than the hours of waiting for the telephone to ring, and a more mature part to play in life than acting the role of a dutiful daughter.

I was sent by Olive Harding to audition for *The Lady's Not for Burning,* a play by Christopher Fry in romantic verse, which had a short vogue in the gloomy postwar years in England. The year was 1949. I had been told that I was to read the part of Alizon Eliot, "the ingenue," as such roles were then called, and that I would be auditioning with another young actor who was also being considered. We were to meet on the stage of the Globe Theatre, on Shaftesbury Avenue, in the heart of London's West End theater district. The actor and director John Gielgud, the actress Pamela Brown, the designer Oliver Messel, and the producer Hugh "Binkie" Beaumont were to be our judges: a very formidable panel. I was so nervous, so determined to get the role that I scarcely noticed the young man. Or so I thought at the time; yet I must have noticed him, for even today I can picture the way he sat in his chair, his rather pockmarked skin, his green eyes. He was an extraordinarily beautiful young man. However, I wasn't interested in young men at that moment, no matter how beautiful, only in impressing my audience. I was there to get a job. We read one scene together; I remember the young man making some feeble joke at the end to cover his nervousness, which was met with a friendly silence. Hugh Beaumont and John Gielgud thanked us both, and said that they would let us know the result soon. I went back to the play I was appearing in on the fringe of the West End theater district, and received a call that very evening from my agent. I had won the role I had tried out for and so had Richard Burton, for that was the name of the young man from Wales who had read opposite me.

I thought little more about Richard, until something happened that I have never been able to explain.

I arrived for the first rehearsal, and was just about to open the door that led to the stage, when I heard Richard's unmistakable voice say, "I was married yesterday." I can remember the moment with absolute clarity, and the dreadful leap my heart gave at the words. Clearly, I had felt the force of his remarkable personality, and was immensely attracted to this unknown and seductive young man with the beautiful green eyes.

The play went on an eleven-week tour, and the younger actors, including Richard and me, booked into the cheaper theatrical "digs" together. Some of these boardinghouses were indescribably vile, cold, dirty, and with the worst of English cooking, while others could be cozy, run by landladies who would make endless cups of tea and spoil the lucky actors for the week that they were there. Long after the curtain had come down, Richard, who had an encyclopedic memory for poetry, would recite poems to me late into the night. He would be seated in my room, very properly, on a chair pulled away from the bed on which I silently lay, fervently listening to the sound of his beautiful voice. We never touched each other, never physically shared more than the rather chaste kiss that I looked forward to every night on the stage; and yet we had unquestionably fallen deeply in love. Sometimes Sybil, his new wife, would come and join the company. I felt no guilt, as I didn't seem to understand my own feelings, and I knew that I had nothing to be ashamed of.

The Lady's Not for Burning opened in London to splendid reviews and played for nearly two years. Richard and I went back to leading our own lives, and, for the time being, our relationship changed into the cooler one of two young actors who were playing opposite each other, who were fond of each other, and sometimes had a lemonade shandy with other members of the company when the curtain came down. At least, I had a lemonade shandy (half sparkling lemonade, half light beer). Richard was drinking seriously even then, although it was taken as normal and rather "masculine" in those days for men to drink. The Welsh had always been known to like their beer, and Richard's father and brothers had been great drinkers. Richard was twenty-three and the disastrous effect this heavy drinking was to have on his future health was unknown to us. Sturdy and barrel-chested, Richard seemed to be indestructible. Drink only seemed to make his conversation more brilliant, and his wit livelier. He would line up glasses of beer interspersed with small glasses of straight whisky, and knock them back in turn. This lethal mixture was called a boilermaker. The other young actors tried to compete in this dangerous game, but Richard could drink them all under the table. Richard, with his Welsh wizardry, would seduce and charm young and old, male and female; onstage and off, we were all under the spell of his magnetic personality.

His presence on stage was hypnotic; one critic wrote that "he carries his own cathedral with him." This was partly the mesmerizing beauty of his eyes, but also a quality he had that was quite undefinable, and that I have never seen in any other actor. His voice, also, had a magnificence that only the Welsh seem to have; it was almost a chant, an incantation. The sense he gave of being utterly at one with himself, certain of his powers and sure of his sexual self, centered and complete within his own magic circle. During rehearsals, when I was still very ill at ease, and nervous of making mistakes, John Gielgud would turn to me and say, "Watch Richard. Why can't you be as simple and natural as he?" Richard, quite simply, *was* and there was no way to copy that. I watched him and I admired him, and knew that there was nothing to be done.

I longed for the hours when I could leave for the theater; I welcomed matinee days. In the intervals I would visit Richard's dressing room, or he mine. Other members of the company thought that we were having an affair; I had never slept with any man, and Richard was faithful to Sybil. I knew Sybil as a bright and resourceful young woman. Outside the theater we saw each other rarely. My friendship was with Richard and belonged in the world of the theater.

But this idyllic period in my life came abruptly to an end. I was offered a leading role in a production to be directed by Peter Brook; the play was Jean Anouilh's *Ring Round the Moon,* and the leading man was to be Paul Scofield; another leading role was to be played by the great comedienne Margaret Rutherford. Desperately as I wanted to perform this much-sought-after role, which I knew would be ideal for me in every way, just as strongly I wanted to stay with Richard and my family of friends in *The Lady's Not for Burning.* Of course I made the decision, which was the only one I could have made, to take the new role. Richard and I parted as friends, but there grew up between us a competitiveness, a jealousy, and almost a dislike of each other, which was only the mirror image of the love that we both felt but had never expressed or even quite understood.

CHAPTER FIVE

Limelight

My life proceeded to follow its own course — normal as far as I was concerned, far from so for any other young woman my age.

I was now, at nineteen years of age, starring in the West End of London in *Ring Round the Moon,* an exquisite and highly praised production. I still lived at home with my mother, and had no responsibility save to appear at the theater every evening six nights a week and twice on matinee days. The small salary I earned was enough to maintain our family, and even pay for most of John's school fees; the rich bride Eddie had gone to South Africa to find had not yet materialized.

I finally had two suitors, both twice my age, both distinguished, but neither of them the man of my dreams. I had as yet received no proposals of marriage, although suitor number one did ask me if I was prepared to give up my profession; to this I replied that I would rather die. That ended the discussion, as he was all set to become an important politician, and to have an actress wife, in those highly conventional days, was not the recipe for success. My mother was upset by my casting off, with so little compunction, such a well-to-do, intelligent suitor. How could I explain to her that I was hoping for a passion that would tear my life out by the roots.

I was an aspiring actress, pretty and talented; there were plenty of other actresses who were both. I had appeared at Stratford-upon-Avon as Ophelia, and had a charming but minor role in *The Lady's Not for Burning;* now I was appearing in *Ring Round the Moon;* that was the extent of my accomplishment. Then, backstage in the intermission one evening, I received a telephone call. It was from Olive Harding, who told me Charles Chaplin had heard about my performance in London. He was in search of a new leading lady; would I send photographs of myself to his studio as soon as possible?

What did I do? Instead of the excitement that I should have felt that this genius had the remotest inkling of my existence, I became paralyzed. For the first and, I believe, only time in my life, my sense of adventure deserted me. I didn't send the photographs. I tried to forget about the phone call. I didn't believe all this could be real. I couldn't face the enormous shift in my life that would happen if, by some miracle, I was cast in Chaplin's movie. I went on with my life as though nothing had happened. This threat of uprooting was so traumatic to me, I had attended so many schools, lived in so many different houses; I longed to keep the small amount of stability I had so dearly won. Of course, stability and an actor's life have never gone hand in hand, although, with all my heart, it is what I longed for.

However, this ostrichlike head of mine, so deeply hidden in the sand, had eventually to be rooted out. A further telegram arrived from Chaplin. "WHERE ARE THE PHOTOGRAPHS? CHARLES CHAPLIN." I saw the name on the piece of paper. Instead of prevaricating an instant longer, I sprang to life. This was serious stuff. I sent the photographs. I realized that what I wanted was to be Chaplin's leading lady more than I had ever wanted anything in the world; more than the Juliet costume that my mother had made for me, more than the role of Elizabeth the First of England. Now I waited every day in a state of tension for an acknowledgment that Chaplin had received the photos. Finally it came. Chaplin invited me and my mother — he had had quite enough experiences of young actresses getting him into trouble — to fly to New York for a week; he would come from Los Angeles to meet us. We were to rehearse together scenes from his new film, which I now learned was to be called *Limelight,* and, at the end of the week, the scenes would be filmed, Chaplin would return with the footage to Los Angeles, and show the tests to his associates there, and I would return to my play.

Two weeks after receiving this invitation, my mother and I were on our way to New York. Although I had not flown in a plane since our flight from Portugal during the war, I was less frightened of the journey than I was of the arrival. The only Chaplin I could imagine meeting was the maestro who had directed and acted in *The Great Dictator, The Gold Rush,* and *City Lights;* that he could be a human being as well seemed impossible to imagine. I was very conscious that I was not well dressed; I knew that I could appear at first meeting to be very withdrawn and inhibited. I was chillingly afraid that I wouldn't make a good impression.

When we came through immigration, Chaplin was waiting to greet us. Neither my mother nor I ever dreamed that he would come to the airport. He looked very tanned, very trim, his blue eyes bright and lively. With him was Jerry Epstein, who was to assist him in directing our scenes together. Chaplin held out a small hand in greeting. "I was worried that I had you fly all this way on my behalf; I was afraid something might happen to you." Chaplin himself, at this period in his life, wouldn't get on a plane, and had taken the long train journey from Los Angeles to New York to meet us.

From that moment on, I was never nervous or shy when I was with him, although I could be with other far less intimidating people. Through the years of my long and precious friendship with Chaplin and with his wife, Oona, I never forgot that I was in the presence of a very great genius. Chaplin himself, modest as he always was in manner and behavior, was also quite aware of who he was and of his unique position in twentieth-century culture.

When we got into the car, Chaplin began to question my mother — only fourteen years younger than he — about the London they both remembered; about the music halls, the eel and pie shops, the vital Cockney life that had all but vanished by the time I was born. Chaplin couldn't stop reminiscing about his life as a young boy in the slums of London, of the workhouse where he and his half brother were sent when their mother became incapable of caring for them, of the poverty, the elegance, the melancholy of the turn-of-the-century London of his youth. My mother, with none of the reserve or nervous self-consciousness that I knew her to be capable of, was vivacious and full of information when talking about the London where they both had grown up, and which Chaplin had not visited since 1931.

Up to this point, I had not seen the script of *Limelight;* I knew nothing of it beyond the fact that Chaplin was to play a clown whose career had faded, and that the role I was trying out for was of a young dancer. Chaplin told me that although I would be given the script to study, I must hand it in to Jerry Epstein at the end of each working session. I didn't understand such secrecy then, but it became clearer to me as time went on. Chaplin had been the subject of vicious attacks by the U.S. press, both for his political position — this was during the McCarthy era — as well as his sexual preference for very young women. Six years previously Chaplin had been the defendant in a paternity suit brought against him by a young woman with whom he had been foolish enough to have a brief affair. Although his marriage to Oona O'Neill, daughter of the playwright Eugene O'Neill, had brought him all the happiness he had vainly sought in one young girl after another, even this newfound serenity was vilified in the press, and made to seem the seduction of an innocent young woman by an aging and lascivious satyr. Chaplin was well within his rights to be suspicious of everyone, even including the little English girl.

Later in the afternoon, still not feeling in the least tired, my mother and I went to change for dinner. In every way Chaplin made us welcome, and treated us to a magnificent week in New York. We were taken to the finest restaurants, where, compared to the austerity of postwar London, the food was so abundant that we were both astonished. I realize only now how courageous it was of him to appear in a public place at that time in New York. People dining at other tables continually looked in his direction, some commenting audibly, and far from kindly, about his political opinions.

Chaplin, who must have been used to this by now, took no notice of any of them, and told us instead about his wife, Oona. He spoke of her loyalty and devotion to him throughout his political ordeal. She was expecting their fourth child, otherwise she would have come with him to New York. He told us that in Oona he had found the woman with whom at long last he was completely happy.

In spite of these evenings in Chaplin's company, the week was one of extreme tension. It was late spring, 1951, and my mother and I would go out to a local coffee shop for breakfast before rehearsals began. There I would question her obsessively about my chances: Was I pretty enough? Did Chaplin like me? Would he choose me? Couldn't she look into some magic glass and assure me that I would be given the role in Limelight and not be cast back to our old life? By now, under the spell of Chaplin's intelligence and glamour, the stability of London was losing some of its old appeal. Both my mother and I knew that a chance had come my way that could change my life; that, should I turn out to be the chosen one, my future career would be assured.

I was told to be in Chaplin's suite for rehearsal at ten. We were to work every day that week until six, chaperoned and directed by Jerry Epstein. Chaplin relented enough to tell me that I could read the full script, not just the scenes that we were to work on, but that I must still return it to Jerry every night. He was a most exacting director, and would give me every inflection, ask me to mimic his every gesture. I, an obedient and captivated acolyte, would obey and copy everything he did. This form of direction, which I am certain I would have resented intensely in later years, was absolutely fine for me at that time. Chaplin demonstrated the least detail with such perfection that I couldn't imagine, when he played my role for me to watch, anyone being more feminine, more fragile, more vulnerable; so I simply observed and tried to copy Chaplin.

We went to Brooks, the theatrical costumier, to outfit me for the test. Chaplin was absolutely precise about what he wished me to wear. "My mother wore a dress like that, she wore a shawl of that color." I realized that it was a composite picture he wanted me to create for him; not only his young mother, lost to him in the past, but also his young wife, Oona, loving and devoted. The two most important female images in his life were to be fused in the one portrait of a young and helpless girl, whom he was now able, in the guise of a film character, to rescue from her fate, and to make whole again.

At some point during this fitting, Chaplin and Jerry must have realized that they had never seen my legs. The "New Look" was then all the rage, and the skirts of that period reached to just above the ankle. An excuse was soon made for me to try on a tutu and tights, although no such scene was being filmed for the test. I understood that I couldn't play a ballerina in the film if I turned out to have legs like a grand piano. Luckily, both of them passed scrutiny.

My mother and I were to leave for London on Sunday, so we did the test on Saturday, at a little-used film studio in Brooklyn. I was close to panic until I realized that Chaplin intended to give me every gesture, every inflection, just as he had done during our hours of rehearsal. Imitating him, I gained confidence. I almost enjoyed myself.

I went back to the hotel full of the day's events, and told Mother I felt that I had done well, and in my big scene, the scene where Theresa finds out that she can walk again, I believed that Chaplin had been pleased with me. I could tell her nothing more.

We all went for a farewell dinner that last evening, and when a friend stopped by our table, Chaplin said that he wanted him to meet a "wonderful young actress." That lifted my spirits somewhat, as, after all the strain and excitement was nearly over, I had begun to feel hollow and depressed. I knew that, in reality, I was only on trial, and that there was still a long time to wait before I would know if I had the role. Chaplin was to take the film back with him to Los Angeles, and he told me that it would be at least ten days before he could let me know his decision.

The return journey was sad and difficult for both of us, as I did nothing but question my mother as to her opinion of my chances, and must have driven her to distraction. We landed in London on Monday morning, and I had to return to the play that night. At twenty I was so young and strong that I didn't feel in the least tired. I wanted to tell everyone in the cast about my week in New York, but, apart from Margaret Rutherford, who wanted to know every detail, no one else was even interested.

Our flat looked poor and dreary after the Sherry Netherland Hotel; my life seemed dull and empty. My brother John came home from school at the weekend, talking incessantly about cricket, and we did nothing but argue. I began to go to the movies every afternoon, in order to escape reality and make the time go faster. Three weeks passed, and then four. I still hadn't heard. Then a wire arrived from Chaplin's business manager to say that I should be hearing further within the next fortnight. This only seemed to increase my anguish, for I couldn't work out whether this meant good news or bad. When, four weeks later, I still had received no word, I felt very desolate indeed. I felt that I had failed, had let down both myself and my mother, that everyone knew of my disgrace and was laughing at me behind my back.

Three full months after I had made the test with Chaplin, a telegram arrived at my agent's office. I was going to Hollywood. I was going to be Charles Chaplin's leading lady in his film *Limelight*. The news took several days to sink in; at first all I felt was an enormous surge of relief that the tension-filled period of waiting was over. Then I realized that I had got the role of a lifetime. I was filled with glorious happiness.

The role of Theresa in Chaplin's *Limelight,* the film performance in which I take the most pride, is that of a young girl who is ready to sacrifice her life for a much older man, a man who had rescued her from suicide and literally talked her back into life again. How, under the circumstances, should she not be willing to give him her youth and devotion in return? The sensible answer to that question is that many young women would be extremely reluctant to do so; they would thank the elderly gentleman, and then get on with their life. Chaplin had chosen me to embody this ideal of pre-Victorian self-immolation, and he had good reason to do so. For he sensed in me an instinctive romantic sensibility similar to his own. I believe that in the stories my mother had quite innocently passed on to me, *The Snow Queen* and *The Little Mermaid,* so innocently read to me years ago in a sunlit garden, stories of one young girl after another who had sacrificed herself at the altar of romantic love, and the story of her own youthful infatuation with an unattainable man, had given me an extremely distorted image of sexual relationships between men and women. As long as I was able to act out these sacrificial fantasies in the roles I played onstage or in films, I was to be fairly safe from harm.

Nora in Ibsen's *A Doll's House,* who changes during the course of the play from a child-wife to a determinedly independent woman, Blanche DuBois in *A Streetcar Named Desire,* whose neurotic fantasies end in the destruction of herself and nearly everyone around her, Mme. Ranevskaya in Chekhov's *The Cherry Orchard,* impractical, vain, and romantic and all too vulnerable — in all of these women I found a common ground;

I felt that what had happened to them in the course of the play could just as easily have happened to me; and Theresa in Chaplin's *Limelight* fitted very neatly into this same pattern.

Into this film Chaplin would bring two characters from his childhood that his memory could never abandon; the defeated father and the broken and unbalanced mother. However, in Theresa, the damaged girl was finally allowed to develop into a mature woman, strong and independent.

In *Limelight* I was given the chance to play out my own childhood dream, inspired by my own broken family — the dream of the fairy godfather. Chaplin, with his deep intuition about human types, had seen that he would be able to focus all that raw hunger into my performance. The dream inherent in the story — of a fairy godfather who comes to the rescue of a young ailing girl, who heals her with his loving presence — this dream was so deeply rooted in my real-life longing that even the youthful crudities of my performance would seem to have been overshadowed by the fervor and conviction that I eventually brought to the role.

But a very important decision had to be made before I left for Hollywood, one that troubled my mother: whether she should come with me on this second journey to America and leave John, only fourteen years of age, behind or whether someone could be found to accompany me in her stead. The filming was to take place over the period of four months, and that was a long time to leave behind a boy whose wishes had always seemed to take second place to those of his older, and often extremely demanding, sister. Apart from the fact that I was deeply nervous of going alone, Chaplin had requested, and indeed offered to pay for, a chaperone, preferably my mother.

Eventually the decision was reached for my mother to accompany me, and for John to board at Westminster School, where he was already enrolled as a day boy; her decision was a great relief to me, but one that she was to question for the rest of her days. I think my mother always felt that, because of the difficulties of my career — the traveling and the nervousness involved in performing, both off- and onstage — she had unwittingly given John, whom she dearly loved, not nearly enough of the attention that he needed. The tension that existed between my dearly cherished brother and myself was a result of those early years, when he must have felt overwhelmed by having a sister whose needs always seemed to come before his own. That he has carved out such a fine career for himself — John is an Academy Award–winning film editor — is a source of immense pride to me, as it was also to my mother. That we have, years ago, reconciled our differences, and that John and his wife, Sheila, are as close to me as it is possible for a brother and a sister-in-law to be, remains a source of comfort and solace.

On the day we were to arrive by train in Los Angeles, I sat on the edge of my bunk watching the sun rise, dressed and ready, waiting to show Mr. Chaplin how right he had been in choosing me.

This time I had no fear at all, only a great sense of anticipation; when the train drew up to the platform and we alighted to meet the representative Chaplin had sent to meet us, I was excited and totally confident. It was the late summer of 1951.

The following morning I went down to the lobby at our hotel, where Chaplin was waiting for me. "You will have to diet," he said; it hadn't occurred to me that I was overweight, but I obviously looked too healthy for a starving girl. "We will both have to diet," he added, somewhat softening the blow. His small, tanned hands never stopped gesticulating, even when he was driving, as he described to me how my weeks in preparation for the film were to be spent. I was to go with his wife, Oona, every morning to an exercise class, then she would drive me back to their house, where Chaplin and I would rehearse our scenes together from eleven until four; then I was to go to a ballet class for the next hour. There was to be no lunch break — this he emphasized — for *either* of us.

This was to be my regimen for the next five weeks, until we

began the actual filming; it sounded wonderful to me. Because he had chosen me, my confidence was, by now, boundless. I only wanted even more tasks to perform for this adored taskmaster.

We arrived at the Chaplin house, and Oona appeared at the top of the staircase, wearing a green velvet dress, whose color complemented her dark good looks; I was astonished to see how alike in type we were. When Chaplin had invited me to come to New York to make the film test with him, he told me that he had done so on the basis of the startling resemblance that the photographs I had sent him bore to his wife. Our close friendship was to last until the end of her life. Even at first Oona and I realized how many qualities we had in common. We both tended toward shyness, and would contentedly sit through a social evening and let others do the talking — especially if the other was the magically entertaining Chaplin. Our reticence drew us together, but our lasting friendship began after I left for England, and we would correspond. Letters enabled these two shy young women to confess how fond they had become of one another, and made it easier to show this friendship next time we met.

Chaplin spoke of *Limelight* as though it were to be the crowning achievement of his career. Listening raptly to this extraordinary man, I abandoned whatever loyalty I still might have had to my own vanished father, and adopted, on the instant, the father I believed I had every right to expect: brilliant, worldly, charming, rich, and strong.

The weather was always fine, and we were able to rehearse every day in the garden. Chaplin was never in repose for a single instant, always demonstrating for me, as he had done in New York, how I was to perform this, what effect I was going to be able to achieve by doing that. Explaining the position of the camera so that when we actually came to film, I would take the camera for granted. Nothing was to be left to chance; there was to be no such thing as chance; there was only his genius.

The rehearsals were intense, and we were all three, Chaplin,

Jerry Epstein, and I, exhausted when the afternoon session came to an end. I then went off to my ballet class, an extremely willing but also very tired pupil.

In the evenings, when I hadn't been invited to the Chaplins', my mother and I would walk down Hollywood Boulevard. We never tired of watching the extraordinary forms of life that were to be seen there; better than going to any movie — it *was* a movie. Every freak in the world seemed to come there, displaying themselves and waiting to be discovered. Would-be stars of every age and description checked their images in the storefront windows as they passed, preened themselves and postured in the hope of attracting attention. Watching them from the inexpensive café where we would have our dinner did nothing to diminish the sensation I frequently had in California: that I was living out a dream, even if it was an exciting and fascinating one.

As the day to begin the actual filming approached, the sense of anticipation I had felt during the weeks of rehearsal and planning changed to dread and apprehension.

To ease me into the filming, we began the shooting with a scene where I was required merely to lie in a coma, so that, when the time arrived for us to begin to film our important work, I had been given the time to feel reasonably comfortable with the camera, and to lose some of the awe I still felt to be performing with Chaplin. Gradually, I gained confidence, and by the time we were to film our important scenes together, I was quite at ease, and saw Chaplin as my supportive and brilliant partner. We played effortlessly together. All those meticulous rehearsals had paid off.

The filming was drawing to its end; above anything in the world I didn't want to be told to go home. I know that my mother longed to get back to John and to her own life; all I longed for was that, in some magical way, the filming of *Limelight* might go on forever.

My dismissal came in a phone call from the Chaplin office; I would be given two extra weeks of expense money, in case I was needed for any looping or postproduction work, but then my job for the Chaplin studios was over. I felt that I was losing the most precious family I would ever have, and although Oona and Chaplin promised to come to London, I dreaded our departure. On February 9, 1952, my mother and I boarded the train for our return journey to England; we had been in America just over four months. I already saw that the months ahead would be a hiatus in my professional life, a time when I would just have to wait for *Limelight* to be released; I had no job to go back to in London, and, after the affluence of the life I had seen and liveliness of the experience I had had in Hollywood, I knew that in contrast my life back home would appear gray and lusterless. *Limelight* was the summit of my early career and far exceeded all my youthful fantasies. But still I was not content.

CHAPTER SIX

The Old Vic

ONE OF THE MOST AMAZING THINGS about myself at this period of my life was that I simply accepted every miraculous offer that came my way as part of the stream of good fortune that was flowing toward me. I was offered, soon after my rather reluctant return to London, the role of Juliet at the Old Vic Theatre; the same theater where, sitting in the "Gods" with my mother, I had seen Laurence Olivier and Ralph Richardson perform their greatest roles.

The Old Vic Theatre was launched in 1880 by Emma Cons as the Royal Victoria Theatre. A devout member of the Church of England, this dour maiden lady determined to give the working class tea and culture in place of the beer and music hall cheer which they had formerly, and understandably, far more enjoyed. By sheer persistence, Emma Cons made her theater into a great success, and was enabled to draw upon a large and devoted following. She was succeeded in time by her niece, Lilian Baylis, and the theater became almost the equivalent of a national theater. Many fine actors performed there, and felt privileged to do so, although the financial rewards were minimal — Lilian Baylis was once heard to pray to the Almighty: "O Lord! Send me a good actor, cheap." There was no finer place in England in which to learn your craft.

The repertoire was grounded in the works of Shakespeare, although the Jacobean and Restoration dramatists were also performed.

When I joined the Old Vic Company, a particular style of verse speaking was expected; all was decorous, well staged, and unremarkable. There was little deep psychological investigation into the motivation of the character — a rehearsal process that is now taken for granted. At rehearsal all discussion was rudimentary or nonexistent; the only interesting conversations were those carried out in the dressing rooms among the actors themselves. Of course, a great actor is a great actor; however Olivier, Gielgud, or Richardson managed to achieve his characterizations, the result was an illumination of the meaning of the text as brilliant and sudden as a bolt of lightning. The blandness of English female acting was at that time almost universal. The need to "be a lady" had hindered the development of English actresses. There were no great Cleopatras, the one great tragic role in Shakespeare equal to the roles for male actors. The finest actress of her generation was Irene Worth, who had been born in America and only arrived in England in her early twenties.

I had no interest in being a lady. Also, my foreign background had predisposed me to reject "Englishness" with a certain amount of scorn. I was fortunate to have been the product of a history and family for whom the world of the arts was a natural arena. My physical appearance and culture singled me out from the other fine young actresses of my generation — Dorothy Tutin, Virginia McKenna, Glenda Jackson, Maggie Smith, Joan Plowright, Rachel Roberts, Jill Bennett, and Rosemary Harris.

I had no idea that I would be breaking new ground when I played the role of Juliet; I just played her as passionately and honestly as I knew how. I didn't worry about the so-called beauty of the verse, only about the clarity of meaning, the expression, the passionate intensity, that I recognized as the center of Juliet's agonizing predicament. I was more fascinated by the journey that she made from a naïve young girl to a desperate and defiant woman, than I was whether I spoke the verse to the satisfaction of the critics.

Although now it has become mandatory for actors to play

roles for which their age makes them suitable, when I appeared at the "Vic" in the early fifties, the great roles were nearly always given to mature actors, no matter how suitable or unsuitable their physical appearance. At the age of twenty-one, it was considered almost impudent of me to want to play the role of a fourteen-year-old girl. It was with great relief that I read the memoirs of the nineteenth-century actress Fanny Kemble; she had been twenty when she first played the part — and was criticized for undertaking the role at so early an age.

We were a company of young actors. Apart from Athene Seyler, who played my nurse, and Sir Lewis Casson, as Friar Lawrence, we were in our twenties or early thirties. Alan Badel was to be a passionate and Italianate Romeo, and Peter Finch a brilliant and incisive Mercutio.

The bus journey across Waterloo Bridge and down the Waterloo Road to the theater was as thrilling to me as though I were Caesar crossing the Rubicon. The views of the City of London and of St. Paul's Cathedral as I looked down the Thames were lovely to my bedazzled eyes, and indeed, in the two and a half years that I worked at the Old Vic Theatre, I never tired of those views down the river; of the good Cockney atmosphere of the Waterloo Road, and the seething atmosphere of The Cut, an outdoor market round the corner from the theater that had been a trading place since medieval times.

Before starting rehearsals, I had gone away alone to a cottage near Stratford-upon-Avon that had been recommended to me by Paul Scofield. There I spent a week studying my text, learning my lines, walking in the countryside, and daydreaming about the romance I might have with either of the leading actors in the company; the fact that they were both married men and a great deal older than I didn't worry me a jot; I never intended my daydreams to go beyond daydreams.

Seated in the circle at the first reading of the play between Finch and Badel, I had little trouble deciding which of them I would choose; Badel was playing Romeo and I was playing Juliet — I still had trouble differentiating the play lover from the real. In any case, having a crush on my leading man certainly wouldn't hurt my performance.

As my turn to speak drew near, all my confidence suddenly vanished, and I became temporarily deaf; I missed my first cue when it came, and was certain that the rest of the cast despised me for my error and thought that I had been cast as Juliet only because I had appeared in a still unreleased film by Chaplin. I was to learn that all actors are terrified of a first reading and that no one has the slightest interest in any actor other than himself.

In the beginning of rehearsal I was more at home with the ardent early Juliet than I was to be in the later, more mature and passionate scenes. I began to reread my notes, and study books on earlier performances of the play, in the hope that I could find some shortcut out of my difficulties; then I decided to let go and throw myself into the part. No footnote was going to help me play the role; what I needed was to abandon myself to the character of the frail yet indomitable girl, and chart her emotional course from the delicate child in the earlier half of the play to the determined and passionate woman she becomes in the later scenes. We opened the production in Edinburgh at the Assembly Rooms, where generations of dour Scottish Presbyterian ministers had convened for ecclesiastical business. Outside, a statue of John Knox pointed a finger toward heaven, bidding the viewers to forsake all earthly delights; nonetheless, our production was never again quite as sexual and delightful as it had been in those solemn and hallowed halls.

The first night of the play in London was the greatest theatrical test of my life, the most intimidating and the most terrifying; it was also the most electrifying and exciting. On the morning of the premiere I felt the dead depression that always descends on me before a first night; I know other actors claim to feel a sense of excitement and exhilaration, but I know many who feel just as I do. But, as the hour to leave for the theater draws near, some kind of adrenaline takes over; the heart begins to beat very fast, and the hands to tremble; a feeling of delicious anticipation begins to flood your entire being. If I had kept a journal of my first night, it would go something like this. It would be more or less the journal of every first night, save that, for the young actress, Juliet is the great test of a career, as important as Cleopatra or Lady Macbeth are to be later in a female player's life.

Monday, September 15, 1952

Rested from two until four. Then tea, a boiled egg, toast with lots of honey for energy. Bathed, dressed, and took a taxi to the theater. The dressing room full of flowers, telegrams piled on the makeup table. Put on a dressing gown, and lie on the floor for ten minutes with the light out, to restore my concentration. I start to make up. Feel much calmer now, try not to worry about whether I will feel as true and alive in the role as I did when in Edinburgh. Try not to worry about anything; to clear my mind. Three-quarters of an hour to go before the curtain goes up. I go to the other actors' dressing rooms to wish them luck. Back to my own room, where I begin to hum my vocal exercises. Think that my mother, in the audience, will be feeling even more nervous than I. Half an hour until the performance will be announced over the loudspeaker. Marie Antoinette on her way to the guillotine may have felt something of the dread that comes over me. The quarter of an hour is called, and my dresser comes in to put me into my opening costume. Five minutes is announced, and the actors who begin the play are summoned to the stage. Suddenly there is silence, and I hear the seats pushed back as the audience rise to their feet for the national anthem. A murmuring of excitement as they take their seats again. Silence, and I know the house lights have gone out. I hear the opening music for Romeo and Juliet. The curtain rises, and the actor who plays the Chorus begins his speech:

> *"Two households, both alike in dignity*
> *In fair Verona where we lay our scene."*

It is happening. I want to go home. I have to remind myself how many years I have wanted this. I go into the wings and find a place where I can sit and listen. Suddenly I feel very young, extremely childlike, very calm. I hear my cue, and run across the stage toward my mother and my nurse. Everything fades save the reality of the play. I feel as though I have a wonderful story to tell.

Alan Badel and I lie dead in each other's arms on the tomb of the Capulets. The lines that have always moved me so deeply are spoken over us:

"For never was a story of more woe
Than this of Juliet and her Romeo."

The curtain falls to a muffled roll of drums. Alan and I scramble to our feet and join the other actors in line for the curtain call. We took sixteen calls; it began to dawn on me that we might be a success.

I cannot remember what happened after the play. I know many people came round to see me, some very famous actors whom I knew only by name; I only recall my mother, looking stunning in a dress bought for the occasion; she was happy with my performance, although she had a few notes which she would give me the following day. As usual, they were accurate. That kept my feet firmly on the ground. In fact, my mother always saw to it that I kept a very level head, and didn't let the success I had that night, or on any subsequent occasion, affect me in any profound way. Not that we didn't both get tremendous pleasure from my early achievements; it was simply that the danger of taking oneself too seriously or expecting that life could possibly continue in this exalted sphere was not being in the least realistic, and only asking for pain and disappointment later in life.

My reviews the next day were everything a mother could wish; even so, one reviewer complained that I had all the requisite passion for Juliet, but had difficulty speaking the verse, while another said that my command of the verse was extraordinary but that I was not yet fully in touch with Juliet's youthful passion. At the close of this remarkable week, two things happened to make my happiness complete. Kenneth Tynan, the most brilliant critic of his day, hailed my performance as the finest Juliet he had ever seen, and I received a wire from Oona to say that she and Charlie were coming to London for the opening of *Limelight,* and that they would arrive in time to see my performance.

Even now it is almost impossible for me to accept the fact that both Oona and Charlie are dead; Jerry Epstein as well, who was so much a part of the story. Of course, I understand that Charlie was born in 1889, and it is ridiculous to wish that he were still here, but Oona and Jerry were only a few years older than I.

In later years Oona had everything in life except Charlie, and nothing would ever make up to her for his loss; neither the love of her children or grandchildren nor the devotion of her friends. Oona had lived through and for Charlie, and although she survived him by several years, her life meant little to her without him.

Mercifully, all this sadness was hidden in the future; now I waited for Oona and Charlie to arrive in London.

About three weeks after the first night of *Romeo and Juliet,* *Limelight* was to open at the Empire Theatre, Leicester Square. Headlines in the London papers, only a few days prior to their arrival, reported that Chaplin's reentry permit to the United States had been withdrawn while he was still on the ocean heading for London. On leaving New York, he had been adamant that he would not embark for Europe until the U.S. Immigration Office had assured him that all his tax affairs were in order, and he would be free to return to the States in six months' time. The main reason he had not visited England for the past twenty years, or even gone abroad, was the fear of being unable to return to his home and his studios in the United States; just as he had anticipated, this was what had happened.

I read the papers with mounting alarm, as I knew the severity of the blows that this news would inflict on two people I had come to love. I also worried — with reason, as it turned out — that however fine *Limelight* might be, it might not get the reception it deserved from the critics or public in the United States. I had witnessed firsthand the baiting of Chaplin while I was there, and knew that the witch-hunt against so-called Communists and other "un-Americans" was far from over. This further strike against Chaplin would give the signal for an all-out assault on him, both as a man and as a filmmaker.

The political persecution that had begun in the mid-1940s was finally to achieve its goal and Chaplin did not return to the United States until 1971; a frail and ailing man of eighty-two, he flew with Oona to Hollywood to accept an Oscar from the Academy of Motion Pictures. It had come to him many decades too late. Privately he told me that, as he took his bows, at each courtly obeisance he would murmur, "Fuck you and fuck you and fuck you." And who could blame him for that.

When I arrived at the Savoy Hotel to have tea with Oona, she was her usual calm and radiant self; she even tried to comfort *me,* by assuring me that there had been a showing of *Limelight* in Hollywood and that the film had been warmly received. However, she told me how much she was dreading the journey that she might have to make back to California to close the house, to dismiss the domestic staff who had been with her for eight years, and go to the bank to bring back to Charlie the contents of a safe deposit box containing all the documents concerning the Chaplin studios and the family's financial affairs. There was no one to do it save herself, and she would be ready to leave whenever Charlie wished her to go. Chaplin arrived back at the hotel a little while later, and was far too preoccupied with the injustice done to himself and his family to take much notice of me; he just greeted me as someone he had seen only a day ago, and that was fine with me.

Some days later, after the first shock had worn off, and Oona was taking an afternoon nap, Charlie said he would enjoy a walk around Covent Garden Market and invited me to go with him. It was a rainy day, gray and fairly depressing, the weather Charlie always liked best when in London, as it evoked for him many of his earliest memories. The word that Charlie had appeared must have gone around the market stalls almost as soon as we arrived, and, very quietly, the stall holders gathered in the rain waiting for him to pass. No one disturbed him, no one asked for Charlie's autograph; they simply waited for him to go by and then murmured, "God bless, Charlie." No reception for a returning monarch could have been more moving, and no greeting more courteous. The Cockneys were welcoming back one of their own. I believe that this meant more to Charlie than any of the adulation he was to receive on later and more glittering occasions, and I know that I have never been as touched and proud as I was that afternoon, when I walked by Charlie's side.

Oona and Charlie came to the Old Vic to see my performance as Juliet, and came backstage to meet the cast, who were all waiting onstage to greet the great man; then Oona had to make the journey that she was dreading so much, the journey alone back to the United States.

She left the hotel on a dark and gloomy afternoon, and Jerry accompanied her to the airport; Charlie didn't want to take the chance of anyone recognizing him if he went himself. This was a clandestine rescue operation, and Oona was the one who had to do it. I stayed in the hotel suite with Charlie after she left, and together with some of his friends, we went out to dinner; the other guests must have wondered why Charlie was so silent. *Limelight* was to open in a few days, and they expected him to be his usual ebullient self, and to regale them with stories of the making of his film, not to be sunk in a mood of such melancholy and bitterness; but Chaplin well knew that this attack on him in the United States would only further harm his image in the American press, and could mean that this film, which he considered his finest, might even be banned there altogether.

Oona came back several days later, having accomplished everything she had set out to do. Charlie visibly relaxed and started to get excited about the opening of *Limelight*. I took the tube to Leicester Square to see the sign outside the movie theater, to find that Chaplin had given me billing almost equal to his own. I tried to concentrate on my performance as Juliet, and not to be too distracted by all the excitement surrounding me. My mother, with her usual cleverness, had contacted one of the leading couturiers of the day, John Cavanagh, and asked him to design my dress and coat for the premiere. This he did for very little money — which was just as well, as we had very little — and it was magnificent. The coat, made of green silk velvet trimmed with white fur at the collar and cuffs, is now in the costume museum at the Castle Howard.

I couldn't attend the showing of the film itself, as I had a performance that night; I was to arrive later, appear onstage, and then be presented to Princess Margaret. Instead I went to view *Limelight* for the first time at a press preview some days earlier. I sat next to Charlie as the film unfolded. It was the most charming film I had ever seen, and the most touching. It not only evoked the magic of backstage theater, but also, with great emotional gravity, documented the ridiculous farce of human breakdown and recovery. It was both funny and, like everything else Chaplin conceived, heartbreaking as well.

The film finished, the lights went on; there was a long silence. Then the audience filed out into the foyer without a sound. Exhausted from watching myself on film for the first time, emotionally drained by the film's tragic close, I simply didn't have the energy to say a single word; Chaplin must have felt somewhat the same, and he too said nothing. We went out onto the staircase overlooking the foyer and saw that the audience had been waiting for Charlie to appear; then they began to applaud and went on doing so, or so it seemed to me, for an eternity. It was all so unexpected, so marvelous, that I burst into the tears I had tried to hold back, and in front of all these strange people, I threw my arms around Charlie's neck, and I kissed him.

My star was at its brightest; it is almost impossible to conceive of any young actress who had achieved so much so soon. As both Chaplin's leading lady and as a rising star in the classical theater, I had become famous overnight. My photograph appeared on the cover of *Time* magazine; I was photographed by *Vogue* and *Harper's Bazaar;* I was invited by society hostesses to attend grand dinners; I went out on deeply boring dates with a variety of chinless wonders; I was taken out to dinner by Prince Nicholas of Yugoslavia. It was all fascinating, but somewhat unreal, and I hoped I wasn't in danger of becoming a sought-out oddity.

My mother, with the money I had earned in *Limelight,* and with total certainty of my bright future, had bought a small but charming house in Chelsea, just off the Kings Road. Not yet the fashionable address it was to become in the sixties, it was, nevertheless, a good investment and one that would give us a more solid foundation than any we had enjoyed before. Moving into the house was exciting and glorious. I couldn't believe that my own money would enable us to live in such splendor. I had my own room, furnished with pale gray silk curtains and rose pink wallpaper, and my mother and John each had their own rooms as well. A housekeeper, Mrs. Ayling, was engaged to look after us, and she cooked dinner and brought me breakfast in bed; all this for remarkably little money. I didn't handle my own bills, all of which were taken care of either by my mother or by my agent, Olive Harding. I didn't know how to write a check. In fact, I was well on the way to being completely incapable of dealing with any kind of life outside a theatrical one; in this rarefied world I continued to flourish.

My life, and my mother's as well, was beginning to achieve some kind of stability. Then, the completely unexpected happened: I came home from rehearsal one afternoon to find Eddie sitting in front of the fire, drinking a cup of tea; as simple as that.

With no warning at all, my father had arrived back in London. His new wife, Bertha, was to follow him to England shortly, but in the meantime, here he was, having a cup of tea as though nothing had happened. My mother didn't know how to handle this situation, or what she was supposed to feel. Knowing Eddie as well as she did, she found it hard to feel anger at what he had put her through; he didn't see things quite as most other people might have done — to him there was something to be commended in marrying a rich woman in order to support your former family. He greeted me warmly and I coolly accepted his embrace; I really couldn't understand what on earth he was doing in the house after all the grief he had caused our family. He tried to question me about my success, of which he must have been very proud; I answered tersely and went to my own room. When I came down again, he had gone.

About three weeks later, after Bertha had joined him, both of them came to see my performance in *Romeo and Juliet*. I should, as a matter of good form, have offered them tickets, but I hadn't. The stage doorkeeper came to tell me that my father and his wife were there to see me; I asked him to bring them both to my dressing room.

Accompanying Eddie was a tiny, rather pretty woman, shy and quiet spoken; he introduced her as my stepmother. Recoiling as though I had seen a cobra, I said that I had no stepmother, as my own mother was still alive. When they invited me to supper, I refused; I had handled the situation as cruelly and stupidly as possible. I went home feeling sad and shaken, full of guilt, and shabby in the extreme. To have brought Bertha to see me perform was something that Eddie must have been promising her for ages. I had humiliated him in front of his new wife, and I wished I hadn't.

Three days later, very early in the morning, the telephone rang. My mother answered, and started to weep, repeating, "No, no." I begged her to tell me what had happened, and eventually she was able to say that Bertha was on the phone. Eddie had died in his sleep during the night.

We rushed over together to the flat that Eddie and Bertha had rented and went up some dark and winding stairs. In the living room, Bertha, looking smaller and more defenseless than ever, was huddled in an armchair. She asked if my mother wished to go and say good-bye to Eddie, who was still lying on the bed. He had died so quietly that Bertha hadn't even known it until she awoke beside him the next morning. My mother went into the bedroom alone, came out, and asked me to come in with her. I had never seen a dead person and was mortally afraid of what I might see. I went into the room; Eddie was lying peacefully on his side, his hand under his cheek; except for the deadly pallor of his face, he might have been asleep. My mother kissed him, and I did the same; his face was cold as ice. I believed then, and perhaps I was right, that it had been my callous behavior in the theater that had killed him; I afterward learned that Eddie had known he had a serious heart condition, and that his visit home had been, quietly, to say good-bye.

I canceled that night's performance; then I picked up and went on with my life.

I remained at the Old Vic to play Jessica in *The Merchant of Venice*, and was invited to return the following season. In the three-month break, I went to Berlin to act opposite James Mason in Carol Reed's film *The Man Between*. Mason proved to be a good colleague and a superb actor, and I was gaining confidence in myself off and on screen. On my return to the Waterloo Road, I was to play the roles of Ophelia, Viola, Helena, Virgilia, and Miranda; my leading man would be Richard Burton.

On the first day of rehearsal for the new season I went up the now familiar staircase to the rehearsal studio; Richard was talking to another actor in the middle of the room. For some reason, someone standing next to me remarked on what a large head Richard had; I wittily replied that perhaps he was growing it in order to play Caliban. Richard caught sight of me, and came over and kissed me; my biting wit somehow forsook me.

So much had happened to both of us since we had been the aspiring young actress and actor playing at the Globe Theatre. Although we were in our twenties — I was twenty-two and Richard twenty-seven — in the terms of our profession we had both reached almost equally dazzling heights for actors so young. However, in our offstage lives, we were very different. Richard, now a married man for four years, had had numerous romantic adventures in Hollywood, and was beginning to get a reputation as a ladies' man. I, on the other hand, was still living at home, very much the talented and cosseted young daughter. But the spark that had only fitfully ignited those few years ago now sprang to flame with an incandescence that astonished us both.

I don't think Richard ever took his courtship of me lightly; we both knew that something very serious had come into our lives.

The courtship was brief. Within a fortnight we had become lovers. We made love quietly in my room in the little house with my mother sleeping upstairs, who may, or may not, have known what was happening on the floor below. I was almost ignorant about sexual matters, and found this first experience perplexing. Richard was tender and considerate, and later we laughed and joked in relief at getting over this first hurdle. Richard left me in the early morning to go back home, and I went to sleep happy and childishly thrilled that I was a "woman" at last. I felt absolutely no guilt about anything, because I knew that to make love with Richard was something that *had* to happen.

I felt a little timid when I saw Richard at rehearsal the next morning, but he tenderly and affectionately joked and made gentle fun of me, and was immensely proud of me. Now, I felt, we truly belonged to each other.

We knew each other so well, were so intimate with each other already, that this further intimacy was just the physical consummation of an already accepted fact. Our joy in each other's presence at rehearsal was obvious to everyone. When free from rehearsal, we would drive to Regent's Park and lie on the grass, talking and daydreaming. I listened, a rapt and adoring audience, to Richard's tales of the Welsh mining community where he had grown up. To his stories of student life at Oxford, where he had been one of the first grammar school boys ever to have been awarded a scholarship. He managed to teach me some songs in the Welsh language — which he had spoken before learning English — and I can remember many of them to this day. Mrs. Ayling helped me to master the simple dishes that Richard enjoyed. My Jewish background appeared to him exotic; his Welsh working-class masculinity and vigor I found excitingly different from the Englishmen I had known.

That year at the Old Vic was, for everyone who was involved, a remarkable season. Richard played Hamlet, Coriolanus, Caliban, Sir Toby Belch, and proved that he was the great young actor of his generation. I played opposite him in five out of six productions we performed that season. Our friends in the company knew of our attachment to each other, but were always discreet and supportive; everyone knew that this was not just an "affair," but something precious and deeply spiritual for us both. Sometimes Sybil would come to the theater to pick up Richard for a late supper party. We behaved on these occasions as colleagues and friends. I have never known how much Sybil knew, or wanted to know. I am sure she knew that she had Richard's love and affection, and that, whatever his relationship was to me, to her he was, in his own way, a loyal and devoted husband. Perhaps we both instinctively guessed that Richard would never be completely true to one woman, and that Sybil and I between us filled the roles that Richard needed most: the mother he had never had and the dream woman that he would search for, and only temporarily find, all the rest of his life.

Sometimes Richard and I would go out to have a drink with the other actors after the play, sometimes he would come home with me, and sometimes Richard and I would go our separate ways; he home to Sybil and I to my house in Godfrey Street. Often, at some hour before dawn, I would hear the sound of his car draw up outside the house, and Richard would let himself in and come up to my room. He always left before it got light, so that he could tell Sybil that he had been up drinking all night with his pals; sometimes that was also true. How much of this Sybil guessed I can never know.

There was one deadly drawback to this first relationship: the secrecy that surrounded our offstage life was necessary but miserable. I came to dread the moment before dawn when Richard had to dress and go back to his wife. There were no answering machines in those days, and often I waited at home already fearing to miss one of his precious visits. I lived with a great deal of tension and loneliness. My mother had moved to a nearby flat, fearing to damage my fragile relationship with Richard. When, for some days, he didn't come to see me, and she was, quite rightly, leading her own life, the house we had bought together felt empty and sad. Then I simply waited for the day to pass, and the hour to come when I could go to the theater; there we were together in our own world.

Our dressing rooms had a communicating door, and we had a private life in the theater we were unable to have outside. We brewed the strong cups of tea we both enjoyed. Exchanged the gossip of the day. Sometimes even our lovemaking took place in the darkened room, between the matinee and the evening performance.

I remember that, somewhat to my surprise, Richard and I were able to go away to the country for a weekend. This was the only time I recall that we actually spent four days continu-

The marriage of my
maternal grandmother
and grandfather, 1901

My mother in her early
twenties.

With my father and mother on Brighton Pier, 1935.

My aunt Mary in the London theater of the early thirties.

Myself, aged six. This is the photo Philip Roth kept on his desk because it amused him.

The serious young actress, aged eight, dressed as Juliet, can be seen on the extreme left.

Peter Brook's production of Ring Round the Moon, *London, 1950. (Houston Rogers, Theatre Museum, V&A)*

With Richard Burton in Edinburgh for the Old Vic production of Hamlet, *1953.*

One of the back-stage scenes from Limelight.

LIFE

CLAIRE BLOOM
IN TV-FILM PREMIERE
OF 'RICHARD III'

20 CENTS

FEBRUARY 20, 1956

REG. U. S. PAT. OFF.

On the cover of Life,
1956.
(Phillipe Halsman,
© Halsman Estate.
© 1956 Time Inc.)

At the circus in Vevey with
Chaplin, 1955.

With Laurence Olivier in the film Richard III.

With Yul Brynner in the film The Brothers Karamazov, *1956*.

As pirate Bonnie Brown in the film
The Buccaneer, *1957.* *Photograph taken*
by costar Yul Brynner.
(Yul Brynner)

With Vivien Leigh in
Duel of Angels,
London, 1958.
(Angus McBean, Harvard
Theatre Collection)

Lunching with
Richard Burton
during the filming
of Look Back in
Anger, 1959.

ously alone together. We went to a hotel in Norfolk, and called ourselves Mr. and Mrs. Boothby. We had a log fire in our room, and spent most of our time there making love — we had never had such luxury before — no strain, no getting up to go home. In less than the year that had passed since we had first become lovers, I had come a long way.

It seemed to me, at the time, that this situation was really quite normal; that we would go on being together always, in spite of the seemingly insurmountable difficulties we faced. But Richard was to go back to Hollywood for three months to make a film, and I wasn't altogether sure what I was going to do next.

At the end of the season, before the company disbanded, we went to Elsinore to perform *Hamlet* in the courtyard of the palace where Shakespeare had set his play; after that, we were to perform at the Schauspielhaus in Zurich.

We all went to Denmark: Richard, Sybil, and I. Like everything else connected to that period, I remember it as a confusing and difficult time. I had come to hate the hiding in corners, the secrecy that accompanied Richard's visits to my hotel room. For Sybil, Richard always had the plausible excuse that he had been drinking all night. In Elsinore, even more than in London, that at least was true. The performance of *Hamlet* would end just before midnight, and the sun seemed to go down for only a couple of hours; by the time we had arrived back at the hotel and had some supper, it was already becoming light. I think the "boys" stayed up many nights without going to bed at all, just continued to drink from one day to the other. Sometimes Richard and I would go back to my room. Our sexual need for each other seemed to increase; I waited only for the times when we could be alone together. As the time to part grew nearer, I began to feel desperate and unsure. The only times I now felt secure and happy were when we were making love. Then everything else seemed unimportant.

Our next stop was Zurich, and we traveled by train. Richard and Sybil traveled in one compartment, and I in another, separated from theirs only by a sitting room. It seems incredible to me now that we got away with this, but Richard actually came into my compartment during the night, and we made love in the moving train.

We separated as planned at the end of the Zurich engagement; Richard and Sybil were to go to London, and then on to Hollywood. I went to Vevey to stay with the Chaplins for a few days, and then to London, to say good-bye to Richard.

Our parting was painful, as Richard had planned to come to my house on his last night in London. I was exhausted with strain and weeping and was also very young. I fell into the kind of sleep only young people can know, deep and heavy with strange dreams. Richard did come to the house, but hadn't his key, and I didn't hear his quiet tapping at my door. I awoke the next morning to realize that I had missed him, and he telephoned in a fury to say that I hadn't heard him, and that he must now leave without saying good-bye. I felt I had failed him miserably. All I could do was wait for his letters, and then for his return.

We wrote to each other every day, sometimes twice a day; Richard sent his letters directly to my house, and I sent mine, covertly, through his secretary. I realize only now, and to my great regret, that these letters would have had enormous meaning for me in later years. On the night before my marriage to Rod Steiger, I tore them up, and threw them into the fireplace.

In 1983, sorting through some papers, I found these letters preserved among them, undoubtedly because of some sloppy filing on my part. Only this one tangible proof remains to me of that enormous bond that held the two of us together all those years, and of the brilliant young man that Richard had once been.

17th Day   10th Sept. 1954

I'm sure I put 17th Day on yesterday's letter, in which case I was premature. They've had a program on TV called

"Mystery Eyes," in which they invite the public to recognize a pair of eyes. The prize for the correct answer was a Cadillac car. Well, the eyes were really mysterious. They were flashed on and off for 17 hours. Last night they were finally and correctly placed. You'd have won the Cadillac easily I hope. They were my eyes. It will take me some time to live it down. We are still doing *Hamlet* but this should be the last time I think. The closet scene being long and violent excited gasps of amazement, awe, and Jeeze how do you remember it all. It must, of course, be bad. We are really halfway through the picture now. Perhaps, who knows, in about 6 weeks I shall be on my way home and into your arms. I am now very thin and hollow-cheeked. I have dropped from twelve and one half stone to 165 lbs which is about 11 stone 10. Means I've lost about 11 lbs. I will lose another couple of pounds and then stop. I have one more scene to do today and then I stop. It's about 5:00 in the a.noon. I'm very tired. Tomorrow should be an easy day. Still no word from you. This must be the longest yet — over a week of silence. I'm sure it's not your fault. It better hadn't be! I'm fed up with filming already and long to go back on the stage and do something fabulous and meaty. I'll have to wait I'm afraid. I love you with awful intensity sometimes when I just sit in a trance staring at a piece of paper, pen poised and immovable, longing for you and remembering you and imagining you. I love you horribly and beautifully.

> All my love,
> Rich

Oct. 7th, 1954

Oh my lovely girl. It's been impossible to write you and even this is difficult. I've been ill in bed for a week — the first time I recollect being confined because of illness. (Apart from appendix removal in 1933.) Hence not able to write and if even so unable to post them. I've had a savage attack of flu. It must have been "Love Pine." Roaring temperatures and complete blockage of nose and chest. But all right now. We have a few days [of] retakes. Then home. I can't believe it but we'll be home. I think I shall do Badet (?) story. I hope that's all right with you. I really expect to be home within three or four weeks. Confined to the house it's impossible for me to read your letters but am going out tonight for the first time and will get to them hail or rain or blood.

I want to make absolutely certain that you get this so will write no more. I will write you better tomorrow. I love you so much. Your sarcastic letters are sweetly funny now that I know you still love me.

All my love.

Rich

November 5th, 1964

My Darling, my own sweet Babilee,

There was a clue in the crossword yesterday which was: "150 artists give you a girl." Well 150 Roman numerals is CL and the initials for artists are A.R.A. (Associate of the Royal Academy) so the answer was "Clara." I couldn't see the paper for longing. Only 20 days left now before I'm home. I'm counting the minutes. Time is so slow. I had a cable from Binkie asking me if I'd be available for a play before Christmas. He didn't say what play. It couldn't be for the two of us? A lovely midwinter with my lovely girl who'd be forced to sleep with me because of the cold. Always couch up to the working class. I would love to do a play with you. A beautiful love story. Heathcliff and Cathy. Working man and lovely Cupboard love! I'm actually in the process of reading a book called "The Lotus and the Wind" by John Masters. My company (our company) will probably do it, Jack Cardiff (the great cameraman) will direct it probably. His first directorial assignment and he might be wonderful. It will be shot mostly in Pakistan and you could so far so easily be the girl. Wouldn't it be odd if I signed for a film. We'd have terrible arguments about money. I'd say 20,000 and you'd say 10,000.

Be a good girl for twenty more days and then you can be as abandoned as you like. I haven't looked at another woman. This has never happened to me before. You have changed me so radically. I have almost grown up. Forgive this horrible biro. Such a slovenly pen. Keep warm and don't catch colds, and don't get wet. Practice chip making and steak and onions. All my love my lovely daughter.

     Rich

These letters are all that remain to me of the bond that existed between Richard and myself.

CHAPTER SEVEN

Lady Anne and Others

Two months passed in a vacuum; I simply waited for Richard's letters, and for the hours when I could reply to them. We wrote to each other sometimes twice a day. Again, the days and then weeks of waiting for the telephone to ring announcing the next job were interminable, and the strain on my nerves was extreme.

An actress, as opposed to a dancer, singer, or instrumentalist, has no way to prepare a new role until the new role comes her way; first there has to be the offer of a part, something which is beyond her control. In those days, in England, there was nothing like an Actors Studio where one could work on solving the pitfalls of certain roles within the congenial atmosphere of a class of actors and actresses. Also, whether I liked it or not, I was very much in the public arena, and had to be careful about the next engagement I accepted.

I received a telephone call. A voice asked me if I had received his letter. That voice belonged, quite unmistakably, to Laurence Olivier.

I didn't know what letter he was talking about — in fact it arrived the next day — and so I asked Olivier, in a confused way, what the letter had said. Olivier replied, "I have written to you asking if you would be my Lady Anne."

I had known that Olivier was making a film of *Richard III,* and rumor had it that his wife, Vivien Leigh, was to play opposite him. That the film should come my way was overwhelming.

Richard and I had been separated for some months, and I was always aware that I had no lasting claim on his affections beyond the fact that we loved each other. I knew that he would never leave his wife for me, that the ties of a shared Welsh background and of their very real delight in each other's company would hold them together more strongly than a more passionate relationship would ever do. I was lonely, sad, and when I started to work on *Richard III* I was extremely vulnerable. Not that, in any way, I doubted my love for Richard, or that everything both he and I said in our letters was not true. I was, at the same time, very unsure of myself, and desperately anxious about the future.

Laurence Olivier, outside his theatrical persona, was far different in character from either Heathcliff or Maxim de Winter. Extremely pragmatic, with a cool and impersonal sexuality that belied his dark and Italianate good looks, he had little interest in anything outside his own particular sphere of genius, and, unlike his more brilliant wife, Vivien Leigh, could even be somewhat pedestrian and dull. However, to play opposite him was like being caught in an electric current. His voice was incisively staccato, like a machine gun in its ability to rattle explosively. His characterizations were never less than extraordinary, and his greatest theatrical creation was Richard III. Lecherous, cruel, crafty, seductive, diabolically intelligent, triumphant even in his last despairing cry, "A horse, my kingdom for a horse," with his lank black hair resting on crooked shoulders, Olivier was the fatal combination of attractiveness and repulsiveness. Thus, in a manner far less aggressive than Richard's when he subdues Lady Anne — while also fulfilling an infinitely more casual agenda — did the actor playing the king seduce the young actress playing his conquest.

Although deeply under Olivier's spell, I was never remotely in love with him, and never, for one instant, confused my feeling for him with my love for Richard. I only confused the great actor with someone who turned out to be a surprisingly earthbound sort of man. In the character of Richard III Olivier was immensely seductive, his gray eyes mesmeric and his invective bitingly incisive. As Olivier himself, he had, by the time I came to know him, a dryness, a lack of spontaneity. Careful, somewhat plodding, full of theatrical mannerisms, he was brimming with a kind of false charm. But I ignored all the evidence; I saw only what I wanted to see, seeking only to continue a romance that was being enacted, considerably more emphatically, onscreen. It was the fascination of the rabbit to the snake. Who Olivier really was, I must confess, I have no idea. I suspect that, like many actors, he wasn't all that sure himself. At that time, he was aware that his marriage to Vivien Leigh was breaking down; perhaps he was trying to show her that he could still enjoy success with young girls. In other words, for our own purposes, we were both using each other: so long as nobody was hurt in the process, there was no harm done.

On one weekend break, Olivier invited me to stay with him in his country home, Notley Abbey. I was extremely nervous about this, lest Richard should find out. Vivien, according to Olivier, was quite understanding of the idea. I didn't know Vivien Leigh at the time, though I was to become her devoted friend some years later. I was flattered and frankly amazed that he should want to conduct an affair with me, for however short a time, when he was married to one of the most beautiful women in the world. I had little idea of the strain their marriage was under, although Olivier had told me a little of his unhappiness over Vivien's mental unbalance.

Olivier picked me up in his car, and drove me down to the country. I felt extremely shy, and wanted to make a good impression. I had never stayed in a grand country house before, and wasn't quite sure what was expected of me. Olivier told me we were dining with his brother, Dickie, and his wife, and I wondered how on earth they would view this interloper. From the vantage point of my experience of such affairs now, I'm certain I wasn't the first young woman Larry had brought down to Notley for a weekend, nor would I be the last.

The house was perfection: Vivien was as talented a decorator and housekeeper as she was an actress, and everything was impeccable. The furniture, gardens, tableware, food. The fireplaces were scented by a burning perfume that Vivien ordered from Guerlain; vases filled with flowers from the garden were scattered everywhere; paintings acquired by Vivien with her fine taste and discrimination hung on the walls. Notley Abbey was absolutely hers, and so was Laurence Olivier, in spite of everything that subsequently happened between them. Vivien loved him until the day she died, and losing him all but ruined her life. I believe, in spite of his marriage to Joan Plowright, a happy marriage to a woman who gave him so much of the domestic happiness and serenity he had been denied by the more mercurial Vivien Leigh, Larry's love for Vivien never died either. I was a tiny footnote in their relationship, and I am glad that I remained only that, and no more.

This brief affair continued for the duration of the film, and then was over; the classic situation of the young actress bedazzled by the attentions of her mature costar ended without any rancor on either side. I had absolutely no further role in Laurence Olivier's life, and the only relationship we had in later years was purely professional.

As I had correctly guessed, the reception of *Limelight* in America was cool, in spite of some magnificent notices. The film was shown in a few major cities, and was not in line for any Academy Award. Although, when *Richard III* appeared, I was featured on the cover of *Life* magazine, I had not become the international star I longed to be. The offers did not appear, and there was no question on producers' lips that it had to be "Bloom or nobody." When I was engaged to perform in *The Man Between,* I had signed a contract with Alexander Korda, and I believe that if he had lived, I might have had films built around me that were suited to my qualities. However, these qualities, whatever they may have been, were not ideal for the commercial film world. I did have the chance, however, to perform in several fairly commercial films, and most of those I enjoyed very much. Among them was the film of *Alexander the Great,* where once again, I played opposite Richard.

In 1955, we filmed for six months in Spain. Sybil was there the entire time and I was alone in my grand suite in the same hotel. It was fine when I was working; however, as in most historical extravaganzas there were long periods when the men performed in battle scenes and the female actors just sat around waiting. I was waiting both to work again and to have time with Richard. For, quite understandably, this time Sybil was more wary, and Richard more careful. I would wait in my room for days on end, in case I should miss one of Richard's visits.

The only way I can come to terms with my passivity at this time is to conclude that my first affair had come fairly late in life; I was completely inexperienced. But there is a missing component in this rationale, a truth which is as old as human relationships: to have an affair with a married man is a recipe for disaster. Even so, if I was handed the same set of circum-stances and given another chance to relive those anguish-ridden years with Richard, I would unhesitatingly choose to do so. He was my first — my greatest — love, the only man to whom I have fervently and completely given all of myself. To feel so much pleasure from the body, mind, voice, mere presence of another is a gift I am profoundly grateful to have received. Even though it lasted only a few years, I realize now how lucky I was. Many women go through life without ever knowing such happiness.

After five years, I realized that I had to break with Richard; there was no future for us: he could not, would not, leave Sybil, at least not for me. I accepted an offer I had twice turned down: to go to the United States with the Old Vic Company, to play Juliet and the Queen in *Richard II.*

Our parting was hard for both of us; neither could bring the other to believe that this relationship was really coming to an end. I would say a final good-bye to Richard, only to find him waiting at the London railway station to meet the train that had returned from one of the provincial towns where we were try-ing out the productions for the U.S. tour. Then he would definitely say good-bye to me, and I would leave messages with his secretary, desperately asking him to telephone. We couldn't let go of something that had meant so much for the past five years. Our final meeting was in Hyde Park.

It had been raining hard, and everything around us was muddy and beaten down; the trees dripped with water, and the ground was soggy. This is the image that I will always carry with me of the end of our relationship. We knew that there was no other way. The rain dripped down, and the sound of it was muted and hopeless. We were not to see each other again for three years.

Hollywood

As the plane took off for the United States, I felt a weight drop as though it was a physical sensation. I knew that however painful the parting from Richard might have been, I had done the only thing possible to protect my future; I was now twenty-six, an age when young women of my generation had already started to think seriously about marriage and children. My mother felt strongly that I was doing the right thing in leaving England, at least for a while; there was no question in either of our minds that this was, however, only temporary and that my real future life and career still waited for me at home.

Before we left London, I had a breakfast meeting with Sol Hurok, the noted impresario who was to present the Old Vic Company on Broadway. When he mentioned that, at the end of the tour, the company was to make a television film of *Romeo and Juliet,* and that the leading players would each receive £1,000, I said that just a few months previously I had played Roxanne in *Cyrano de Bergerac* opposite José Ferrer for the same TV company and had received $10,000. Sol said, most disarm-ingly, that he couldn't ask that fee for me alone as he would have to ask the same for the three other leading players. "But," said Sol, "at the end of the tour, I will give you a magnificent present." When we performed in New York, I would walk on Fifth Avenue wondering which of the magnificent rings or bracelets on display Sol had in mind to present me with. I needn't have wasted my time: at the end of the tour, Sol gave me his intended gift — a magnificent nothing. If I had been Elizabeth Taylor, I would have demanded some trifle as my due; as it stood, I was quite amused at my own naïveté.

New York in the mid-fifties shone with a luster that was in marked contrast to the gray pall that still lay over postwar London. In the vibrant atmosphere of that city I felt free: liberated from the image of a demure cutout doll, an image foisted on me by the British press; and one I knew to be very far from the complex and troubled young woman who existed beyond their simplistic vision; from the role I had most willingly played as my mother's dutiful daughter; from the turmoil of my five-year relationship with Richard. The Old Vic tour completed, I decided to stay, if only temporarily, in New York and try my luck there. Very shortly after this decision, I received an offer to go to Hollywood. MGM invited me to play the role of Katya, Dmitri Karamazov's rejected fiancée, in a film version of *The Brothers Karamazov* starring Yul Brynner.

I received this offer with great enthusiasm; I saw it as an entry into the mainstream of filmmaking, as opposed to the very specialized films I had been making until then. That a film based on a novel by Dostoyevsky might not be precisely the key to popular success didn't even enter my mind. That a bowdlerized version of a great and highly complex novel would appeal neither to a discerning elite nor to the vast majority of the public who wanted to enjoy a good time at the movies became all too clear when the film was released. Still, carried away by my excitement at appearing in an American film at last, I was determined to enjoy my Hollywood adventure.

When I arrived to begin filming, I had taken the kind of

grand apartment in Beverly Hills that I thought appropriate to the role of a glamorous movie star. Temperamentally unsuited to life within the publicity machine, never having been taken into the heart of the chic film community — that position had already been filled by the infinitely more glamorous Audrey Hepburn — I was often numbingly lonely; I remember, with some sadness, a long Fourth of July weekend — production had been halted for the holiday and it was too hot to venture out-doors until after sundown. I wasn't able to drive, and the shops were closed. Lying on my sofa, in my ridiculously luxurious apartment, I read Dostoyevsky's *The Insulted and the Injured,* presumably to cheer myself up. By the end of this wretched time, I knew that I would have to alter radically my new mode of living.

Still, I was lucky to have made it to Hollywood in the closing gasps of the days of the great studios. MGM may have been past its halcyon days, but enough of its atmosphere lingered for me on the soundstages, in the commissary, in the dressing rooms, to give some idea of what those palmier times must have been like. The dressing room once occupied by Garbo was preserved as pristinely as the bedroom of the long dead Prince Albert had been by his widow, Queen Victoria. At lunchtime the commissary was crowded with film stars whose names and faces had been familiar to me since childhood.

The very young Elvis Presley was making one of his earliest films on an adjoining soundstage and I would see him pass, surrounded by a phalanx of "cousins," their rather thin and pasty faces decorated with sideburns, like those of the famous icon himself; all dressed identically in sober, tight-fitting black suits. In the midst of them, for all the world like a young Roman emperor, walked Elvis. To my surprise, I was informed by the publicity department that Elvis had expressed a desire to meet me, and had invited me to come and watch the shooting of his new film.

In person, his magnetism was as considerable as his unmistakable aura of sexuality. There wasn't a great deal of subtlety about Elvis; his manner was direct. Somewhat at a loss as to what to say to the man who was a living deity among women of my generation, I feebly remarked that the car I had noticed him driving around the studio was of a type I had never seen before. Elvis replied that he had bought it directly from the showcase window. "Because, honey," said he, looking steadily into my eyes, "when I want something, I want it QUICK." He must have thought I was a terrified virgin of twelve as I made for the door with alacrity, muttering something about being needed on the set. Alas! A chance missed, but one that I have lived well without.

My Hollywood adventure, as I saw it, would not have been complete without a glamorous and romantic affair. I thought I could change my nature, and I might be capable of enjoying a sexual relationship without any emotional repercussions. I went out on Hollywood dates with several rapacious theatrical types, and felt completely out of my depth. I couldn't wait for these evenings out to be over so that I could be alone. I was immensely homesick, and utterly out of my depth.

But as the filming got under way, I found one man with whom I could talk about books, and theater, and music — all the things that interested me. This remarkable new relationship came in the extremely unlikely person of the King of Siam.

Yul and Me

Yul Brynner was an unusual, interesting, and intelligent man. He was a fine musician and photographer as well as a movie star. He was an absolute self-invention. He had contrived to manufacture from his past, which would have been compelling enough without so much elaboration, an intricate pseudo-history, which he adapted to each listener at will.

Sometimes claiming to have been born on the island of Sakhalin — I immediately looked this one up in an atlas, and found it to be the name of a Russian criminal settlement off the coast of Japan — he did indeed have the features of a latter-day Tamburlaine the Great. Perhaps some of his stories were true, perhaps not; it didn't matter to me as he spun each tale with an endearing belief that I would hang on every word, which I did.

Yul was very magnetic, his body as stocky and powerful as the trapeze artist he sometimes claimed to have been. Perhaps he *had* been in the circus; he backed this invention with another invention equally plausible, until you ended up believing either everything or absolutely nothing. No matter; he played the guitar divinely, sang Gypsy songs to me in either Russian or Romany — I never quite knew which — I was in Hollywood, and I too was acting a part. Peering deeply into my eyes, Yul would say to me: "You are my people." I didn't have the slightest idea what he meant, but I loved it anyway.

The only problem was that acting a role *offstage* was rather more difficult in my case; however much this delicious nonsense suited Yul, the other side of this adventure for *me* was aching loneliness. When I wasn't working, I was either waiting for one of Yul's unannounced calls or, as was often the case, I was quite alone.

Against all the warnings I had so strictly given myself not to fall in love with Yul, I suppose I did anyway. When, many years later, a Russian friend remarked that Yul had told her he had been truly in love with me, I was immensely surprised. Although I think I knew Yul was very fond of me, and considered me to be an odd, and charming, departure from his usual women, I never had an inkling that his affections ran any deeper than that; perhaps they didn't.

However he may or may not have felt, Yul, not unlike his counterpart in *The King and I,* needed to be surrounded by an adoring harem of women. Toward the close of filming, after a relationship of three months, Yul's visits to my apartment became less frequent, then finally stopped altogether. I felt enormously let down, and asked my mother if she would come and keep me company, which she did. I wasn't naïve enough to suppose this relationship could have ended any differently; Yul had never promised me more, and I never expected anything else.

Mother and I tried to have a good time in Tinseltown, but it was hard going. I had to accept the fact that I didn't fit the required mold; I was not going to make either my career or my life in the competitive world of movies.

Having finished *The Brothers Karamazov* and, as I had understood the situation, finished my romance with Yul, who had succumbed to yet another charmer, Kim Novak, I had to stay on to appear opposite him in *The Buccaneer*. The unlikely role of Bonnie Brown, pirate, is the only role I have ever won by influence. At the height of our affair, Yul had wanted to keep me in Hollywood, and had insisted that I appear in this film opposite him. Although he may by this time have somewhat regretted his action, I did not, at least on professional grounds. A role of this kind was quite different to the doomed and fragile heroines I seemed fated to play; certainly Anthony Quinn, the director, resented having had me forced upon him, and never addressed a single word to me during the entire shoot of the film. I couldn't have been less interested, for I enormously enjoyed throwing knives, shooting pistols, and physically overpowering large and beefy male actors; above all lunching with the great Charles Boyer, a fellow pirate in Jean Lafitte's crew of buccaneers. Near the end of all this wonderful nonsense, however, I received an offer to return to the London theater to appear with Vivien Leigh in Jean Giraudoux's play *Duel of Angels.*

Yul, having almost ignored me during the filming, which I had found painful and humiliating, to my immense surprise invited me, at the end of shooting, to accompany him for the weekend to "Paradise" the appropriately named ranch owned by Cecil B. De Mille.

Although De Mille was nominally the producer of *The Buccaneer*, I had met him only once before, when all the leading actors were presented for inspection. We were lined up to receive his greeting as he made what can best be described as a royal progress. This had scarcely prepared me to be a guest at his house; I was still immensely drawn to Yul. I wanted to spend this last weekend in his company, and I wanted to see what a trip to "Paradise" entailed.

Cecil B. De Mille was, by the time I met him, a courtly and elaborately charming older gentleman; as he bent to kiss my hand in greeting, it was difficult to envisage the despot he was reputed to have been in his younger years. Yul showed him the deepest respect and affectionate regard; De Mille's attitude toward him was not unlike that of a Victorian father with a wayward son. Brynner owed his success in film to the unwavering belief in him shown by De Mille; although already a star on Broadway, Brynner was considered too exotic a type to play the lead in any important film; De Mille changed all that by casting him as the Pharaoh in his production of *The Ten Commandments*.

There was one rule very strongly enforced in this Paradise: only unmarried couples were invited to spend the weekend. For many decades De Mille had spent his weekends in secret isolation in this lonely and beautiful place with his lifelong mistress, the actress Julia Fay. As De Mille had made his career producing films based on biblical subjects, it would hardly have done for him to have had an open liaison with someone other than his lawful wife. Yul, who had surely visited the ranch before with several unofficial partners besides me, showed me to my room, which was adjacent to his. No servants were in evidence; everything was exquisitely organized by unseen hands. As in the Cocteau film of *La Belle et la Bête,* invisible hands had turned down our beds, had served the dinner before we arrived in the dining room, were invisible to us throughout our stay. There were several buildings on the estate, and after dinner, Julia Fay and De Mille would walk off hand in hand to an unseen destination, while we went our own way to our own.

At the finish of this extraordinary weekend, Yul and I separated, I to go back to London and the theater, and Yul to Hollywood and more screen glory. And that, I thought, is that. To my surprise, about a week after I returned home, Yul telephoned me from Paris, to ask if I could meet him there. I was already in rehearsal for the new play and had only one night to spend with him, but, somewhat to Vivien Leigh's amused chagrin, I went anyway.

After I had checked into the hotel, Yul called me from his own room to tell me we were to spend the evening at a nightclub owned by the family of Gypsy musicians who had brought him up. When we walked in, Yul was greeted with high emotion — embraces and kisses were given and received. To speeches of welcome Yul replied in what I presume to be Romany; whatever else he may have embroidered onto the true details of his early life, the affection and honor with which he was regarded by this family was far from any fantasy; songs were sung in his honor, glasses of vodka raised in a toast, then flung at the wall to break against it in the finest Russian tradition. Yul borrowed a guitar, and played and sang; he had a warm and expressive baritone and indeed had supported himself in this way for some time when he first came to New York.

My adventure with this wandering spirit left me in the final analysis relatively unwounded; I was left with an immense affectionate regard for Brynner that I never had any reason to change. Although we sometimes appeared at theaters in the same city in later years, I never made any attempt to reach him nor did he me. This affair had its place and it was over.

I thought it very dashing at the time I knew him that Yul smoked black Sobranie cigarettes, and smoked many packs a day. It was his death sentence. This unique man gave a TV interview from his hospital bed, warning people to take note of his example and to give up smoking. He died as he lived, a gallant and indomitable spirit.

Home Again

After all this heady excitement, I returned home in 1957 to London and to the theater. I seem to have a pattern of always returning home; a need to rediscover the kind of domestic peace I cannot seem to find in any other city. Timid and insular as the English may sometimes appear to be, there is a stable society in London to which I always long to return and to which, in spite of my years of wandering, I still, in some mysterious way, belong.

The play in which I had been asked to perform with Vivien Leigh, *Pour Lucrèce,* written in French by Jean Giraudoux and translated into English as *Duel of Angels* by Christopher Fry, was set in a provincial town in late-nineteenth-century France. It told of the battle of wills between the stubbornly virtuous Lucrèce, the role I was to play, and of the wearily disillusioned Paola — played by Vivien Leigh — whose hatred of the heroine's rigid morality is the center of the drama. As well as the excitement I felt over the prospect of acting with Vivien Leigh, I had another reason to wish to appear in this play, for it was to be directed by Jean-Louis Barrault, France's leading classical actor. As the mime Baptiste in Marcel Carné's film *Les Enfants du paradis,* his portrayal had made him a figure of mythical significance to many actors of my generation; he had directed *Pour Lucrèce* in Paris, with his wife, the great actress Madeleine Renaud, as Lucrèce; he was to re-create the same production for me and Vivien.

Vivien Leigh came to the first rehearsal with every gesture, every nuance, as perfectly formed as it would be on the first, and on the last night. I doubt if my guess that she had been coached, again and again, by Olivier, was far off the mark. Perhaps her rigid self-control, her obsessive need for order and organization, was an effort to keep chaos and disorder at bay and counter the torment of a mental illness that constantly threatened her fragile existence.

At the time that we performed together in *Duel of Angels,*

Vivien Leigh was in her mid-forties, and I was twenty-seven. A gap in age that, in an actress less generous than Vivien, might have given rise to jealousy and dislike. In spite of my brief affair with her husband some five years earlier — which was tacitly understood but never mentioned — there was never any tension or rivalry between us; Vivien never showed me anything save the greatest kindness and affection.

We had dressing rooms redecorated especially for our use; a large pink pattern of full-blown roses had been used for both, although in larger quantity in Vivien's room, which looked a little like Titania's bower; we even had rose-patterned divans on which to rest, the whole effect being feminine and charming, However, one day, after her afternoon rest, Vivien felt a little itch, which developed into a very nasty irritation the next day. To her horror, the doctor told her that she had been bitten by fleas. Our theater was in Soho, the heart of London's prostitution district, and the stage doorkeeper had made a fair amount of cash on the side by renting Vivien's ravishing dressing room out to punters for a night's "classy entertainment." Vivien and I both thought this hysterically funny; I was thankful that my dressing room had not been made quite so ravishingly attractive as hers.

Vivien Leigh's beauty was absolutely radiant, her elegance phenomenal. She was extremely cultivated, discriminating in her choice of paintings, furniture, beautiful objects; she was a highly gifted actress, a brilliant comedienne. She was also, at the time we worked together, a terrified woman; it was clear to her that Olivier's affections were drifting and that their marriage was steadily disintegrating.

The previous five years must have been unbearable for them both; Olivier had become deeply involved with Dorothy Tutin, who, with her piquant charm, bore a fleeting and troubling resemblance to the younger Vivien Leigh; and Vivien had, with Olivier's compliant agreement, carried on a long and passionate affair with Peter Finch.

Vivien, who always kept her emotions in public tightly

under control, only twice showed me the extent of her haunted inner life; once I went into her dressing room and found her in tears. But Vivien in tears was not like anyone I knew; no red nose, sniffles, swollen eyes. She simply sat at her table, in her beautiful scarlet costume, and diamond tears rolled down her cheeks; her beauty was undiminished, her makeup untouched. The other time was infinitely more serious.

I had left the play after the eight months specified in my contract to take part in a film. I was asleep in my bed at about three in the morning when the telephone rang, and half asleep as I was, I recognized Vivien's voice, and the desperation behind it.

Vivien had canceled her performance that night, and her understudy had performed her role; this was already serious, for Vivien, an obsessively responsible actress, would never have been "off" for any trivial reason. "Would you come over at once," she cried, she was "quite alone"; she went on to say that she had put the lavender bath salts I had given her in her bath and had tried to drown herself, holding her head under the lilac-colored water. Thoroughly alarmed, I threw on some clothes, and took a taxi to her home on Eaton Square. When I reached her apartment I found that, far from Vivien being alone, a lively party was in progress. She opened the door herself, and I saw that her lovely face was puffy and swollen, almost unrecognizable. One record player was blaring away at one end of the room, and another one at the other. Vivien had been drinking, and so also had most of her guests; all were people I had never seen before. Her doctor was trying to calm her and get her to go into the bedroom for a sedative injection. I waited, but knew there was no way I could be of any help. I went home extremely disturbed and worried. It was a glimpse into the anguished world of Vivien's mental imbalance, a glimpse into the kind of hell that the Oliviers' life together must have become.

The film project for which I had left the successful run of

Duel of Angels was to be a film version of John Osborne's play *Look Back in Anger.* Osborne, whose play had had such a sensational impact on audiences at the Royal Court Theatre, was the first in a new, and long overdue, wave of sociorealist dramatists who had let some badly needed fresh air into the rarefied atmosphere of the London theater. The plays in which I had appeared until this time were charming, beautifully mounted costume dramas, with no relevance whatsoever to any contemporary situation; there was no voice to express the revolution that was taking place in the London of the late fifties; no playwright before Osborne to illuminate the extremely uncivil war that was taking place between the middle class and the "working" class. Into this genteel, hidden society strode the angry Jimmy Porter; spewing out, with brilliant venom, his loathing of everything that represented middle-class morality. I had felt very much excluded from this youthful movement, and feared that I was considered to be part of the genteel West End theater. My relief was immense when Tony Richardson offered me the role of Helena in Osborne's film version of his play; the only drawback was that Richard Burton had been engaged to play Jimmy Porter.

Richard Burton was still an adventurous actor; he wanted, as did I, to try new fields of work. Our careers were still running on parallel lines; Richard had recently returned from New York, where he had appeared in a translation of *Time Remembered,* by Jean Anouilh. His costar had been the young Susan Strasberg.

Although Richard was still married to Sybil, his name had now been linked to many young women, and to many Hollywood starlets. We had not seen each other for nearly four years; I was very defensive at our first meeting, a rehearsal in a dingy pub near the Royal Court Theatre. Richard appeared very nervous. His hands were shaking, as were mine. I was determined that, whatever happened, I was not going to be caught in his spell — neither to be hurt again nor made emotionally vulnerable. As our mutual caution disappeared, we began our conversation where we had left off some years before; we knew each other so well that we were still able to talk in a kind of shorthand. Our old intimacy quickly came back: too quickly. I viewed the resumed affair this time with some suspicion. Richard's former, youthful charm had become somewhat spurious; it was too facile, too widely spread. I no longer saw the talented and handsome young boy from Wales; although only just over thirty, Richard already had some of the airs of a practiced roué. This suspicion proved only too well-founded. On one occasion, at the close of the day's work, I wanted to say goodnight; I opened Richard's door without waiting to knock, a custom we both had followed. I saw him wrapped in a fervent embrace with Susan Strasberg.

At that time, she resembled me so much as to be almost my mirror image, and for one stunned moment, I stood frozen in the doorway, thinking that it was I whom Richard was embracing and that I must be outside of myself watching this. They were also frozen, looking toward me, Richard's arms still around Strasberg; she was wearing a white chiffon head scarf and looked like a young nun. I finally pulled myself together, and summoning all my formidable verbal ingenuity, invited them to "Fuck off, the pair of you!" I left, slamming the door behind me.

This encounter marked the end of another phase of our involvement. Although, on the surface, more for the sake of our work in the film than anything else, we remained on speaking terms, the tie that had bound us, even before we technically became lovers, for almost six years, was finally broken.

I was left with a profound sense of loss, of panic and humiliation. I was extremely angry at myself for resuming my affair with Richard, an affair that should have died out naturally. I made a vow that I would never, never again have an affair with a married man.

Whatever our personal dramas, *Look Back in Anger* I consider to be one of the finest films in which I have appeared; surely it was one of Richard's most exciting performances; only in his later roles in *The Spy Who Came in from the Cold* and *Who's Afraid of Virginia Woolf?* did he live up to the level of brilliance he brought to the role of Jimmy Porter. As Jimmy, he was able to draw on his own sense of social injustice, to remember the Great Depression, the poverty of his family, the illnesses suffered by his brothers from the years spent underground in the Welsh coal mines. Richard was always extremely aware of his own good fortune in escaping from such physical labor; however, I always thought that he suffered from a feeling of inadequacy in the face of his family's stoic endurance; that he believed the life of an actor was "cushy," and that he had been emasculated by his profession. All these powerful emotions, all his anger, he was able to use when he created the role of Jimmy Porter.

We rehearsed in the same house where the film was to be shot, and lived in it as though it actually *was* the home of Jimmy and Allison Porter. The director, Tony Richardson, who had also directed the stage version and whose first film this was, gave the actors every encouragement to be as natural as possible, answering our questions with a noncommittal "I have no idea; do what you like." This, drawled in Tony's deliberately offhand manner, was a great release of energy for me. Instead of feeling I was in the control of my director, however clever he might be, it was now up to me to invent, to discover. I believe that, in this film, I gave my first fully adult performance in a movie.

The role of Jimmy's wife was played by Mary Ure, repeating on film her highly praised performance on the stage; she was, at the time, married to John Osborne. Mary's beauty was as soft, as delicate, fair, and ephemeral as spun sugar. Mary's life, like that of many actresses, ended sadly. Her marriage to John Osborne became a torment to her, and she was "rescued" by the equally difficult Robert Shaw. At first content to be the mother of his children and the center of an extended family, she flourished. But the British film industry failed to see the fine talent and delicate beauty that Mary possessed; she began to regret the passing of time, and the talents that had never been realized. Mary began to drink, and to withdraw into herself. She was about to undertake a play in the West End when her life ended in 1975. She was only forty-two.

The film was finished. Richard and I went our own ways. We never said good-bye, but parted on terms of mutual animosity. I had reached an age where I began to fear I would be "left on the shelf." I was in an impossible profession. To meet a man who was neither married nor gay was extremely difficult. I had wasted too many years of my life in relationships that had led absolutely nowhere; it was high time for a change.

CHAPTER EIGHT

Rodney Stephen Steiger

THE YEAR WAS 1958. I still owned my house in Chelsea.
However difficult it might be, I hoped I might be one of those
fortunate women who were able to combine a family life and a
career. I certainly had no intention of stopping work, but was
open to a new way of life. If the right candidate should come
along, I was willing to give him a chance.

Looking back on it today, I am not certain whether it was a
husband I was searching for; perhaps it was an amalgam of
father-lover-friend. I was searching for the paternal masculine support of the kind I had been deprived of when I was a
child — the support that Richard, because of his marriage to
Sybil, had not been in a position to give me. Somewhere in the
back of my mind was my mother's voice telling me, at a delicate
stage of my development, "One can only fall in love once."

Having experienced a first adult relationship with Richard,
I was willing, and possibly even relieved, to settle for something
far less demanding.

My idea was to remain in London for longer periods of time,
try to forge a normal life, and discover a wider circle of friends;
above all, my intended course was to stop hiding behind an
all-absorbing work schedule.

Actors have always been at the mercy of the unexpected
telephone call. Scarcely had I completed *Look Back in Anger*
than I was offered a role on Broadway in *Rashomon,* based on
the film by Akira Kurosawa, which had been adapted for the

stage. I was asked to play the role of the nobleman's wife; my costar playing the bandit would be Rod Steiger, the actor who had recently achieved international success as Marlon Brando's brother in Elia Kazan's *On the Waterfront*.

I accepted, packed my bags, and flew to New York. Impressive as I had found Steiger's performance in the Kazan film, I was convinced there would be no question of falling in love with *this* leading man; he was both too tough and too prosaic to appeal to me romantically.

Steiger was a different man from the image he brought to the screen. With a certain formality on our first meeting, he kissed my hand; he politely escorted me home to my apartment after the pre-production party. Wearing a camel hair coat and sporting a floppy black fedora hat, he appeared to be more a figure out of the nineteenth-century theater than a product of New York's Actors Studio. He seemed to have a great knowledge of painting and was surprisingly well read. I soon discovered the tough-guy exterior was a cover-up; in reality he was sensitive, sentimental, kind, even if, like many actors, somewhat self-involved.

Despite the obvious differences in our natures and backgrounds, we got on surprisingly well. I came to rely on Rod's kindness and solid support more and more; he offered me much of the warmth, tenderness, and protection I so badly needed. His companionship became very dear to me. We began to be accepted as a couple.

We must have appeared to outsiders to be an oddly assorted pair: the classy actress from London and the method actor from New Jersey. In fact, these distinctions were just as ludicrous as such generalizations always are.

After the run of the play, I stayed on in New York and moved into Rod's Greenwich Village apartment. We went on vacation to Sicily, and I returned two months' pregnant. Rod without hesitation offered to marry me. Our wedding was held in the Malibu sheriff's office, near Rod's beach house. I was twenty-eight and Rod thirty-four.

The marriage offered us the shelter and affection we were seeking after errors in previous relationships — in my case Richard, in Rod's his first marriage to Sally Gracie. If our priorities were more need than passion, our relationship gave us many years of supportive family happiness.

One important event bound us closely together as nothing else could: the arrival of our daughter, Anna.

Her birth, far from the trauma that many women describe, was the most triumphant experience of my life. There were some moments of terror at midnight in the labor ward; I was feeling apprehensive but excited when I arrived at the hospital. The room I was put in to await the delivery room's next shift was dark and the woman next to me was screaming in agony. She had a long and painful labor; for the next three hours that I shared the ward with her, I listened to these sounds with mounting anxiety, but my own labor was relatively easy, and my baby was delivered at eight the next morning.

Seeing this little creature emerge from your own body, with toes, arms, and legs, is a miracle in itself. I find it difficult to convey the immediate surge of love I felt at the first sight of my daughter. We named her Anna Justine; she was born on February 13, 1960.

Rod had not been allowed into the delivery room, but he was there as Anna and I were wheeled out. The only blot on those transcendentally happy days was that I was rarely allowed to hold my daughter; there was an outbreak of Asian flu in Los Angeles and the fear of the babies' being infected was extreme.

My mother had come to America for the birth. She was waiting for us when we brought Anna home. Rod's burly frame was touching in contrast to the tiny bundle he carried so carefully.

I bought a mobile toy, which I hung over my daughter's bed; it played tunes as it revolved. She would watch with fascination as the colored figures turned round and round, reaching her arms toward them and smiling with delight. Anna was always surrounded by music, whether it was charming Swedish children's songs or nursery rhymes.

Eight weeks after her birth, with Rod's full approval, I went back to work. We went together to Berlin — not the easiest place to take a baby — where I was to appear in a film opposite the German star Curt Jurgens.

There I was joined by the woman who became a part of my family for the next thirteen years: Hélène Morand. Several years older than I, she came from Gruyère in French-speaking Switzerland. She was too highly qualified to be simply a nurse to Anna; Hélène had, in fact, run her own travel agency in Lausanne, but had suffered two recent tragedies that had radically altered her life: first, her mother died painfully of cancer, then her fiancé was killed shortly after in a car crash. Hélène left Switzerland — and her life there as a professional woman. Tall and blond, she was a highly attractive woman, and her personal and social abnegation couldn't have been easy. She went to England to care for an elderly couple.

Disappointed with that position, she applied to a nursing agency, and so came into our lives. Together with my mother, we formed a strong female triumvirate; whether I was working or not, in those early years Anna never lacked for care and affection.

Rod was happy in his life in Malibu, then a small beach community about an hour's drive up the Pacific Coast Highway from Hollywood. On the whole, I found my two years there deadly dull. The inescapable discussions regarding which actor was to play which role in which film drove me to distraction. I had always lived in a city, enjoyed going to the theater, to museums, to exhibitions, to concerts. Also, I couldn't drive, which was a major drawback, for to be able to do so would certainly have lessened my sense of isolation. I missed Mother and John; I missed my friends in London and New York; I missed my earlier life.

Professionally we both did well; we made some interesting films and Rod was twice nominated for a best-actor Oscar.

Rod was an actor before all else, taking his profession with a seriousness that I could never match or even begin to appreciate. My lighthearted jokes about our melodramatic scenes in *Rashomon* had confused and annoyed him a great deal. He was utterly absorbed in the roles he played, and I couldn't understand how anyone could take himself so seriously.

In spite of his certainty about himself as an actor, the real Steiger was just as insecure as the rest of us.

The great difference was that he was able, anytime he played a role, to really believe that he, Rodney Stephen Steiger, *was* Terry Malloy's brother, Charlie, Marty the butcher, or Mr. Nazerman, the pawnbroker; Rod was most sure of his own very existence when he was playing someone else.

At the first Academy ceremony we attended, Rod was up for *The Pawnbroker,* a serious film, and lost the award to Lee Marvin for *Cat Ballou,* a lark. As we entered the theater, the waiting fans cheered Rod, calling his name and wishing him good luck. We were photographed, Rod was interviewed for television and radio, then we were formally escorted to our seats. After Rod didn't win, we left the auditorium unnoticed; we couldn't find our driver, and when we arrived at the party, we were led to a table hidden in the deepest recesses of the ballroom. Naturally, Rod was immensely disappointed at having lost, but the absolute disregard with which losers were treated in that city came as a great shock to both of us. Such is the price of glory in Hollywood.

Rod and I were both presenters the night he won the golden statuette for his performance as Sheriff Gillespie in *In the Heat of the Night.* The film took best screenplay, best actor, and the most important award of all, best film of 1967.

I was dressed rather unassumingly for that kind of occasion, in a black-and-white chiffon dress. When we arrived home, we found Anna in tears. She had watched her father win his award on television and stayed up late to greet us. She said that she had waited and waited for us to come on, and when we did, I was dressed as I was every day. I asked Anna what she had wanted me to wear, and she described a crown of diamonds and a glittering white gown with a crinoline skirt — the dress of a fairy princess from one of her children's books. I promised her that I would remember it next time.

Rod had won the most coveted award in the world of film. Understandably, he expected that offers for work would never cease coming in. He was not to receive a single offer for the next twelve months. There was absolutely no explanation for this; it is just the luck of the game.

The worst aspect of any actor's career is being out of work. When you aren't in demand or haven't a job in sight, you suffer a severe loss of self-confidence. This happens to all of the unemployed, but the problem in this profession is that unemployment recurs on a regular basis. It happens to the best actors as well as to the mediocre. You can be a triumph and win every prize, and then you can be out of work for a year, as Rod was. You may be offered parts, but none of them seems right, so you turn them down and wait. This waiting goes on all the actor's life.

Rod lay on the sofa in the living room, and watched sports programs on TV. He was never unkind to me or Anna; he simply was unable to communicate with us, or with anyone; he couldn't rouse himself out of his near-catatonic state. There was very little I could do to help. I tried to keep up a cheerful front for Anna, but it was a dreadful time.

After a year of this depression, Rod's career gathered momentum, but I had seen up close the wounded child-man that lay behind all the bravura. His childhood had been miserable and lonely; his mother and father had parted before he was born, and his mother had become an alcoholic. Though we were together as a family, Christmas was always a hard time for him, a period of deep melancholy, which is a common side effect in children from broken homes. This time of the year would bring in the old ghosts: his mother was on a drinking binge; there was no food in the house; the heating bill hadn't been paid. The effect of those early years couldn't be overestimated and they were always a miserable, dark part of him.

I sympathized with his suffering, but a healthy, vibrant part of me — call it the survivor — longed to get away. Early in our marriage, long before Rod's depression, I had attempted to find a balance between my past in England and the new opportunities of a family and working life in America. The isolated life in Malibu made our situation difficult; there was no distraction from the grim atmosphere at home. I felt I was out of tune with California both personally and professionally. I was aching to do something worthwhile. Something that would restore my confidence as an actress. Something in the theater.

On a brief visit to London in the early sixties, I was contacted by Laurence Olivier. He asked me to join the company he was forming as new director of the Chichester Festival — this was widely known to be a "dry run" for his directorship of Britain's first-ever National Theatre: the actors, in all likelihood, would form the nucleus of the company he would eventually be taking with him to London.

Rod appeared to be extremely threatened by this new development; he made it clear that it would distress him greatly if I accepted the offer, an engagement that could take me away from the U.S. for a long period of time and would mean an enormous change in our lives. But I wanted to seize this opportunity, a brilliant chance to find my way back into the heart of the English theatrical world in which I felt I had lost my place. This situation triggered all my insecurities; instead of behaving like a rational woman, I got frightened. Then I did the one thing I should never have done.

At our meeting, Olivier told me that he was offering two roles; his young wife in a Jacobean drama, *The Broken Heart,* and another as the heroine of a farce entitled *The Chances.* I asked what other plays were being performed that season, and Olivier replied that the third play was to be Chekhov's *Uncle Vanya.* "Who is to play Yelena?" I asked.

"I have promised that to Joan Greenwood," replied Olivier.

"And who is to play Sonya?"

"I have promised that to Joanie," replied Olivier, referring, of course, to his wife, Joan Plowright. Ever since that time in New York when I first saw *The Three Sisters,* I had dreamed of appearing in one of the great Chekhov plays; I would have loved to play either of the female roles in *Uncle Vanya.* Suddenly, I found that I had a way to resolve my ambivalence, and blurted out these ten reckless words:

"Then I don't think I want to come to Chichester."

Olivier's face became stonelike, his basilisk's eyes impenetrable as granite. I had done something irreparable. All he said at the time was "How wonderful of you to have been so honest with me." What he actually meant was "You will never work for me again." Laurence Olivier never forgave a slight.

After Olivier had assumed the leadership of the National Theatre a few years later, I heard that he was going to play Othello, and wrote him a rather amusing letter suggesting that I was ready and willing to play Desdemona. I received a cold and wounding reply in which he stated that he was sorry to disappoint me, but as I had disappointed him in the past, he had to tell me that Desdemona was already cast.

I had been faced with a choice millions of women make every day, a choice very few men are asked to make — career versus family. If our roles had been reversed, I would have followed Rod wherever his work had taken him. Admittedly, he was the financial support. The money I earned was used for my personal needs. I feared that Rod might be right, and that I would do harm to our relationship by going away to England for such a long time.

However, this episode caused me such anguish that even to this day, I cannot look back on the decision I made without feeling remorse at the lost opportunity to act at Chichester opposite Olivier, one of the greatest actors of our time.

Nevertheless, there was one production of that period of

which I remain proud: Chekhov's *Ivanov,* with John Gielgud. We had worked together many times before: in *The Lady's Not for Burning,* he had been both director and star — a man in his mid-forties while I was just eighteen. Then I was his Cordelia in George Devine's production of *King Lear* with Japanese costumes and sets. By the time I played Sasha to his tortured Ivanov in 1965 in London, I was a much more experienced actress and all his hallmarks — the personal beauty, lyrical voice, intelligence, and nervous sensitivity — were undiminished.

In the final scene prior to the wedding, when a headstrong Sasha has forced the aging, ruined councilman to marry her, Ivanov enters dressed as the bridegroom, only to tell his bride that he is an old man with gray hair, a failure, and he cannot marry her. There was something about Gielgud the minute I saw him that made me want to cry; John cries very easily, but I don't, yet in that scene, we reached an emotional pitch I have never felt with anyone else. It was the last time we were to perform in the theater together.

On the surface, Rod's life and mine went on as before. We traveled to many places and worked in movies, either in his films or mine.

Rod made two films in Rome, and then stayed on while I made two more. I felt at home in the warm, informal atmosphere of that enchanted city. My close friend Gore Vidal was living there at the same time, and we would go for day trips to some inaccessible places, where Gore, an indefatigable scholar of ancient history, would read to me passages from the Greek military historian Thucydides, and teach me about obscure periods of the Etruscan and Roman past. Although I had left school at fourteen, I was insatiably curious about the classical world; to be with Gore on one of those trips was better than any formal education.

Gore and I first met at a New Year's Eve party at New York's Plaza Hotel in 1956. We were seated next to each other and struck up a conversation. We ignored the other guests and continued talking. Then we left for a nightclub, where until the late hours we sat, still talking animatedly. By the end, there was still more to say — by which time we had become friends.

When I got to Hollywood later that year, Gore was already there working on a script for Bette Davis. On weekends he would visit my apartment, bearing bottles of champagne and tins of caviar — all, according to him, so he could get me into bed. He might have fooled me. Despite his great intelligence, wit, and undoubtedly seductive charm, I never considered Gore as a possible romantic partner. His frequently declared homosexuality, over which he was unusually frank given the conservatism and repression of the time, had made me believe he wasn't remotely interested in a relationship with a woman. However, he has recently gone on the record maintaining that sex and affection are mutually incompatible, so I can only be grateful for my shortsightedness.

Our social life in Italy was far different — and far livelier — than in Malibu. Anna was happy as a clam and enjoyed our expeditions to the Roman monuments and the terrific restaurants of the Trastevere quite as much as we did.

Richard Again

In 1964, I was asked to appear in a film version of a novel by John le Carré, *The Spy Who Came in from the Cold*. The director of the film, Martin Ritt, for whom I had worked previously, offered me the role of the idealistic young librarian Nan Perry. The film was to be shot in Dublin over a period of three months. I had read the novel and admired it enormously. I couldn't put it down. Richard Burton was set to play the role of the disillusioned spy Alec Leamus.

Due more to the enormous publicity surrounding his recent marriage to Elizabeth Taylor than to his undeniable magnetism as an actor, Richard had now reached the pinnacle of his career. His fees were stratospheric and his power was enormous. He could certainly have vetoed my appearance had he wished; I was surprised when he chose not to. Also, to Rod's credit, he said there would be no question of my turning this part down because of my earlier romance with Richard. In fact, he was insistent that I accept it.

I had mixed emotions about making this movie; I knew my feeling for Richard was still strong. I had to face the simple truth that where I had failed, another woman had succeeded. A woman who was able to give him the opportunities for glamour and fortune he had secretly coveted all his life. That Elizabeth Taylor was considered to be one of the most beautiful women in the world made her no small trophy; Richard believed that he had won a paragon among women. During filming he told me more than once that to wake up and find Elizabeth on his pillow was like having Christmas every morning — a sentiment that raised in me urges akin to murder. In the studio, Richard and I behaved with the greatest circumspection; even so, as I came to learn much later from various printed accounts of their lives — and with some pleasure, I must admit — Taylor was extremely upset by my reappearance in Richard's life. Subsequently, she was always on hand during our scenes together. Her commanding, if unmusical, call for "Richard!" sent him scurrying to her side. She had originally offered to play the part of the innocuous librarian herself, but the appearance of a star of her magnitude would have unbalanced the stark tone of the film. She settled for feeling extremely uncomfortable having me around.

I believe that Richard, during those early days of their marriage, was terrified of his wife. Certainly he behaved in ways unlike his former self. He was still drinking very hard. A slight tremor in his hands early in the morning was always lessened by that first cup of "coffee," sipped from a mug emitting a whiff of something stronger. That was around nine; at noon he was drinking Champagne in his dressing room, followed by several bottles of wine, which he consumed with his cronies at lunch.

By late afternoon, Richard was pretty well out of commission. When I held his arm in our first scene together, it wasn't the powerful arm I remembered holding not so many years before; like the spirit of the sturdy miner's son I had known and loved, the muscle tone had vanished.

Richard's role in *The Spy* was considered to be among his finest, but his performance was held together, strangely enough, by the editor, Anthony Harvey. Though Richard's memory for poetry had been phenomenal when he was slightly younger, he now had trouble memorizing the script. The final scene of the movie, which should have been shot in a single night session, extended over three nights. Unable to remember his lines, Richard ended up having his part written on cue cards and stuck all over the interior of the car in which we were shooting.

I saw Richard socially on only one occasion during the entire three months that we spent in Dublin; it was understood that his wife didn't wish to attend any event to which I had been invited.

David Cornwell, the real name of the author John le Carré, came to Dublin on a brief visit to watch the filming of his book. We were both invited to the Burtons' hotel suite for dinner.

There ensued a scene that neither of us has ever forgotten.

The evening began with enough civility. Richard, a terrific raconteur, related extremely witty stories which David, a better storyteller and an even finer mimic than Richard, was always able to top. Whether this — coupled with the fact that she was not the center of attention — triggered the lady's annoyance, I don't know. But she left the table and went to her room, unremarked by her husband. Through a speaker system connecting the bedroom and the living room, Taylor started to summon Richard every five minutes to come to her.

Richard continued having a good time. Then Elizabeth Taylor appeared, like some spirit of vengeance, and a shouting match began. I thought this might be a good time to leave, and, saying goodnight to David, I quietly left the room, hoping that this might calm things down.

When David also slipped out of their suite, the heavyweight contest was still in progress. Despite such lively scenes, life chez Burton must have had many satisfying moments or their marriage wouldn't have endured as long as it did. I can only report, admittedly with some relish, what I witnessed.

At the close of filming we parted coolly. Our paths never crossed again. Twenty years later, Oona Chaplin was returning to Switzerland on a flight from London; on the plane was a gray, deeply lined man whom she didn't recognize at first. When he spoke to her, she knew his unmistakable voice; it was Richard, whom Oona had met with me in London many years before. He asked her if she was still in touch with me and she replied that she was.

"Then," said Burton, "please give her my undying love."

When Oona told me about this, I was dumbfounded and made a cruel remark — that he must be at death's door. He hadn't spoken to me, indeed had no contact with me at all, over the intervening years. My callous remark turned out to have some truth. Richard died of a massive stroke two years later at the wastefully early age of fifty-nine.

I was more saddened by his death than I could ever have believed possible. Even after so many years, I realized what a large part Richard, even the memory of him, had played in my life. He had always understood my ambitions and desires; in those early years, we had had so much in common. I wished we could have met once more, if only to say good-bye.

After the announcement of his death, there were tributes to Burton on radio and television. One program touched me. It could not have been recorded very long before his death. Richard was asked what, if anything, would he have changed if he had had his life over again. He replied, "I wouldn't change anything. I have had the most incredible life."

That was his epiphany: the young boy from Wales truly

believed that he had married the most beautiful woman in the world, and that his subsequent life and career in the public eye had been the fulfillment of all his youthful fantasies. If that was the case, what might have seemed a life of wasted opportunities to those of us who loved and admired him must never have seemed so to him.

CHAPTER NINE

The Unmentionable

SOMETHING UNSETTLING had been growing between Rod and me, an emotional drawing-away on Rod's part, and an ever-increasing restlessness on mine. I felt that my best years were being passed in an emotional vacuum. Rod sensed my growing dissatisfaction. What altered in our relationship is hard to define; perhaps it is as simple as stating that a marriage between two actors is a high-stakes gamble guaranteed to produce more losers than winners.

Although outward appearances might belie this, both of us were dominating personalities; Rod openly so, while I hid my strength under the cloak of compliance and patience. We had never completely understood each other, either professionally or personally; we had married because I was pregnant. That inauspicious beginning had grown into true affection, but it was not enough to hold us together permanently.

We increasingly began to get on each other's nerves. When Rod was performing Benito Mussolini or Al Capone at a film studio, he seemed to think it necessary to play Mussolini and Capone at home; whatever I happened to be playing, I would bring back to our home my fear of failure and nervous tension. Our last film together had been *Three into Two Won't Go* in 1969, the story of a marriage that has reached the end of its run — an unhappy coincidence.

Into this highly charged atmosphere came a street-wise and charming opportunist.

Hillard Elkins was a skillful theatrical producer whom Rod had met at a party and found to be extremely shrewd and flamboyantly amusing. They soon became friends. Elkins began to be a frequent guest at our house. Although I sensed that he only wanted Rod's friendship for material reasons — he almost immediately asked Rod to invest money in his next production — I found him an intriguing figure, extremely different from anyone in our group of friends. But then, Elkins was unlike anyone I had ever met.

Elkins was an average-built man with impeccably manicured nails and a perfectly trimmed goatee. His red complexion was not the product of a Caribbean holiday, but of many hours spent under the sunlamp. Dressed in a far too youthful manner for his age, he had the frenetic air of a ringmaster added to a threatening and intimidating sexuality. Despite the salesman's confidence he exuded, there was also an air of fearful anxiety; the cornered look of a huckster waiting to be caught out. At the time, I didn't know that his outlandishly extravagant style of living kept him only one step ahead of financial ruin — not unlike my father.

Strangely, Hilly had some of the same features as Eddie — certainly the same weak mouth. Still more bizarre, they even shared the same birthday.

He was invited to our house several times for dinner, and always arrived on his motorcycle, like some middle-aged urban cowboy. Some weeks after he made his auspicious entry into our company, Rod was due to leave for Russia, where he was scheduled to make the Sergei Bondarchuk film *Waterloo*. To my amazement — and in my presence — Rod telephoned Elkins, asking him to take me out while he was away. I was understandably angry: I didn't wish to be disposed in this way; I also knew this situation to be potentially dangerous — for Elkins was a known womanizer. I told Rod so, adding that I strongly objected to his interference in my affairs — that I didn't require a stranger to take care of me in his absence and was perfectly able to take care of myself. However, behind my apparent reluctance lay a far deeper apprehension; I knew I was powerfully drawn to the blatant sexual drive in Elkins.

Rod left, and Elkins called; we went out to dinner.

I had met a man who was a buccaneer. He vigorously pursued me, and I found myself impelled toward what my good sense told me was a hazardous path. Even though I was thirty-eight years old, and approaching the years when — for an actress certainly — middle age is just around the corner, I was not a developed person in certain ways. I had been a professional actress since the age of fifteen. I had no real adolescence, no grace period in which to try out the role of woman and make my big mistakes early on. Despite my one important love affair, my sexual life had been only partially fulfilling. In my marriage to Rod, the relationship of father and daughter had superseded that of husband and wife. I was acutely aware that something was missing.

On my second date with Elkins, we went back to his house and smoked marijuana. Though I had never touched pot before, I found that it made me much less self-conscious, indeed released all my inhibitions. A sexual liaison with Hillard Elkins featuring one or two joints was my introduction to the decade of the sixties; as the year was 1969, my long-awaited education took hold just in the nick of time.

I quickly became turned on to the excitement, and even, briefly, to the neurotic turmoil that was Elkins's life. I knew that this should be simply an affair, but my needs overwhelmed my knowledge.

I was immensely flattered to be so fiercely desired. Elkins was determined that I leave Rod and marry him. Initially, I said that perhaps it was better for us to continue the relationship as an affair, but he replied that, in that case, the affair would be over: it was marriage or nothing. I pondered the gamble and accepted, despite the pain I was sure to cause Rod and the disruption to Anna's domestic security, despite the anguished pleas of my mother and warnings of friends who knew of Hilly's reputation. Elkins had made me promises of a happy future together, and I hoped to make a good life for Anna as well. The difficult task that lay ahead was to tell Rod that it was all over.

On a miserable, thunder-laden afternoon in Rome, that is what I did. It was a dreadful confrontation; Rod was furious, understandably so. Some part of me hoped he would do something to avert the situation or make it impossible for me to go ahead with my plans, but he simply accepted everything. Perhaps, in his deepest self, Rod wanted the separation as well. Perhaps the surprise of my affair with Elkins immobilized him. Perhaps he also needed a wife rather than a daughter, just as I needed a husband rather than a father. Happily, Rod would find his true love much later, in a successful marriage to Paula Ellis.

The only thing that saved me during my marriage to Elkins, and I do not in any way belittle it, was that Elkins was a fine theatrical producer. I worked ceaselessly and hard, both because I wanted to and because I was the main source of support for our household.

During the period I was performing in New York I lived with my daughter and Hélène in Elkins's house on the East Side of Manhattan, a house of faux-Napoleonic grandeur as though purchased, top to bottom, from the basement of Bloomingdale's. Hung throughout with crimson velvet draperies, the hallway contained a golden harp whose purpose was indecipherable, as there were no harp virtuosos to be seen anywhere near the premises. A portrait in oils of Bonaparte graced the formal dining room. The initials "H.E." were as prominently monogrammed and displayed throughout the home as any at Malmaison.

The effect of all that red velvet was to evoke an atmosphere somewhere between MGM Studios and a provincial bordello. The phone rang continuously. On the other end of the line would be Hilly's reluctant business associates, Marty, Jerry, or Mel, who would listen to his overenthusiastic pitches, but would never quite come through with the thousands of dollars he expected.

Food disappeared into his mouth more as fodder for his manic energy than anything to be savored and enjoyed; appropriately, he kept a small refrigerator in the bedroom for his midnight snacks of lox and bagels. He owned more shoes than Imelda Marcos and more suits than Liberace. The seventies style of clothing was flamboyant; Hilly dressed for the decade.

Time was always of the essence to him, although what it was he was hurrying toward was never quite certain — not to me, not to Anna, not to my mother, not to anybody. He drove his motorcycle the way he devoured food and women, always on the run. Sometimes the police would stop him for speeding, and Hilly, never missing a beat, would smile and offer the officers free tickets to his Broadway-hit revue, *Oh! Calcutta!*

Life with Hilly had its perks: I was given a weekly allowance drawn from my theater salary; I never saw the rest of my earnings. My money ostensibly went to pay for the rent and the housekeeping. Luckily for me, Rod always provided generously for Anna and also paid for Hélène.

This marriage had all the high living and dangerous excitement of a pulp novelette; but sadly, it was all too real. For Anna this was a very unhappy time; not only did she miss her father, but she loathed "the unmentionable," as Hilly was later to be called by those of us who survived him. Neither Rod nor I had ever let on that our life together was not as happy as it appeared to be. Perhaps we should have tried to prepare her for something that — at least in my mind — was unavoidable. Our divorce and my quick marriage to Elkins came as a terrible shock to her, and the manner in which it was handled is something from which I know she feels she has never completely recovered.

Hélène was always a stable figure, as was my mother, who helped in raising Anna. I was working so hard that I was able to see very little of my daughter; she would come home from school just when I was about to leave for the theater. I rented a house in Wilton, Connecticut, for a few months, but I could only get there after my performance on Saturday nights; Anna had to be back at school on Monday mornings. We did the best we could under the circumstances, but this was a hard life to impose on an only child, especially one who had recently had her stability taken away.

As an adult woman with life experience to draw upon, Anna has reached some acceptance of the issues surrounding my breakup with Rod. At the time of my second marriage, she was understandably hurt and resentful; and the anger she carried against me made for some very turbulent years.

Elkins's entire being was centered on sexual gratification; his fantasies were alternately voyeuristic and sadistic. Inexperienced and sometimes apprehensive, I was a willing partner to his games stretching the boundaries of physical experience. But this was my trial by fire and I wanted to live every moment, to enact what had previously been the stuff of youthful imagination; to actualize what had only existed within the comfortable secrecy of books. I understood even then that my own brand of liberation — as brought about under the tutelage of Elkins — one in which I took a momentary pride, was no more than the belated growth process of a child-daughter into a more sexually aware adult.

To the outside world, I was a normal woman — a mother, and a well-known actress. But, step by step, I began to feel that I was losing my identity. There was more than a little guilt preying on my mind: as a mother, the knowledge that I had dealt my daughter what might be a crippling blow; as a wife and friend, the realization of having wounded Rod deeply; as a daughter, the certainty that I had disappointed my mother. The sense of dangerous adventure that I had reveled in earlier with Elkins turned into self-loathing. These waters were plainly out of my depth; in order to reclaim my life, I determined to work harder than ever on my career. Acting had been my sanctuary in times of uncertainty or distress; now it would be a safe haven once again.

The rescuing hand came, ironically, from Elkins himself; although he had never produced a "straight" play, he had proved himself a uniquely gifted theatrical producer. Although he may well have seen me as a commodity for making money, he also knew my worth as an actress, and wanted to be accepted as a serious producer.

Elkins produced two Ibsen plays for me in New York: *A Doll's House* and *Hedda Gabler*. I had suggested *A Doll's House* to other managements many times before, but Elkins was the first to recognize its timely importance to the women's movement — and therefore, its wonderful money-making potential. First produced in 1879 three weeks after its publication, at the Theater Royal Copenhagen, this play about a young wife who leaves her protected and comfortable home to find her independence was considered revolutionary. The sound of Nora's final slamming of the door to her husband's house had been called the sound that echoed around the world. The play had not been revived in New York since Ruth Gordon had last performed it in 1937 — an extraordinary lapse of time for so important a work.

In the final confrontation between Nora and her husband, Torvald Helmer, there was one line in particular that always had moved me profoundly: in reply to her husband's statement that no man would sacrifice his honor, even for love, Nora responds, "Millions of women have." To my astonishment, and that of Donald Madden, who was playing Torvald, at our first preview in New York this statement was greeted by prolonged applause; when the curtain fell, many members of the audience came down the aisles and stood at the foot of the stage, voicing their approval. When I performed the same scene in London with a different cast, the reaction was basically the same, except that where the New York audience had applauded, the London public audibly drew in its breath. The shock of Nora's truth was almost palpable.

In Nora Helmer I was able to fuse two conflicting sides of my nature — the spoiled child-wife and the determinedly independent woman. Nora's painful journey toward freedom was one that I was able to make, although the implications of that concept would take me another twenty years to fully understand. Just as the role of Juliet had come to me at a moment in my life when I was a very young woman and was beginning to find my own emotional identity, *A Doll's House* came when, like Nora Helmer herself, I was forced by the circumstances of a disastrous marriage to reexamine many of my own choices.

To my great joy and relief, the success of *A Doll's House* in New York led to an offer to film the production in Norway and England and then a six-month engagement to perform the play in the West End. Although Elkins and I went to London together, to escape that bizarre house on East 62nd Street was sweetness itself, and to be able to go with Anna and Hélène back to the safety of London was a benediction. Although Hilly's "generous" financial arrangements continued — he deducted the rent and housekeeping, leaving me an allowance from my own salary — I was now in my own home environment, and therefore better able to have some understanding of how my money was being administered.

The successful run of *A Doll's House* was followed by a magnificent revival of Tennessee Williams's *Streetcar Named Desire*. Blanche DuBois had been suggested to me by my friend and agent, Robbie Lantz. I was forty-two years old, a perfect age to play her. However, it was a daunting task to follow the performance of Vivien Leigh, who had made the part so much her own in 1949 on the stage and in the Elia Kazan film of 1951. Twenty-five years had passed since she played Blanche. I had reached a point in my career when I wanted to meet a big challenge. Elkins contacted Tennessee and invited him to come to London, meet us, and approve his producing *Streetcar*.

Extremely apprehensive about this meeting, I asked Gore Vidal, an old friend of Tennessee's, if he could join us for this all-important first dinner. As Blanche had to puff nervously at a cigarette during the course of the play, I thought it might impress Tennessee if I did the same. I was not a smoker and this was not a good idea; Gore told me later that he had fully expected me to place the cigarette between my eyes, taking a drag of it that way. I asked Tennessee what happens to Blanche after she is led away from Stanley and Stella at the end of the play — I asked because I was curious, not because it necessarily makes any difference to the approach an actress takes in the part. He seemed surprised by the question — indeed, he said no other actress had ever asked him that — then gave us a wonderful postcurtain scenario depicting Blanche's phoenixlike ability to rise from the ashes. It made sense, because Blanche has suffered losses and humiliations before the play begins, and still she clings to her illusions of love, gallantry, and vindication during its course.

I firmly believe that I would never have understood Blanche DuBois without the experiences of the last year in New York; that without Elkins the dark part of my sexual nature would never have come into being.

Women of my time and upbringing were offered very few opportunities for sexual exploration or expression, something our brothers and fathers were brought up to believe was their birthright. I was given the chance, albeit by the most manipulative of men in hardly the easiest of circumstances, to tread on that forbidden ground, and examine an area of human development we had been told to accept as terra incognita by our mothers and grandmothers. Between the Judaic abjuration of sexual pleasure and the Victorian stricture against anything sexual whatsoever, my generation of Jewish women were thus doubly trapped. The only way out of the prison was to break out of it. That is what I tried to do.

It is both shameful and courageous to take a record from life and use it as a means to an end. The painter Claude Monet, to his own shame, looking at his adored young wife on her deathbed, could not help recording the changing color of her skin and the dissolution of her once-beautiful face. But he went on to use this image in his work. In a similar fashion, I could not avoid taking mental notes during my adventures with Elkins and later applying many of them to my performance as Blanche DuBois. There are outlets for life's unwelcome pitfalls that a creative setting — in my case, Blanche and *Streetcar*—can effectively unleash.

The ladylike behavior of the Southern Woman is, in Blanche's case, a defense. Within this lies the hidden need to obliterate a transparently false facade, with the intervention of a man, in a moment of reckless passion — this was something I could well relate to. I was also aware of Blanche's extreme terror of abandonment and her craving for protection. Her neediness only brings suffering; it is accompanied by resentment, in the anger she expresses toward Mitch and Stanley; for there are no such saviors. Neither of these archetypically male figures is remotely capable of understanding her search for that "corner of the world I can hide in," nor her pursuit of magic at the expense of reality. That is the ultimate irony in *Streetcar:* at the end, the man toward whom she bestows the most famous line of the play is in reality a doctor leading her away to a mental institution. And she follows, transfixed and happy.

On the morning following the opening night, Elkins awakened me by bringing in the daily newspapers; the reviews were unanimous both in their praise of the production and in their approval of my performance. So brilliant, in fact, that I had a momentary feeling of terror. I thought: "I will have to pay for this."

The role of Blanche has had a notorious effect on many actresses who have played her; like the emotionally draining role that ruined Aunt Mary's health, there is no other way to play Blanche than to spill your guts out every night. Vivien Leigh took months to recover from the strain it placed on her fragile psyche. I was made of far stronger stuff, but the exhaustion that followed our eight-month run of eight performances a week certainly contributed to my subsequent nervous collapse. However, there is no other role that compares to it in the entire canon of twentieth-century theater; whatever the cost to my physical and mental health, I wouldn't have missed the opportunity to play Blanche DuBois for anything in the world.

My glimpse into the future turned out to have some substance; I was at the apex of my career. Blanche had brought me all the rewards any actress could desire. In 1974 I received the prestigious Evening Standard Award, plus the Variety Award. I had more than revived my place on the London stage.

I had also taken back into my own hands the responsibility for my daughter's and my own financial future by investing whatever money I had managed to secrete away in a substantial house in London, the purchase of which would guarantee us somewhere permanent to live. Whether a move of this kind was what Elkins was waiting for, or whether he had taken his decision to leave me some time before, I have no way to know.

Elkins became remarkably involved in the redecoration of the new house; he even took time out from his incessant telephone calls to bring back to me samples of fabric from a local decorator's shop. He was eager to introduce to me the talented and attractive owner, Tricia Guild, and I engaged her as my decorator. I noticed that she appeared to be on very good terms with my husband.

I received a message in my dressing room some weeks later, just as I was about to put on my makeup before the performance. The caller was a film producer whom I recalled meeting a long time ago; I accepted the call. The heavily accented voice told me that this was not a social or professional call; he announced that his wife and my husband were in Sardinia together, and that he could furnish me with incontrovertible proof that they were having an affair. If shocked, I was not very surprised. I knew Elkins had gone off to attend a film festival in Corsica — a somewhat unlikely setting for such a celebration — from which it was not too hard to picture adultery in

Sardinia. He went on to tell me that my decorator was an old friend of his wife's, and that she had been their go-between. Being my decorator had made it unnecessary to explain the frequent telephone calls she made to my husband. This was the only way our relationship could come to an end. One week later, Elkins returned to New York with his new conquest; they were eventually to marry, and the fourth oh-so-lucky Mrs. Elkins was to divorce him within three years.

My second marriage had lasted almost five years.

Anna and I now found ourselves caught in the symbiotic relationship that had formerly existed between my mother and myself; we were two women against the world. We shared a room on the upper floors of what would eventually become our house until other rooms were completed below. We became almost like sisters, arguing over our territorial rights, squabbling over clothes. Anna was my confidante, often my adviser. I became her playmate, her friend; our roles as mother and daughter were confused. In this chaotic house, in this dangerously precipitous financial climate, we clung together for support. Now Anna had to grow up as quickly as I had done during the months of my mother's illness in America, when our roles became reversed and I had, at the age of eleven, to take responsibility for the welfare of my brother. No young girl of fourteen should have to feel such responsibility toward a mother of forty-three.

I will always be grateful to Elkins for what he did for me as an actress; he had the faith to produce two plays by Ibsen in the New York theater; Ibsen at that time had the reputation of an author whose plays open on Monday to close on Tuesday. Against all odds — Jane Fonda, rather mysteriously, suddenly decided to film *A Doll's House* at the very time Elkins and I were planning our own production — he had raised the money for the film and cast it meticulously with Anthony Hopkins, Ralph Richardson, Anna Massey, Denholm Elliot, and Dame

Edith Evans. A finer cast could not have been assembled anywhere. He had won the right from Tennessee Williams to produce *Streetcar;* the production of which was perfect in setting, costume, cast, and direction.

This marriage had been a misbegotten adventure, a torment to my daughter and mother, and it was now finally over. I was forty-three; my future was up to me.

I was on my own for the first time in my life. And there were problems. My new house was a heavy financial burden; each morning another hefty bill appeared in the letter-box. After a highly successful run, *Streetcar* abruptly closed; my salary stopped as well.

For several weeks I was extremely uncertain of myself. I rose late and went to bed early. No work came my way, and although I badly needed the income, I didn't want any. I only wanted to be left in peace. The blow to my ego, the uncertainty of my economic position, and this hiatus in my working life contributed to a steadily increasing depression. Still physically exhausted from the run of *Streetcar,* I was also deeply beset by guilt over the pain my marriage to Elkins had caused Anna. From looking far younger than my years, I began to look years older. Painfully thin when I began to play Blanche DuBois, I now appeared almost emaciated. I often had the sensation that I was spinning out of control. This second desertion made me revisit the fear, sadness, and insecurity I had felt when Eddie left to go to South Africa. Two irresponsible yet important men in my life had disappeared, making me feel rejected and alone.

Hélène, whose father had recently died, left to go home to Switzerland; this was a further blow to Anna's delicate sense of stability; in recent years, Anna obviously no longer needing a nurse, Hélène had become housekeeper and support to us both. I missed her as well.

I started to recover my health and mental equilibrium. New friendships entered my life. Work began to appear and my monetary position improved. The delicate balance between a mother and daughter, which had been disturbed for five years, was reclaimed. I began the process of psychotherapy, commencing the inner work I should have started years before. It was time to look to the future and move on.

Quinn and Company

There was one shadow that still hung over me from my professional association with Elkins. I had been contracted several months before, while we were still together, to appear on Broadway in a project he was to produce: a new play by Tennessee Williams, *The Red Devil Battery Sign*.

When Tennessee had come to London to approve our production of *Streetcar*, he had invited the same team — Ed Sherin, Elkins, and myself — to be director, producer, and leading actress of his play.

Even at the first reading, I could see that my role was not only going to be difficult to grasp, it possibly lay outside my field of experience or expertise. With a role designated only as "The Unknown Woman," any experienced actress could have seen the uphill work involved to create a fully evolved character from a past that doesn't seem to exist; but the opportunity to appear in a new play by Williams made any misgivings seem inconsequential.

The male leading role had been conceived specifically for Anthony Quinn. Although I recalled that he had resented my being foisted on him by Yul Brynner in the film *The Buccaneer*, I thought this must have been long ago forgotten.

I wanted nothing further to do with Elkins, but I was a professional and I had to do my job, even though he was nominally one of the producers of the play. I returned to New York, and booked into a hotel. Seeing Elkins for the first time since we went our separate ways meant very little to me; it only showed me how meaningless our relationship had been.

Since our work together in *Streetcar,* Ed Sherin had become a close and trusted friend. He had written affectionate letters — of his admiration of my work, of his longing to work with me again — and together we had agreed on the interpretation of the role I was to play in *Red Devil.* Or so I thought. Before my arrival in New York, he had apparently come under the not inconsequential influence of Anthony Quinn, and together they had worked out a very different view of my character. Where Tennessee had described the role as a woman who was lost, mentally wounded after the assassination of her husband — a woman bearing a strong affinity to Jacqueline Kennedy, at least as she was presented to me — the team of Sherin and Quinn reinvented her as a closer sister to Martha Mitchell, the wife of President Nixon's convicted attorney general, John Mitchell. Also known as "Big Mouth" Martha, this abrasive woman who kept the press and nation in stitches during the Watergate scandal was a far cry from the woman I had been cast to play. Their views seemed solar systems away from the picture I had previously drawn from either Sherin or Tennessee.

I had received no hint from Sherin's letters that Quinn was resentful that I was playing opposite him or that he thought an American actress could have better played my role. Given his view of her, this suggested not only a difference of nationality but an entirely different type of actress. He may have suspected, as I was the then producer's wife, that I was being forced on him as I had been in *The Buccaneer* all those years ago. Whatever the reason, I began to see that what I had looked forward to playing was now moving far beyond my real capabilities and that I was likely to make a real fool of myself if I attempted to play it in their way.

To play the role as Quinn and Sherin now visualized it was to begin on the note of C major, with drums pounding and trumpets blaring, and sustain this throughout the evening. Sherin was now adamant that this was the only way to balance the role played by Quinn. I began to study tapes of a Texas accent. I hoped that, in rehearsal, I would be able to reach some kind of compromise between my view and my director's.

A cocktail party was given to introduce the members of the cast to one another. Later in the evening, Quinn invited a number of us to a local Greek restaurant for dinner. He suggested that we all enter by the back entrance, so as not to attract undue attention. This entrance led naturally onto a small stage, which we all crossed as unobtrusively as possible. All except Quinn, that is. He appeared last and the audience burst into excited applause: Zorba the Greek — in the flesh — was gracing their dinner tables. The bouzouki band struck up the familiar tune composed by Mikis Theodorakis, and Zorba began his slow dance. Skipping and hopping with complete abandon, by the time he reached his climax, throwing his head back with arms raised, he displayed an ego of such dimensions as to make the Acropolis look like a village taverna by its side. He waited for his adulation and, of course, he got it.

A spent and sweaty Zorba then joined the rest of us mortals at the table and calmly ate his moussaka. It had been quite clear to me — and was not lost on the other members of the cast, either — that all this energy had been expended to prove who was the real star of the show. Fair enough, I thought. What I found hard to understand was why anyone should need to go to such extreme lengths: to bring Italy to its feet as Mussolini had done employing similar gestures, perhaps it might have been necessary; but for a play, even one by Tennessee Williams, it appeared a trifle overdone.

The rehearsal period was hell for everyone except Quinn, who thrived on discord and control. He was also obviously going to give a splendid performance; the role he was playing suited him perfectly. I was tied up doing my impersonation of a tough cookie, and had lost my always-supportive Tennessee. Each rewrite he presented was rejected by Sherin and Quinn, who now appeared to be the self-appointed codirector; the author fled back to the safety and tranquillity of Rome. On one occasion I became so incensed by Quinn's unsolicited direction that I threw my script at his head. It missed, but then he turned toward me, arm raised, ready to strike. Luckily for him, he thought the better of it.

One week before we were due to leave for the tryout in Boston, I received a note at my hotel; it was from a man I had met several years before, the author Philip Roth. He suggested that we meet for a Chinese dinner. Although pleased at the invitation, I was so wound up in my vain attempt to find the key to the unplayable Unknown Woman that I put his note aside, unanswered. The company left for Boston as planned, and I never did find time to reply to his invitation.

At the opening performance, I looked around to see where Quinn had got to; he was standing so far behind me — an old actor's trick — that I couldn't find him. This maneuver meant that, in my confusion, every line I spoke had to be thrown upstage, and so made me inaudible to the audience. The critics were understandably confused by the play. Quinn telephoned both Gena Rowlands and Faye Dunaway, who came to Boston with an eye to taking over my part. Both intelligently passed on the opportunity, obviously far better than I was at recognizing a dud role.

Elkins had, by then, been edged out of the picture by the other producer, David Merrick, who wanted only his own staff in charge. The stage was now set for me to enjoy the full Broadway experience; each player in the game would now try to jettison the other, in the heartwarming ritual that is frequently enacted before many Broadway openings.

Merrick wanted to sack Sherin; Quinn wanted to sack me. I was desperate to sack myself, but was told by my agent that I had to wait patiently to be dismissed; in that case, I was contractually bound to be paid so long as the play ran. Quinn joined Merrick in a cabal against his old pal Sherin, and soon wanted to take over the direction completely. When that point was reached, Sherin wanted to fire Katy Jurado — the only person who had kept her head and had consistently given a fine performance — and it was obvious that this disastrous production could not go on much longer.

I longed for an evening out of this Hellzapoppin' madness. I suggested to Quinn that my understudy go on in my place; that way he and Sherin could evaluate together if a replacement would make a telling difference to the play. I wanted out. Later the same evening, I was invited unexpectedly to Quinn's apartment and told that I was irreplaceable, but to realize that they had to see a very different type of actress play my part.

I felt, for a brief moment, relieved, even grateful. The outside world had faded from reality, all that remained was the play and the players. Quinn then proceeded to seduce me, and I complied. My mistake, his power trip. I found myself in bed with a man I found dangerous, destructive, and whom I had come to despise prior to this encounter. The following morning I was full of remorse: I was also astonished at my lack of judgment, my abdication of self-preservation. This was my only one-night stand. It goes without saying that I was as furious with myself as I was with him at having succumbed to Quinn's ludicrous macho display.

However, the next day, Quinn was up to other tricks. He and Sherin had found new targets to shoot at: they were now engaged in a plot to replace the unhappy young actor playing Quinn's son. I was, mercifully, for the moment, forgotten. Not that our brief interlude did anything to dampen Quinn's enthusiasm to replace me. It only gave him a further handle through which to exert his control on us. He knew that I was an appalled but sometimes amused observer of his machinations. He once said, "You look at me with those big brown eyes, and all the time your little mental computer is noting everything I say." He was correct.

Although Tennessee sent us several more scenes from Italy, the play was, by this time, irretrievable. There were two separate plays being performed, and they didn't add up to a complete evening. My story told of the wife of a murdered president from an unspecified country hiding out in a border hotel, who falls in love with a waiter who is, unfortunately for her, dying from a brain tumor. The waiter's story tells of a man, his wife, and his daughter, with whom he is — or perhaps is not, it is never made clear — conducting an incestuous affair.

There were flashback sequences featuring a girl dancer, decked out in Spanish gear, loudly stamping her feet and dancing flamenco. Other scenes introduced troupes of mariachi players noisily strolling across the stage. Somewhere, deeply hidden amidst the fanfare, were some very fine passages of dialogue by Tennessee. Merrick closed the play only ten days after we opened in Boston. And that was that.

The Red Devil Battery Sign has never had an important revival and must be counted as one of Tennessee's later failures. I had been saved the humiliation of being replaced by the skin of my teeth. I returned home to London, the entire experience having been ludicrous, upsetting, artistically disappointing, and almost disastrous financially.

CHAPTER TEN

The Writer

THE NEXT FEW MONTHS were, happily, quiet and uneventful. Pleased to be home once more with my daughter — and with my mother close at hand — I wanted nothing more. I just wanted to be at peace. I hadn't been offered a film for some time; during my years with Elkins I had been so absorbed in the theater that I had appeared on screen only once. Now an offer came to appear in an adaptation of the last, uncompleted novel by Ernest Hemingway, *Islands in the Stream*.

Though the book's events take place in the Bahamas, the project was to be filmed on location on a small island off the coast of Hawaii. I was to play the estranged wife of an artist played by George C. Scott. The enigmatic role could have been tailored to suit me; altered from the larger-than-life star, she now corresponded to two women in Hemingway's life — his third wife, Martha Gelhorn, and his widow, Mary — to both of whom I bore a passing physical resemblance. Scott was an actor I had always admired; the money was more than welcome. The thought of three weeks on an island in the Pacific was almost too good; I felt my fortunes might be about to take a favorable turn.

In order to select my costumes for the film, I had to stop briefly in New York on my flight to Hawaii.

Our meeting was typical of us and ridiculously simple. I was walking up Madison Avenue to have tea with my yoga teacher; Philip Roth was walking down on his way to a session with his psychoanalyst. Philip was looking very professorial behind his glasses, and bent over to kiss me on the cheek. I told him I was on my way to Hawaii to make the Hemingway film with Scott, whom I predicted would be a monster, like most of the testosterone-driven leading men I had recently had the pleasure to come across. Philip silently pondered this for a moment, then said, quietly but firmly, "Not all men are."

We had first met in East Hampton, Long Island, in 1966. Rod and I had taken a house for the summer months, and we had a good time there with Anna, bicycle-riding, swimming, performing a host of healthy summer activities. Neighbors invited us over for a drink; one of their houseguests was Philip. Already a highly acclaimed young writer — the author of *Goodbye, Columbus,* a fine volume of short stories — I recognized his tense, intellectually alert face immediately from photographs. Tanned, tall, and lean, he was unusually handsome; he also seemed to be well aware of his startling effect on women. I was immediately attracted to him, and he would tell me years later that he also had felt the same toward me. We were both attached — Philip to a beautiful young socialite, Anne Mudge, and I to Rod — but neither of us forgot that meeting.

A few days after our Madison Avenue encounter, I went to Philip's apartment for coffee; we both sat checking one another out. I had dressed as attractively as possible, and was determined to be at my most charming and witty. Philip was very seriously considering me from behind his glasses, sizing me up in a manner particular to him, taking every detail in, with intense concentration on each intellectual, psychological, and sexual aspect of the woman in front of him. To have such a mind as Philip Roth's fixed on your every word and gesture is both daunting and extremely flattering; but it was difficult to read his intentions from the emotionally neutral and sober expression that followed every comment I made. Though he had it to an immense degree when the mood took him, his brand of seductiveness wasn't charm; it was intelligence, the sort that passes as acute sensitivity by dint of an astonishing facility for under-standing. He made no effort to conceal the caustic and judg-mental sides of his character; as a result, I felt that I would never be able to measure up to the high standards he demanded both of himself and his friends — and especially of the women with whom he became involved. But, confoundingly, he also ap-peared capable of great kindness and depth of feeling.

I gave Philip my address and I took his. We agreed to write. I had to leave for Hawaii the following day, and I promised to telephone him when I knew I was coming back to New York.

I flew on to fulfill my professional commitment, the area in which I had always felt most secure. Scott, far from being the monstrous egomaniac I had suspected him to be, was an ex-tremely good colleague and we played together very well. Granted, he didn't have much to say to me; we stood in silence between takes. I became quite tongue-tied and couldn't think of anything interesting to say; he, meanwhile, didn't utter a word. He did become quite jolly around 6 P.M., when he was brought a glass of what might conceivably have been water; then he would gather all the men on the crew together, and laugh and tell stories. His burly build, gravelly voice, and stern-ness of manner suited the role of the great novelist's final alter ego, Thomas Hudson, to perfection; I also believe I was success-ful in the part of a real "Hemingway woman." However, the film was not a financial success and has since been completely overlooked, which is a pity, as it is one of the more successful adaptations of a Hemingway novel.

I had been the first to write to Philip; I had written to praise the book he had given me on parting, his novel *My Life As a Man*. This work catalogues, in hilarious yet savage terms, Roth's marriage to Margaret Michaelson, his shiksa to end all shiksas, and details his involvement in a violent and grotesque marriage.

Under Roth's brilliant inventiveness, beneath his diamond-sharp observation, was a deep and irrepressible rage: anger at being trapped in marriage; fear of giving up autonomy; and a profound distrust of the sexual power of women. I noted the warning signals; but of course the situation would be different with me. So most women imagine it will be with them, as they enter a new and challenging relationship.

The first letter in my possession, dated December 4, 1975, begins with a careful "Dear Claire." In this letter Roth states how glad he had been to hear from me — because he had wanted to hear from me. That it had been terrific to see me in his apartment and he hoped there would soon be a next time.

He goes on to say that he had been interested in me for a long time, but that every time we ran across each other, "you had a husband and I had a wife-candidate and we are both such good children that propriety prevailed." He closed by saying he wished I could have remained longer and asking me to write again. The letter was signed "Yours, Philip."

I wrote to Philip accordingly, and received an enthusiastic response.

I had arranged to narrate a voice-over that would bring me to the United States for a brief visit, and arrived back in New York on February 16, 1976.

There were flowers at the hotel to greet my arrival. "Welcome, Philip." Very careful and correct. It had been arranged that we have dinner at his apartment on this first evening. Philip went to great trouble to entertain me properly, to regale me with good food and wine. I was jet-lagged, and promised to return again the following evening. Our conversation had been light and easy; the rapport between us as strong as on the previous occasion we met. We dined together the next evening and the next, and on the fourth evening we went back to my hotel room and made love for the first time.

A week after, we admitted we were in love with each other. Philip spoke first, and his voice was suffused with pain and a kind of suffering; it was as though it hurt him to declare his love for me. I stayed in his apartment that night and for the nights afterward. By now I had only ten days left of my stay in New York.

To my surprise, I overheard Philip talking on the telephone; from his end of the conversation I gathered that it was with a close male friend; they arranged to leave together in a few days' time for a vacation in the Caribbean.

This arrangement was a great surprise to me after the eager tone of his letters and the affection he had shown since my arrival. I had expected to spend the time I had left in New York with him. This was my first glimpse of Philip's rigidity: he had arranged to go, and he was going. I suspected at the time that this trip might have been worked out some time before my arrival, perhaps as a safety valve to avoid becoming too emotionally involved; I thought it was even possible he now regretted it. But whether he did or not, he was going through with his original plan.

A few days later, Philip left as arranged and I went on to do the narration that had originally given me my excuse to come to New York. I made my own plans to leave, but I felt that I had been treated in a strange and offhand manner by the man who had declared himself to be in love with me not long before.

One may well ask why I said nothing to him of my disappointment — and, indeed, resentment — at being treated in this patently cavalier manner. The answer is that I was intimidated: Philip always gained the upper hand in any argument, and with his razor-sharp wit could easily say something amusing and cutting to make my position appear futile and humiliating.

Underneath his impeccable manners and serious demeanor, I sensed a profound nervousness and fear of commitment.

I arranged to leave for London; three days before I was to fly home I received the following telegram:

3.22.76 ST. MARTIN

WILL BE RETURNING SATURDAY OR SUNDAY STOP WILL YOU STAY
THROUGH THE WEEK END SO I CAN SEE YOU STOP CABLE ME ST.
MARTIN PHILIP.

3.26.76

ARRIVE SATURDAY EVENING NINE FORTY FIVE LOVE PHILIP.

I stayed and we had one night together. I had to leave for
London the next day.

The tone of Philip's letters had changed. Gone was the old
guardedness. A letter dated April 5, 1976, tells me how nice it
was that the urgent need to write letters was over, as we now
spoke regularly on the phone.

Several weeks and many, many letters later, Philip invited me
to come to Connecticut and stay with him for three weeks (the
three weeks were stated very clearly). The pattern of our life
together during that time, when we were happy in the newness
of our relationship, had its share of unfair compromises, at least
for me. There was a deep ambivalence in Philip toward full
commitment; he had a long-established fear of giving away too
much to a woman; however much he loved her, he felt that he
could lose a vital component of himself. From the beginning,
the scrutiny I was under was considerable, making me feel as
though there was a trial under way and I was the defendant. I
was eager not to disappoint him intellectually; I knew how little
patience he had with his friends in this regard. And yet, despite
some infrequent flare-ups, during this period we were in close
harmony. We read the same kinds of books and loved to walk
together in the country. I had found in Philip a brilliant and
attractive partner. His rigorous lifestyle may sometimes have
made me feel lonely during the day, when, my short visit notwithstanding, he disappeared into his studio for the lonely business of writing novels. But when I was reunited with him at the
end of the day, I was captivated by his penetrating mind and
depth of sensibility.

All in all, our first foray into domesticity was a success. There was an antique brass calendar on the mantel that had to be turned manually with each passing day; I hated to see the days skip away, measuring the time I had already stayed against the time I had left. I knew, of course, that I had to go home to address my other responsibilities, but I didn't want to leave. What I wanted was to stay and make a life with this difficult but remarkable man.

Once again I returned to my house in London, to my daughter, my family, and my friends. It was comforting to be home, but I missed Philip all the same. We wrote frequently, reporting and discussing every event that happened to us during the time we were apart; no definite plans were yet made to meet again.

Only a week or so after I returned from my New York visit, the salutation "Dearest Love" shows that Philip had made an almost reckless step forward from the careful "Dear Claire" of his earlier letters. The next letter begins with the words "Dearest, dearest" and ends "I love you." A further letter began "Dearest Thesp of mine." He wrote of his longing to have me back and of the preparations he would make for my return. He also notes: "A skunk crossed my path; or, as the skunk would say, a Jew crossed my path."

Soon after I arrived back in London, Harold Pinter had invited me to appear on Broadway, under his direction, in a stage adaptation of Henry James's great novella, *The Turn of the Screw;* the title of the play was *The Innocents.* The chance to return soon to New York and be once again with Philip seemed to be nothing less than providential. I had always admired Pinter, both as playwright and director, and been fascinated, since my teenage years, by the James story of psychological terror and erotic possession; I knew the central character of the Governess would suit me well.

But there was even more to delight me. The rehearsal period was to be held in London, and Philip suggested that he join me there, and then we could return together to New York.

Although it was a joy to have Philip so unexpectedly with me in London, some of the problems we would subsequently have to face must have been almost immediately apparent to us both.

Anna was now a young woman of sixteen. Emotionally fragile as a result of my second marriage, she was deeply distrustful of the strange new man in my life and full of anxiety, lest the damage done to us both by Elkins should be repeated in yet another painful relationship.

Those four weeks in London were both tense and happy. I recognized how skeptical Anna was about Philip. After Elkins and the horrible aftermath during which she was my main source of emotional support, she probably found it difficult to trust another man in our house. They viewed one another with civilized caginess and without much instant rapport. Knowing Philip better, I can look back and honestly say that, during this early attempt at family life, he tried to treat Anna with understanding; but he had already made his position clear about living in my house with my daughter.

Philip and I returned to New York at the close of rehearsals for the opening of the *The Innocents;* Anna and my mother were to follow. I rented an apartment on New York's Upper East Side; Anna and my mother would live there, I would ostensibly live with them; it was, however, understood between my mother and myself that I would spend my Sundays, when I would be free from performances, with Philip in Connecticut. Just how I intended this juggling act to go off without a hitch, I wasn't entirely sure; somehow I hoped I could please everyone. Anna was entered in school, and was miserable about yet another adjustment period being foisted on her. Meanwhile, I prepared to go on tour with the play for six weeks prior to our Broadway opening.

I knew well that this arrangement might be hard on my mother and on Anna, that my absence would leave them lonely and disoriented. I planned to come back to New York on the brief weekend breaks whenever possible. Philip understood my desire that he call my mother and Anna from time to time while I was away, and take them out to dinner or to a movie — but he never did. Knowing that they had no other contact in New York and that I had asked him to keep an eye on them, he could easily have made this relatively simple gesture. My mother felt he had showed little interest in my family, and this distant manner convinced her that he had a very cold and detached temperament. Admittedly I was disappointed that he had proved emotionally incapable of including my family in his affections. He had shown me, and not for the first time, that he would do things only his way, and do them as and when he wished.

The Innocents played on tour in Boston and Philadelphia. Philip came several times, at my request, to see the production in both cities. His notes at my performance were incisive, sometimes brutally critical, always completely accurate.

With Harold Pinter's guidance and the help of Philip's revealing comments, I interpreted the elusive character of the Governess; I allowed the audience to form their own conclusions, although in my own mind, I had, of course, to form a concise picture of her inner life.

Henry James's great story of psychological possession, of the past colliding, in almost tangible terms, with the events of everyday life — an unknown man looking in at you from the window; a shadowy figure only faintly glimpsed on the farther side of the lake; a strange woman surprised in midafternoon sitting at your own desk, who turns toward you a despairing and desperate face — James makes of these visions that haunt our collective imagination a brilliant and horrifying narrative.

My task, and that of the director, was not only to preserve the psychological line necessary to clarify the plot to a theater audience, but also to preserve that elusive energy that has made the story so gripping to readers of Henry James. I had decided the Governess is motivated by a very clear set of sexual impulses, and I hoped to interpret her in that way; if the audience wanted to read anything other into my interpretation, that was all to the good. The play was a puzzle that should never be completed.

Both Harold and I had immense confidence in this production. The music by Harrison Birtwistle contributed to the eerie atmosphere; the two children were both extraordinarily talented; Mrs. Gross, the housekeeper, was played by the superb Irish actress Pauline Flanagan.

I looked eagerly forward to the opening night, impatient to begin my life with Philip and to have much more free time to spend with Anna and my mother. So convinced was I of the high quality of this production, I thought I had only to wait for the official opening of the play in New York to be able to settle down to a long Broadway run.

The Innocents, so well received in Boston and Philadelphia, opened to lukewarm reviews in New York; Clive Barnes, then the theater critic for the all-powerful *New York Times,* began his review with the inspired sentence, "How time jets." He must have been up all night to have invented such a telling phrase. This near-perfect production, which would undoubtedly have run in London for ten months, closed on Broadway after a run of only ten days.

I had allowed myself to be lulled into a false sense of security, and security has no place in the life of an actress. I had expected the play to succeed, and made my plans accordingly: let my house in London and rented an expensive apartment in New York. I had entered my daughter in school and hoped that my stay in the States would be long enough to form a permanent relationship with my new companion. I thought I would be able to fulfill all my obligations. Now it was obvious that the failure of the play would bring everything to a crisis.

Reliant on my theater salary, I was now going to be very short of funds. Philip gave me two thousand dollars toward the rent, which was more than generous; the estate agent agreed to search for another tenant for the apartment. My house in London, now occupied for the next six months, was unavailable to me. My mother thought it best to return with Anna to London, where my daughter could live with her for the moment; she suggested I try to sort my life out with Philip and join them later.

The chasm that was to come between my family obligations and my desire to be with the man I loved was beginning to show itself.

The evening preceding their departure was wretched beyond words; Anna, furious and justifiably hurt, said that I had once again chosen a man over her, which made me feel compromised and guilty. I feared Anna was right — perhaps I was unconsciously sacrificing her in favor of Philip. I wanted desperately to keep what I knew could be the first complete relationship of my life; I understood that my true chance of happiness was with Philip, and that I couldn't give him up.

Mother and Anna left for London the next day, and I went to Connecticut to begin my new life with Philip Roth.

The house of gray clapboard lay just off a dirt road, behind an orchard of apple trees Surrounded by open meadow, which must at one time have been heavily wooded, the house appeared as orderly and sober as the writer who worked within it, and as austere and beautiful as the New England landscape in which it was set. The interior, furnished with country pieces suitable to this late-eighteenth-century farmhouse, had retained original chestnut floors now scattered with colorful rugs. Very few ornaments or paintings were to be seen, only books — books piled high on the tables, stacked on the floor, overflowing the ceiling-tall bookcases.

The sweetness and simplicity of the life we led there in those early days more than compensated for any sense that my other life, that of an actress, was in danger of getting lost. There were, nevertheless, times when I questioned whether I had the inner resources I would need to live in such an isolated and withdrawn manner, even with so stimulating a companion as Philip.

I was happy and cheerful in the mornings, until Philip left to go to his studio; then I began to wonder how I was going to get through the day. I took long walks, planned elaborate menus, I read; but my time was really passed in waiting until Philip came back in the late afternoon.

One concern was constantly with me: the knowledge that, by staying with Philip in Connecticut, I was neglecting my daughter. Mother was now in her early seventies, and although I flew to London every six weeks, the care and supervision of a sixteen-year-old was far too large a responsibility for her.

To my great relief, a few months after we had begun our life together, Philip suggested that we try spending six months of the year in London, and the other six in the United States. I knew what a difficult decision this must have been for a man of Philip's temperament, that for a writer to change the place where he creates his work takes enormous courage. Philip was chained to his writing habits; he had never neglected to sit down at his typewriter even in the first days of our relationship. I was deeply appreciative of this gesture. There was, however, one provision: he made it clear that he had no intention of living together in the same house as my daughter.

This mixture of kindness and cruelty, this coupling of gener-osity and selfishness, made me frantic with confusion. I told Philip that what he demanded of me was an impossibility; there was plenty of room in my London house for the three of us to live quite comfortably together. Eventually, Philip agreed to see if some form of family life would be possible for him.

We moved to London, and at first all was peaceful. Philip found a studio to work in; Anna had her own space upstairs, and we occupied the lower half of the house. I have no doubt whatsoever that this new existence must have been strange for Philip, who was used to living alone; now he was forced to share his life with a mother and daughter whom he viewed as too needily interdependent.

Anna was just beginning to embark on her singing studies,

and was as ambitious and self-involved as only a teenager could be. The dinner conversation, when the three of us were together, centered around her progress at the Guildhall School of Music. I was blind to the degree that this made Philip feel excluded and of the frustration and jealousy that was gradually building up in him; that he was becoming both bored and angered by our obsessive discussions.

I tried hard to expiate the guilt I felt toward Anna because of my former involvement with Elkins. I wanted, in every way possible, to show her how profoundly important her welfare was to me. The more I tried to make up to Anna for my past mistakes, the more Philip resented the attention I paid her. I knew that if only there could be some leeway from either of them, somehow I might be able to handle the situation. But I was up against two very strong personalities, and neither side would give in to the other. It was like having two children who were terrified of losing their mother's love. And I became a third child, terrified of losing the love of either of them. Many times I went to my mother or my brother and sister-in-law's house, weeping and distraught. I also was in fear that I had no way of keeping my other self, the actress, the woman, alive under such strain. All I wanted to do was to preserve some kind of peaceful coexistence in my own home, and even that seemed to be almost impossible.

There is no need to chronicle the life we led from day to day. There were happy times, and times of great anguish. The tension between my daughter and my companion began to accelerate, and somehow in the middle I was running from one to the other, trying to placate them both. I distinctly recall taking a walk, and stopping in surprise because I heard myself sing. I didn't recognize this response. It had been so long since I had been free of worry, I was caught unaware by this woman who sang so cheerfully.

In 1977, the second year of our life together in London, I was offered a role I had long wanted to play: the strangely single-minded and haunted character of Rebecca West, the woman at the heart of Ibsen's great masterpiece, *Rosmersholm*. I embraced this offer eagerly; as always, it seemed a way out of my labyrinth. I hoped that with the concentration I needed to play such a remarkable role, all my other worries would just go away, and everything would work itself out for the best. But the production was not a success.

The translation was execrable, the director uninspired, and between the leading man and myself, no love was lost. Although the play ran for its allotted four months, it was a grave disappointment to all concerned.

Even so, I would return from the theater high and excited; I wanted to drink, to gossip, to have supper, to unwind. Philip, who had been working since early in the morning, would be reading; he needed quiet and serenity. Often there had been some problem between Anna and Philip, something that seemed fairly petty and tame. The radio may have been playing too loud or Anna was playing the piano upstairs. To me these were minor annoyances, but they were anything but minor to Philip, for whom even moderate disturbance was almost a torture.

I decided that after *Rosmersholm* closed, I would do no more theater, but stick to the far easier television or occasional film role. It would take less of a toll on my personal life.

CHAPTER ELEVEN

Transitions

ONE EVENING, while we were living in London, I returned home after the theater to find Philip in a paroxysm of silent anger.

Anna and a college friend were in Anna's room on the top floor of the house, laughing and talking. He protested that their noisiness interfered with his concentration. I asked him why he hadn't gone upstairs to complain; he replied that it was my job. I obediently walked into Anna's room and asked them to be quiet; the girls apologized and complied. When I came downstairs, Philip refused to talk to me.

In the morning, after a strained breakfast, just as he was about to leave for his studio, he thrust a letter into my hand.

This missive, one of many I was to receive during the course of our years together, contained the following conditions: He wanted to continue his relationship with me, but under no circumstances would he again live in the same house with both me and my daughter; unless Anna agreed to move elsewhere, he would return to New York; we would spend the agreed six months of the year in Connecticut, but in London I would be alone.

He closed by repeating his intention not to end our relationship.

Although Philip's dislike of my daughter was transparent, as was his fierce competitiveness for my affections, I hadn't recognized how deep his prejudice ran where she was concerned. I was caught in the middle, with emotions and responsibilities tugging away on both sides; it was a no-win situation. Placing Philip's needs over Anna's meant hanging on to an important relationship at the price of my daughter's trust in her mother's protection; putting Anna's first meant keeping faith but surrendering a bond I felt with all my heart I couldn't live without.

It was a choice between the security of a companion and the welfare of a daughter. Anna was asked to move out. She was eighteen.

The circumstances were terrible: Anna witnessed someone she viewed as an outsider calling the shots in her own home, and her mother unable to set any boundaries; understandably, she felt angry and betrayed. In addition, Henry Wood House, the student hostel, was located across the Thames in one of the least salubrious neighborhoods of London.

But Philip had his way, and it has taken me a long time to accept the repercussions of his calculated move barely two years into our relationship. It wasn't about hatred for my daughter, though animosity may have been the catalyst — it was about control. Philip made character assessments the way surgeons make incisions. He knew I would make any compromise to support our relationship. If I was willing to jettison my own daughter in this manner, what could I ever deny him?

I know I was diminishing my own character with each successive act of capitulation. These confrontations left me debilitated and unsure, and were to shape many of my future decisions.

He also understood that part of me that was afraid of him. I had once seen a facet of his character that shocked me deeply. Angry over something I frankly no longer remember, he turned toward me with the face of an uncontrollable and malevolent child in a temper tantrum; his lower jaw thrust forward, his mouth contorted, his dark eyes narrowed. This expression of out-and-out hatred went far beyond anything I could possibly have done to provoke it. I remember thinking, with total clarity, "Who is that?"

That feral, unflinching, hostile, accusative, but strangely childlike face would appear increasingly in our years together, sometimes without warning, frequently without provocation, always out of proportion to the events that had given rise to it.

The power Philip held over me wouldn't have existed without his ability also to be a tender, thoughtful, and understanding man. Just as I feared the appearance of this "other" Philip Roth to such a degree that, in order to avoid him, there was almost nothing I wouldn't have done to make him disappear, I also feared to lose the Philip who was my dearly loved companion.

After a spell, the situation between Anna and Philip seemed to improve. When her father underwent a second heart-bypass operation in 1980, Philip was extremely helpful; he behaved as if he had put away his anger. Anna moved back home eventually, and there was one brief moment when I almost believed our life together might come to resemble that of a proper family. But it was not to be.

Years later, when Philip accused me of having an unhealthy preoccupation with Anna, neurotically attempting to make up for what I had failed to do in the past, he was correct. I cannot recall my actions during that time without experiencing an unrelenting feeling of guilt.

Although young people often leave home for college at Anna's age, I have to be extremely clear on this point: my own history had predisposed me to react in panic to any threat of abandonment, leaving me with few weapons to fight for what was right — in this instance, that my daughter remain at home until she and I decided otherwise. Undoubtedly, many women would have reacted to Philip's letter very differently; the truth is that I was unable to oppose him.

This painful passage coincided with a fortunate turn in my career. At the age of forty-nine I was offered the role of Lady Marchmain in the television version of *Brideshead Revisited,* Evelyn Waugh's lyrical evocation of a lost aristocratic domain between the world wars. I nearly turned it down, which is paradoxical, since it was to reestablish me in film and television after a few years' absence. The thought that I should play a matriarch with a grown-up family was something I initially found unacceptable.

There comes a time in every actress's career when her chronological age defines her public identity, thus limiting her ability to attract new offers; consequently, she desperately tries to cling to her youth. I've heard it said that, in the current film world, this dynamic has changed, but my impression is that, some notable female initiatives apart, there are as many insecure actresses today as before. Unlike men, the roles for women alter radically after fifty. Gone then are the lovers, the suitors. Now, in steady succession, come the mothers, aunts, spinsters, and only with the lucky ones who stay to the bitter end, the grandmothers, the crones. A painful transition for any woman.

With *Brideshead,* I had the sense not to allow my vanity to overpower my reason. Nonetheless, at my first costume fitting, one of the younger actresses greeted me with a cheery "Hello, Mum." The dowdy 1920s costumes and the fusty hairstyle did the rest to plummet my rapidly sinking morale.

I was about to play the wife of an expatriate aristocrat played by Laurence Olivier, a man who has distanced himself from his country, family, religious heritage, but above all from his wife's devout adherence to the moral disciplines of the Church: Lady Marchmain is a descendant of generations of Catholic aristocracy. Her whimsical youngest son, Sebastian Flyte, is the most sympathetic character in the novel — a casualty of his religion and class — whereas tradition-bound Lady Marchmain is in some ways the least. Therein lay the challenge for me.

The class system that prevails in England will more than likely persevere so long as the nation remains a monarchy. Actors and artists have historically been able to cross this divide at will. I made several forays into that stratum of society when I was a young and sought-after actress — and always felt out of place. But, quite recently, I had made a new friend who inhabited this old, alien world like a comfortable pair of slippers:

George Howard was the owner of Castle Howard, the setting of Evelyn Waugh's novel and, happily, also the location where the fictional Brideshead was to be brought to life before the cameras. The coincidence of my returning to play the chatelaine of that great house where I had already stayed twice before, as a guest, seemed almost incredible. I remained at Castle Howard for the entire time we filmed. If ever I was to entertain any serious delusions of grandeur, I might well have come to believe Lady Marchmain and I were one and the same.

Fairly late one evening, I was having dinner with Simon Howard, the third of George's four sons, and Jeremy Irons, who played Charles Ryder and was also staying at the estate. They decided to go out to a party. As I had an early call the following morning, I thought it best not to join them. What I didn't realize was that I would be utterly alone in the vast, hushed emptiness that was Castle Howard.

Thinking I would feel less isolated in my own room, I gingerly walked down the long corridor lined with antique statues to arrive in my room, with its stately four-poster bed and dim light.

A gale was howling in my corner of the building, not unlike the wind-swept moors depicted in *Wuthering Heights*. I turned the radio on for company, only to hear a bulletin pronouncing that the "Yorkshire Ripper" was believed to be about his business somewhere in the vicinity. That was enough: I took a sleeping pill and hid in bed, with my head pinned under the covers. The sun rose the following day to find me still among the living.

The filming at Castle Howard continued for several months, and often Philip came to stay for the weekend. He found the very idea of this nice Jewish couple visiting Castle Howard hilariously implausible — fertile Philip Roth territory.

"Try not to feel the curtain fabric and don't ask how much per yard," he warned. "Above all, Claire, don't say 'very nice stuff.' And remember: No Yiddish before breakfast."

With a wonderful cast and its wealth of vivid characters, *Brideshead Revisited* was an all-round success, capturing the spirit of an expansive book while being scrupulous in its attention to detail. I still find it puzzling when I am told I played a manipulative and heartless woman; that is not how I saw her. Lady Marchmain is deeply religious, and her dilemma includes trying to raise a willful brood of children on her own, while instilling them with her rigid observance of the Catholic code. Sebastian is both an alcoholic and a homosexual, and from her point of view, he lives in a state of mortal sin. She has to fight for his soul by any means in her power, with the knowledge that her efforts may eventually lead to his destruction. A born crusader, the marchioness confronts her difficult choices head-on; her rigidity of purpose, which I don't in any way share, is understandable in context. The aspect that rings most true is her sense of being an outsider, a Catholic in Protestant England. Not such a leap from being a Jew in Protestant England as one would imagine.

Domestic Life

Even though I sometimes felt my own career was not as fulfilling as I had hoped it would be at this period in my life, I found great compensations in the growing achievements of Anna.

In her third year as a student at the Guildhall School of Music, Anna was selected to perform a concert with the school orchestra conducted by Stephen Barlow. She sang Ravel's *Shéhérazade*. Before my astonished eyes, a young woman walked onto the platform, elegantly dressed and disarmingly self-assured. Anna held the stage as though she had inhabited it all her life, and met the sensuous music's demands with surprising maturity and an acute feel for the nuances of French poetry; Anna's years at the Lycée and with Hélène paid off. Hélène had always spoken French to Anna, and it came as naturally to her as English. For me, it was difficult to reconcile this passionate young artist with the amusingly grumpy daughter I had eaten breakfast with that morning. The first time my mother saw me act must have been similarly jarring for her; on this occasion, she attended and savored Anna's success at the Guildhall with a satisfaction and pride to match my own.

While still a student, Anna won the 1982 Sir Peter Pears Award for young singers. When she graduated from the Guildhall in 1983, she was invited to become a member of the Glyndebourne Festival Opera Chorus — then, as now, a major gateway through which many great British singers have passed. At Glyndebourne she won the 1985 John Christie Award as the most promising chorus member of the year. Over the next three years of her apprenticeship, she was given small roles and eventually promoted to soloist. In 1985, she won the Richard Tauber Prize, which carried with it a recital at the Wigmore Hall.

Anna was an understudy during the 1986 season when Maria Ewing sang the title role in Monteverdi's opera *L'Incoronazione di Poppea*. She was upstairs taking a bath when I picked up a message left for her on the answering machine: Ewing was ill — Anna was to call the theater immediately.

I ran upstairs and told her the news. Draped in a bath towel, she came and sat on my bed. "How do you feel?" I asked.

"I'm very nervous, but I think I'm going to be very good," she replied thoughtfully. And she was! I was amazed at the confidence and accomplishment of her performance, not even taking into account the fact that she was only starting out as a singer. Anna's Italian was as fluent as her musicianship, and she enjoyed a great success as Poppea. Only with her first curtain call did she betray any sign of inexperience, bowing so quickly I wasn't sure I had seen her, a minor flaw she had corrected by the next performance. Anna's career was off to a flying start.

During this brief period, Anna and Philip appeared to be getting on well, even enjoying their time together. Anna always relished his humor — she was an enthusiastic audience. When they first met, she was in her teens and was insecure about writing even so much as a Christmas card to Philip, given his reputation as a man of letters. When I mentioned this to him, he wrote her a letter teeming with typographical errors and dyslexic, ungrammatical English. It was a thoughtful gesture she appreciated enormously.

The three of us had some good times. We sat together in London to watch the 1978 Academy Awards, when Laurence Olivier received the "lifetime achievement" Oscar: he proceeded to give an interminable speech full of hyperbole, thanking everyone under the sun, with more than one reference to a "firmament," presumably a marquee in the heavens over which his name featured prominently. The television cameras caught Jon Voight, a contender for best actor that year, transfixed and tearful. After Voight won his award, almost choking on the words, he thanked Olivier for his speech. "Why was he so moved?" asked Anna.

"Firmament," said Philip, "is the longest word he's heard since *refrigerator.*"

Philip could be devastating in a concert hall. After the Barbican Centre in the city of London was completed, Anna, Philip, and I went to hear an internationally famous — and, it must be stated at the outset, extremely overweight — American diva perform in a song recital. We listened to her singing attentively, at least until the encores, by which time Philip had had quite enough. Each of these encores was preceded by the arrival of a new bouquet of flowers presented by the house manager, whereupon she sang her piece, bowed, disappeared, came back empty-handed, and the cycle continued. More flowers, more bowing, more singing.

"You know why she keeps on getting flowers, right?" Philip said wildly. "She's eating them! What do you suppose she did during the intermission? She must have had to send out for a triple steak and fries. And look at her! She's still starving!"

Another time, Philip had graciously offered to buy a bed for Anna's room. With his payment came a theatrical tirade worthy of Sophie Portnoy: "Here is money for the whole bed. But if I ever hear that a goy is sleeping on the other half, I swear to you that I'll jump out of the window. And then you'll live with that for the rest of your life and you'll see how much you'll enjoy the bed. You'll hate the bed, you'll be sorry you ever saw the bed, you'll wish the bed had never been made! This is my warning to you. If you have any feeling for me at all, KEEP ALL GOYIM OUT OF THE BED!"

When Philip and I were alone in Connecticut during the years we spent the winter months in London, our time together was often sweet and gentle. There were good spells and there were bad, as in every relationship. When he left the house in the morning for his studio, I occasionally felt lonely and isolated in the depth of the country. But I found ways to make life more interesting. My friendship with Francine and Cleve Gray, our neighbors at the end of the road, became important and precious to me. There were projects to work on, walks to be taken, meals to be discussed and prepared, and yoga lessons, with Francine, to be learned and practiced.

Late in the afternoons, Philip would leave his studio, take a long walk, and come into the house to light a log fire. Frequently, he would open a bottle of red wine, and quietly read while I prepared dinner. Afterward, Philip methodically cleared away and washed the dishes — a task I resisted — and the evening would come to a close with more reading, this time by both of us, beside the hearth. The warmth of the room usually lulled me to slumber; then Philip would wake me, and drowsily, like a child, I would follow him upstairs to the bedroom.

Reading books, exchanging books, discussing books: this was an essential method of communication between us in all the years we were together. My reading was mainly for my own pleasure, for historical research, or as a distraction from ordinary life. But, for Philip, it was his most vital and consequential activity. We both shared a profound seriousness regarding the rewards of this occupation, and our choices were voracious.

Philip introduced me to the works of Milan Kundera,

Tadeusz Gronowski, Bruno Schultz, Jiri Weil, and other Eastern European writers whose works he not only admired but had been instrumental in introducing to the English-speaking world in an innovative series of books entitled *Writers from the Other Europe.* He encouraged me to explore Céline and Kafka, his literary idols, far more exhaustively than I would have done on my own, along with American authors I had formerly acknowledged in a cursory manner, such as Hawthorne and Melville. We shared an admiration for Colette, Chekhov, Conrad, Tolstoy, and Dostoyevsky. Some of the English nineteenth-century writers I had read over and over again — Dickens, Eliot, Hardy — never really found an important place in Philip's lexicon; try as I might to spark his interest, he preferred the more intricate, trenchant austerity of the twentieth-century style.

When I came to prepare, a few years later, dramatic readings of Charlotte Brontë, Henry James, and Virginia Woolf, our immersion in those works came to life in a remarkable way. With Philip's advice, I prepared each performance with great care, and he proved to be a brilliant interpreter of character for theatrical presentation. To this day, I approach reading in the same scrupulous manner he spurred in me.

Sometimes during the writing of a new book, Philip would invite me to read the unedited material. This timing varied according to his enthusiasm, or the degree to which he needed a patient listener on whom to try out a new idea. The genesis of each book followed no particular pattern: sometimes he discussed his plans in a detailed way, other times he preferred to keep them a secret, even from me, until he was certain of his direction.

If he reached an impasse with a female character, we would sometimes play games of improvisation in order for him to find a fresh approach. Occasionally, I would hit on precisely the right turn of phrase; then Philip, after some adjustments, would use it.

I was always careful not to spoil the process with early or harsh criticism. At the same time, I didn't want him to feel I wasn't being as frank with him as he habitually was with me — or, indeed, other writers. He had an uncanny knack for detecting meaningless, easy praise, and his scorn in such cases was quick and unmitigated.

The definition of truth was always a cardinal aspect of Philip's character. He could be brutal when faced with the task of critically assessing his own — or any writer's — work. On one occasion, Bernard Malamud read to us from a manuscript that was to prove to be his last book, and Philip's response was a surgically precise and unemotional condemnation; his verdict was that it shouldn't be published. Bernie was an old, valued friend, and at this point in his life, it was clear that he was a dying man. I could see that his wife, Anne, was appalled — and could understand her, although I hadn't admired the writing any more than Philip had. It was a difficult, uncomfortable, unhappy visit.

After we left, Philip asked me whether he had been too hard. I said, "Yes": I believed it wasn't necessary to attack an old man in the twilight of his career. He argued that he could never be anything less than honest where writing was concerned; he was sorry he had hurt Bernie, but he was compelled to tell the absolute truth when asked to do so by a fellow writer.

Despite the view that Philip's gifts shone most brightly in the realm of the savagely amusing, there was a tenderness that wasn't often remarked upon: the first book he dedicated to me, *The Professor of Desire*, in which he described his life in the country with a former companion, Barbara Sproul, was much more lyrical than many of his later works. *The Ghost Writer*, the first of three books tracing the life and interior progress of Philip's alter ego, Nathan Zuckerman, and also set in a fictionalized version of the Connecticut house, was a beautiful chronicle of the reclusive life of an author. Although publicly Philip maintained it was an amalgam of Malamud's and Saul Bellow's personalities, the writer on whom the portrait was most clearly modeled was, of course, himself.

The Ghost Writer provided one instance where I was instrumental in the conception and development of a character. One evening, Philip came in unexpectedly early from his studio and asked me if I was prepared to let myself go — to describe to him what it was like to live with a writer in the country. I couldn't wait to provide the material, and was off like a horse through the gate: "We don't go anywhere! We don't do anything! We don't see anyone!" And so it went: wearing the mask of Hope Lanoff, the writer's wife, I savored each moment. Although we both laughed at the self-evident truths in my diatribe, Philip must have recognized their validity: they appear almost verbatim in the book.

There is a perfect example of the game Philip loved to play with public perceptions and interpretations of his work. *The Ghost Writer* was made into a television film some years after its publication in 1979, and I was cast as Hope. Despite the obvious differences — she is a Wasp from an old family, has lived her life solely through her husband, and given him many children — there were our relationships with a writer, and our objections, in common.

Another layer of insinuation, because the character is English, was that the *Zuckerman Trilogy*'s Maria was inspired by Philip's relationship with me. In reality, that tender and loving portrait was based on the beautiful, gifted novelist Janet Hobhouse, with whom Philip, the year before we met, had had a brief and intense relationship. Prior to her tragically premature death in 1991, she had written a subtly disguised but sharply observed portrait of her affair with "a celebrated author" in her extraordinary, posthumous roman à clef, *The Furies.*

Still another, and in this instance quite correct, was the evocation of Anne Frank, which was based on my physical appearance as a young woman — the girl from "The Country of Fetching" as she might have been had she survived the war years. Anne Frank and I were born a little over a year apart. The photograph of her that Philip kept on his desk stood next to one of me taken at roughly the same age. The similarity between us as children is striking; it isn't unrealistic to imagine us resembling one another as young women. But with this modest exception and despite some elements of my personality finding their way into his work, I don't believe any of his women were based directly on me.

There seems to be a balance of power struggling away in Philip's fictional men and women. Neither the maternally nurturing young American women of his domestic portraits, nor the sexually available Eastern European women of his erotic imagination, can hold a candle to their male counterparts in intellectual vigor. There is one picture of clear-cut negativity in *My Life As a Man:* the destructive, almost Kali-like figure of Philip's deceased first wife, Maggie.

As re-created, she emerges as the archetypal shiksa, one lacking any sense of moral responsibility, whose sole genius is to possess and destroy. Even though Roth, in a fictional sense, beats the daylights out of her and breaks away from her fatal lure, he never gets rid of her. Here lies a common element that appears and reappears in his later works: the need to escape from a woman at the moment when he realizes his affection makes him vulnerable to her. Implicit in this notion is the sense that, through a woman's dangerous, clandestine power, she is bearer of his physical and mental castration — possibly, even, his death.

In his near-demonic spouse, he created the polar opposite of his own overweening mother, whom Philip would come to depict more compassionately in *The Facts* and in *Patrimony:* no longer Sophie Portnoy, but a passive, good-natured Jewish parent, the fountain of strength and pillar to a close-knit community of first-generation American Jews from whom her introspective son drew much of his writerly fuel.

Acute as Philip's study of Maggie is, I often wondered

whether the former Margaret Michaelson didn't get bad press in this book. Whatever self-fulfilling prophecy made him marry her in the first place, she became only the first in a long parade of women over whom he exercised his considerable power to transform through his writing. The dead woman has gone into the realm of Roth's fiction; the truth about her real self has been left far behind.

A frequent source of strain between us during those country months was that, from time to time, by the very nature of my work, I was forced to travel. There was an ambivalence on both our parts where my career was concerned. Philip's help was invaluable to prepare my work for the stage, and he was immensely proud of my success as an actress; he also admired what he viewed as my courage in facing an audience. But he resented my absences from home.

Even when you love someone deeply, it is hard to give something up that has defined you since childhood. In addition, had I given up my career entirely, I would probably have lost a great deal of the allure I was able to exert in his mind. Had I turned into the maternal figure he so longingly had described to me — preparing tuna fish sandwiches for him to take to school and waiting with a steaming bowl of Heinz tomato soup when he got home — it wouldn't have taken him long to rebel against that particular incarnation of motherly care.

Ultimately, though, it was for myself that I continued to work and strive to keep the important roles in my life — partner, parent, professional woman. My mother and I had sacrificed a great deal for this career. I felt I had years of good work ahead.

CHAPTER TWELVE

Departures and Arrivals

DURING THE PERIOD after *Brideshead Revisited* my mother, although still an extremely self-reliant and independent woman, began to show signs that time was finally catching up. She was approaching eighty.

I understood, although I was unwilling to face the fact, that my mother, in her own way, was slowly saying good-bye. Her last spring was marked by almost perfect weather. There was a lilac tree about to come into bloom outside her window; I often caught her gaze fixed on that tree, as if every moment of its growth and beauty was increasingly precious to her.

She didn't seem any weaker than usual. Uncharacteristically, the night before she died she asked me to buy some food for dinner; it was unusual because she always insisted on doing everything herself. Even then, she didn't allow me to stay and prepare it; she told me to get on with my own evening. I kissed her goodnight, and left for a dinner party.

The telephone rang early the following morning, and I heard the voice of my sister-in-law, Sheila: "Come over quickly. Nanma has had a stroke." I ran downstairs, saw Anna's frightened face, and shouted that I couldn't talk. I rushed over to my mother's house. Outside her door, two burly ambulance men tried to bar me from getting in. I punched one of them on the arm with all my strength, and they let me by.

Mother was seated in an armchair. Her head rested against her side. She had been dead about three hours.

The grief I felt was terrible. I kissed her bare feet and begged her not to go. Sheila was also distressed — she, too, had loved my mother, and had been loved in return — so, together, we cut some of her white hair to keep as a remembrance, and picked bluebells from the garden to lay about her body.

Then, being English, we had several cups of strong tea.

Anna arrived, and I summoned all the strength I could muster to tell her Nanma was dead. "I want you to come and see her," I remember telling her. "Then you'll realize there's nothing to be afraid of."

Philip came from his studio and sat with us next to my mother's body, comforting us both. It took courage on his part to do this, taking into account his inordinate fear of the dead. Philip also performed one other, utterly thankless task: he called John, who was working in Los Angeles, to break the news. Neither Sheila nor I could face doing it ourselves.

I shall always be in Philip's debt — and Anna's, too — for their forbearance in allowing me the freedom to do something I was unable to explain at the time but was compelled to undergo: for the next three days, I sat in the room beside my mother. I silently returned home only to sleep and eat; then, quietly, in the morning, I would return to her. My mind was filled with sounds and images and memories of our life together. Finally, on the third day, I allowed them to take her away. I have absolutely no belief in any form of afterlife, but I am certain my mother was with me during those three days in some indeterminately peaceful, close, and happy communion. Then she was gone.

She was cremated after a simple service attended by our family and a few close friends. Aware of her Nanma's deep and abiding love of Mahler, Anna chose the radiantly peaceful slow movement of his Fourth Symphony to be played.

On the evening of her grandmother's funeral, Anna fulfilled an obligation to give a concert at Kent University. Philip and I went to hear her. The piece was Benjamin Britten's *Les Illuminations*. Anna appeared white and strained, but managed against enormous personal odds to give an incandescent performance. A work of art can take on a deeper meaning when placed within a new context, and Anna's interpretation of the music — but even more, of Arthur Rimbaud's vivid, elegant, and melancholy poems, for which she had always felt a strong affinity — made an unforgettable memorial for her grandmother's death. The final song, *Départ*, reemerged as the most personal of farewells:

> *Seen enough. The vision has been met*
> *everywhere.*
> *Heard enough. Sounds of towns, at night*
> *and in the sunlight, and always.*
> *Known enough. The obstacles in one life. O Murmurs*
> *and Visions!*
> *Leaving into new affections and sounds!*

The period after my mother's death was a time of hard adjustment. At an airport, I had to stop myself before buying a carton of cigarettes to bring home to her. I sometimes had the feeling that we were due to meet for lunch at the Daquise, a small Polish café she loved, located up the road from her house. I couldn't pass Walton Street without the sensation that she was there. It took me a long time to accept the fact that she wasn't, and never would be again.

The year before my mother died, Philip had gone to the United States to visit his father, and while there received his yearly flu shot and medical checkup. There was bad news: he telephoned me to say that three of his arteries were shown to be partially occluded. Though Philip was prone to endless problems with his back, his knee, and a host of other upsets — some real enough, others less so — what had previously seemed to me no more than hypochondriacal fantasies had suddenly metamorphosed into reality. Now it was life-threatening.

He flew back to London to be with me. We determined,

with his doctor's encouragement, to attempt to stave off open-heart surgery for as long as possible. Each year that passed would bring further refinement to already existing methods to prevent an operation. There was medication with miserable physical side effects. I learned to cook low-salt, low-fat, high-fiber meals. Philip exercised more and tried to work less. He was rigid and disciplined — part soldier, part monk — in keeping to his new regimen. Always lanky of build, he became increasingly lean. Gradually, our initial fears subsided and, over the next few years, we learned to live with the situation.

Unquestionably, this news awakened in Philip a dark anxiety. He became extremely sensitive to anything that disturbed him; any minor mishap would cause him to become irritated, usually with me. Instead of keeping my head and remaining calm, I allowed my insecurities to show in ways that only distressed him further. Behind my deceptively frail exterior I knew I was capable of being reliable in a crisis; but I fear that Philip only saw my anxiety and came to lose faith in my steadiness and support.

From the success of *Brideshead,* I was hopeful that film offers would pour in. Even when they didn't, I still had plenty of work. My career was not at a standstill, but I felt it had no direction. For example, I never received an invitation to join the National Theatre — though, even if I had, my personal circumstances would have made it next to impossible, as this would have required at least a full, one-year commitment to London. However, the fact that I was overlooked for parts that would have suited me became more and more disheartening — the actor's perennial lament.

But there were high points. In 1984, the BBC sent me the treatment of a screenplay to be presented as part of a series of programs dealing with religious subjects. Despite my extreme skepticism regarding anything religious, I agreed to be a part of the project at this early stage of its development. The television film that came about, *Shadowlands,* dealt very poignantly with a late-blooming bond between the Christian author and scholar

C. S. Lewis and his wife, the converted Jewish-American poet Joy Davidman. This was a wonderful role that conveyed the sensitivity of an intelligent woman dying from an incurable disease, and C. S. Lewis was to be played by my old friend Joss Ackland.

In the 1985 British Film and Television Awards, *Shadowlands* took home every important prize in each category, with one sad omission: for his beautiful performance, Joss received nothing. In my acceptance speech I was determined to praise and thank him as best I could.

But the life of an actor is peppered with blows to the ego. I believe our production of *Shadowlands* was unsurpassable, yet Joss and I saw in subsequent years a theatrical version based on the same material with other actors; and also, quite recently, a film directed by Richard Attenborough, again utilizing virtually the same script, with Anthony Hopkins and Debra Winger — younger and far more successful film performers — playing our roles. Over the years, you must learn to let go.

In 1985, a challenge of another sort presented itself. One of the most peculiar roles I have ever been offered was that of an Indian woman in the American television adaptation of Michael Korda's fictional account of Merle Oberon's life, entitled *Queenie*. Oberon's mother had been a poor woman from Calcutta, while her father was an Irish worker who disappeared soon after her birth. When she became a star in Hollywood, the fact that she was half Indian was hidden, lest letters protesting her acting opposite "white" actors flood in. Her dark-complexioned mother came to be by her daughter's side, posing as a maid.

Fitted in a fine sari, my makeup tinted a very becoming shade of golden brown and my eyes heavily outlined in kohl, I thought myself pretty exotic and surely irresistible — a sexually alluring figure from the *Kama-Sutra*. That is, until I returned home one day after filming some interior scenes in a London studio prior to traveling to India. Philip greeted me with a simulated airport public announcement: "Dr. Shapiro! Dr. Shapiro! Please go to Gate 10. Your wife is waiting for you." What I resembled, said Philip and Anna, laughing, was a nice Jewish snowbird returning from wintering on Miami Beach.

Finally, in 1986, a splendid film role came my way. After the success of *My Beautiful Laundrette,* Hanif Kureishi wrote another screenplay in his collaboration with director Stephen Frears, and the part I played was the only one that has ever been written expressly for me. The provocatively entitled *Sammy and Rosie Get Laid* was a fascinating study of London's class and race barriers, one that offered a biting overview of Britain's disenfranchised youth. I played Alice, an elegant woman past her prime, unmarried, who has let herself go ever so slightly, and whose life is momentarily lifted from resignation and tedium by the rekindling of a romantic flame from many years earlier. My partner in the film was the great Indian actor Shashi Kapoor. Despite positive reviews on both sides of the Atlantic, the film went relatively unnoticed.

Highs and Lows

After his diagnosis of occluded arteries, I hated to leave Philip alone in the isolation of the house in Connecticut. Before each trip, I called our friends nearby so they would check up on him every so often, which they conscientiously did.

In 1987, Philip once again paid a visit to his father, and once again he telephoned me with disturbing news. I was in London appearing in a television film.

Before he traveled to New York, Philip had been suffering from an inflamed knee joint. He rang to say that the day before, without informing or consulting me, he had checked into a hospital and had his knee operated on for what the doctor described as a "medial meniscus tear." It seemed like a fairly standard procedure, but during the course of the operation, the doctor decided to shave away some of the frayed bone fragments of Philip's knee joint.

I was aghast that Philip hadn't waited to seek my advice first. Also, it was uncharacteristic of him to take such a drastic measure without a second doctor's opinion. As it was too late to say otherwise, I told him I was certain he had done the right thing. Privately, I was by no means sure.

Once more he flew back to London, and I met him at the airport. He was seated in a wheelchair, grim and pale. The pain in his knee had not abated; it was worse than it had been prior to the operation.

When we got home, Philip told me he was sorry he let the eager young doctor perform the operation.

We remained in London for two weeks, after which I was free to accompany him back to New York. The pain by now had become unbearable. We went from one doctor to another, each more curt and unpleasant than the last. In the silence of Connecticut, Philip began to have nightmares, which were to continue for the next few months. Terrible, complicated nightmares: in one he described to me, a frieze of the alphabet that had circled the walls of his bedroom when he was a child came to life and tormented him. It might have seemed innocuous enough, but it was a life-or-death matter, for the alphabet was Philip's very existence, the key to all the words that eventually made up each book he read or wrote. During his conscious, working hours in the studio, he was able to exert control on them. Now, in his tortured unconscious, the instruments of his craft turned against him. Other dreams were too painful for him to revisit; my only notion of their horror was the high-pitched cries he emitted in the night.

He began to suffer from insomnia, lack of appetite, difficulty in concentrating on his work — even to the layman, textbook symptoms of anxiety and depression. He became more and more exhausted and, in the end, completely collapsed.

He went to his psychoanalyst, who prescribed two drugs, Halcion and Xanax. Initially, Philip felt some relief, and was able to sleep without the dreams that had recently haunted him for long hours. At this point he began a harrowing, regressive slide back into his early childhood. Philip's mother had died in August, 1981, and now, suddenly, he became her little boy again. He clung to me in a way he never had before, his entire body trembling with the desperate need for maternal comfort and reassurance. It was a beautiful summer, and the house was filled with brilliant sunlight. "Why don't we walk in the fields?" I asked. "Why don't we go for a swim?" He had become terrified of the water, and made slapping movements with the back of his hands like a child's first, awkward paddle. "No, don't make me stay in the pool," he cried. There was nothing I could do to help. Philip disintegrated before my eyes into a disoriented, terrified infant.

Neither of us connected this breakdown with Halcion; it had, after all, been prescribed as a safe drug by his trusted doctor. First a questionable knee operation, now a possibly drug-induced depression. So much for trusted medicine and other oxymorons.

To my knowledge, Philip had never experienced a depression of such intensity. Had the doctors diagnosed his condition during the first episode and treated him with the appropriate medication, I believe he might have been able to control this devastating illness.

We had little help and no advice; alone in Connecticut, we spent the better part of three months hoping against hope that his despondency would somehow come to an end by itself. From my point of view, Philip's mental coming-apart is almost impossible to describe; but from his, there is a grueling and sobering account in his 1993 novel, *Operation Shylock,* which is neither inaccurate nor overblown; it was just as he recorded it, with the added factor, unmentioned in the book, that I was dangerously close to going down with him.

There was one occasion when I lost my grip. Before joining Philip in Connecticut, I was alone in London, and had made a swift — and, it is now clear to me, panic-driven — decision to sell the house and look for an apartment with no stairs to climb, my reasoning being that Philip's knee should not be aggravated

My mother on her houseboat on the Thames
(at Chelsea Reach).

Dressing room photograph
with Rod, 1966.

On holiday in Capri with my daughter, Anna, 1966.

Anna Steiger as Maddelena in Rigoletto, *1995, Monte Carlo Opera. (C. Mac Burnie)*

As Blanche DuBois in
A Streetcar Named Desire,
London, 1974.
(John Haynes)

With Philip outside the house in Connecticut, 1986. (Richard Stem)

As Irene in When We Dead Awaken, *with the great Norwegian actor Espen Sjonberg at the Almeida Theatre, London, 1991.*

Our wedding, April 19, 1990.
(Dominique Nabokov)

As Mme.
Ranevskaya in The
Cherry Orchard,
American Repertory
Theatre, 1993.
(Richard Feldman)

My brother, John.
(Sheila Bloom)

With my
sister-in-law, Sheila.
(Sheila Bloom)

Filming Daylight *in 1995 at Cinecittà with Sylvester Stallone and director Rob Cohen.*

As Mary Tyrone in Eugene O'Neill's
Long Day's Journey into Night,
performed at the American Repertory Theatre,
Cambridge, Massachusetts, 1996.
(T. Charles Erikson)

in any way. I must have known that Philip would be angry at an excessive, over-emotional reaction to his problems, because I never informed him of these plans.

In Connecticut, I received a call from the real-estate agent, which Philip overheard; he was predictably furious. I told him I was only trying to be helpful, but his anger persisted. The real reason for his anger, unbeknownst to me at the time, was a secret agenda concerning our life in London.

I felt unfairly misunderstood and just started screaming; I ran out of the house into the fields and refused to come indoors. Eventually, I calmed down and, reluctantly, went back inside. My strength — no, my endurance — was fading fast. Philip suggested asking his old friend Bernard Avishai, a fellow writer, to come from Boston and stay with us for the next few weeks, and I agreed.

I am convinced that Bernie saved Philip's life.

Less than a year before this episode, Bernie had suffered a similar breakdown. He also had been prescribed Halcion, and had become suicidally depressed as a result. Philip, who had feared he was losing his mind, was relieved to hear that his terrible situation could possibly have been drug-induced. For, in that case, he could see some end to the labyrinth in which he had become lost. Bernie put him in touch with his own doctor in Boston, who confirmed the hypothesis. With the encouragement of our longtime friend and doctor, C. H. Huvelle, Philip agreed with Bernie that the only way out of the inferno he was experiencing was to go "cold turkey" that very night. Bernie offered to stay with Philip during the next seventy-two hours, which he warned would be agonizing for Philip to endure — and, he stressed, for me to witness.

My first reaction was distrust: I didn't know Bernie well at the time, and was extremely protective of Philip. But the situation was desperate. I moved out of the bedroom and let Bernie take over his care.

Philip spent the next three nights alone with Bernie; in the morning, they both emerged from their sleepless ordeal drained and shaken. I don't know what Philip experienced during those nights; he never spoke of it. By the time Bernie left us a week later, Philip, although still weak and frightened of a relapse, was already on the path to recovery. We spent some time in Martha's Vineyard with William Styron and his wife, Rose. For Philip to be with such an old friend helped restore his spirits.

In *Operation Shylock,* Philip suggests that Halcion only exacerbated the suicidal course of his depression, but that the real cause of his breakdown arose from something deep within him, which may explain his fear regarding committing himself to a mental institution.

The Trappist seclusion of our country life had become a threat to us both. As an outcome of Philip's illness, the comfortably quiet life we had found so satisfying had turned into one of constraint; both of us were afraid of being alone together.

I agreed that our six-month period in London had come to the end of its purpose. From my standpoint, Anna was now out in the world, my mother was gone, I could work on either side of the Atlantic, and Philip vowed never to live in England again. He now claimed to find the English anti-Semitic, boringly predictable, and offensively insular. I was struck by a great sense of disappointment and loss, because Philip and I had enjoyed some of our happiest days in London. He had come to my country a healthy and vibrant man. We had many friends and an active social and intellectual life; he wrote the Zuckerman Trilogy and *The Counterlife,* arguably his defining achievements as an author, during that time. He had felt free and happy in London for many years.

There is one anecdote that displays all too graphically Philip's mounting frustration and displacement in London. On our last visit together there, we had gone out to dinner at a local restaurant. We could overhear a conversation at a neighboring table: a woman was recounting to her companion that she had bought her ring from "a little Jew" who had "naturally" cheated her. It was like a scene out of one of Philip's novels. I listened and couldn't believe what I heard. Philip went over to their table, called the woman a "scumbag," and then left the restaurant. I was left at the table near the anti-Semitic patrons, presumably convicted of guilt-by-nationality. My attitude toward that brand of prejudice — which I believe to be less common in England than it is in the United States — has always been to stand against it, vote against it, and otherwise put it in context simply as an ugliness of life. After I made my way home, Philip's response to this rationale was to accuse me of "criminal indifference."

So we began the move to New York, and the search for an apartment in Manhattan. Almost immediately I hit upon one I thought was ideal. Philip agreed, and we became residents of New York City's Upper West Side.

I was delighted with our new apartment; I loved the view from our sixteenth-floor bedroom window looking southeast over to the Citicorp Building. I watched the sun cross its white facade in the early morning, a transformation that revealed hues from pale rose to deepest scarlet. It was the first home Philip and I had chosen together and was in every sense our own. After searching for a special piece of furniture, we would then sit and gaze with pleasure after each new article arrived. Philip showed an unexpected knack for polishing, and used to make me laugh at the thoroughness he brought to performing this ordinary household task. In polishing as in writing as in every aspect of his life, Philip's way was dedicated and, to a fault, serious.

My career took a satisfying turn that presented opportunities for me to play before live audiences, something I've always loved. In 1981, with Philip's help, I had devised several one-woman performances of Shakespeare, initially studies of Viola, Volumnia, Katharine of Aragon, and Juliet, which I entitled *Then Let Men Know*. Over the course of the decade, I started to obtain bookings all over the United Kingdom and the United States, where the programs concocted by both of us became even more ambitious: two further Shakespeare presentations, *Sisters and Daughters* and *Women in Love,* where I played roles I had never had the experience of performing onstage — Lady Macbeth, Cleopatra, Imogen, Titania, Rosalind, and Isabella. I adapted readings from Charlotte Brontë's *Jane Eyre* to Tolstoy's *Anna Karenina* to Henry James's *The Turn of the Screw;* and one of my most challenging recitals, a program of poems and settings in music by two of the century's boldest voices, Russian poets Marina Tsvetaeva and Anna Akhmatova.

This collaboration brought together readings in the original language by one of Russia's paramount classical actresses, Alla Demidova, followed by translations of these poems read by me, interspersed with musical settings by some famous Soviet composers sung by Anna with piano accompaniment.

The bulk of my time was spent making short trips — none of them keeping me away from Philip for more than a few days — throughout America and occasionally across the Atlantic to fulfill an artistic endeavor I loved and he supported entirely. My life suddenly became very happy.

I enjoyed being in New York with our friends. I've often felt it was a city that boosted my energy when I was strong, depleted it terribly when I was down. This was a strong time: we gave weekly dinner parties; Philip was teaching literature at Hunter College, a branch of the New York City University system; I was offered a job there, too, and found I had some talent for teaching aspiring actors how to approach Shakespeare. I enjoyed the company of my young students, and they seemed to enjoy mine.

Sometime after Philip had recovered from the breakdown, he began sporadically to write again. He started on a new book; it was to be called *Deception.* Although his usual custom had always been, when he was enthusiastic about his work, to discuss it openly, this time the book was barely mentioned. I had no idea what he was writing about, nor any suspicion that he might have a reason to be less than informative about the contents of the new book.

I rarely visited his studio, which was only two blocks away from our apartment. I always respected it as his private territory. On one occasion I received an unexpected piece of good news in the mail, and ran excitedly, letter in hand, to visit him. His reaction was cold, alarmed, and unwelcoming. I told him I would never interrupt him there again, and left.

When he completed *Deception,* he didn't invite me to read the material, as he had previously done with other books at this stage. The manuscript sat on his desk for three weeks; then, early one morning, he brought it to me before he left for the studio.

I eagerly opened the folder. Almost immediately I came upon a passage about the self-hating, Anglo-Jewish family with whom he lives in England. Oh well, I thought, he doesn't like my family. There was a description of his working studio in London, letter-perfect and precise. Then I reached the depictions of all the girls who come over to have sex with him — in the most convoluted positions, preferably on the floor. As Philip always insisted that the critics were unable to distinguish his self-invention from his true self, I mindfully accepted these Eastern European seductresses as part of his "performance" as a writer; but I was not so certain. Finally, I arrived at the chapter about his remarkably uninteresting, middle-aged wife, who, as described, is nothing better than an ever-spouting fountain of tears constantly bemoaning the fact that his other women are so young. She is an actress by profession, and — as if hazarding a guess would spoil the incipient surprise lying in store — her name is Claire.

I no longer gave a damn whether these girlfriends were erotic fantasies. What left me speechless — though not for long — was that he would paint a picture of me as a jealous wife who is betrayed over and over again. I found the portrait nasty and insulting, and his use of my name completely unacceptable.

Far earlier than usual, Philip returned home, carrying in his pocket an exquisite gold snake ring with an emerald head from

Bulgari on Fifth Avenue. I was waiting for him, shaking with rage. I told him he had used me most shabbily. I told him I wanted my name out of the book. I told him that was the end of that; there would be no discussion. He tried to explain that he had called his protagonist Philip, therefore to name the wife Claire would add to the richness of the texture. I replied I didn't care whether it did or not. I reminded him that, like him, I was a public figure also and would seek any means at my disposal — even legal means — to have my name removed. For once confronted by my opposition, Philip agreed to remove it from the novel. Then I accepted his guilt offering. I wear it to this day.

In 1989 we returned to Connecticut for the summer. Philip appeared in very good health and we were planning to spend time alone without any of the tensions and extremes of the past year. One August evening we went out to dinner at the Hopkins Inn and took an outside table; we ordered a bottle of wine and sat enjoying the warm summer evening air. Suddenly Philip's face turned white; I felt his brow, which was covered in cold sweat. He said he felt terribly ill. Leaving our bill to be settled later, we went straight home. The next morning, Philip said he felt much better and went about his day; I accepted his explanation that the glass of wine he had taken on an empty stomach had made him feel sick. Later that day, however, as he was taking his usual solitary afternoon swim in the pool some distance from the house, he had an alarming experience; unable to draw breath, he clung to the edge of the pool. For some reason — perhaps because he was already scheduled to visit the Waterbury Hospital the next day for a checkup, possibly because he did not want to alarm me further — he didn't bother to mention the episode in the pool.

He visited the hospital and later telephoned me to say the news was not good. The electrocardiogram had shown his arteries now occluded to an alarming degree, some as much as eighty percent.

Totally shocked, I sat down, and attempted something no degree of acting prowess would make any easier — to make my voice sound steady so as not to upset him. Here was the moment we had feared for so long. Philip told me he had been advised to return home and wait for three days to repeat the tests. The results were being faxed to Dr. Smithen, his cardiologist in New York.

Less than ten minutes later, I received a call from Dr. Smithen. He said that Philip was to come to New York immediately; they were scheduling emergency open-heart surgery for the following day.

Mechanically, I began to pack his overnight bag. He called from the local market to ask if we needed anything and I had to break the news that his doctor had called and insisted he must go immediately to New York Hospital. He met this information, as hard for me to break to him as it must have been for him to hear, with great calm, and came home immediately.

We left for New York straightaway. Philip insisted on driving himself. While on the road, he dictated very calmly several things I was to take care of when we arrived. I was to call his brother in Chicago and ask him to come as soon as possible. I was to inform his close friends what was about to happen. I was to take the car to the garage.

We checked into the hospital and were ushered into a room that was quite shabby and far from clean; the nurse who showed it to us said, with an evident air of importance, that this was the room in which Andy Warhol had died not long before. I didn't want Philip to stay in this room, so we asked for another. I went down to arrange for a private nurse and to see that the television set was turned on; then I went into a phone booth and made the necessary calls. On Philip's instructions, I called his father, Herman, and told him that Philip had unexpectedly had to leave for a book tour and would call him in a few days. This fiction was kept up by Philip to the end of his convalescence; the reason being that Herman was in his eighties and dying of an inoperable brain tumor. Philip had wished to spare his only remaining parent the shock of his own impending operation.

In his room, I sat beside Philip while he ate dinner. Over his shoulder I could see the scanner monitoring his heartbeat — rising, falling, rising in a rhythm that, even to my eyes, was unmistakably erratic. Philip's anxiety was illuminated on the screen, but outwardly he appeared composed. We were told that the operation would begin at 7:30 A.M., and would take several hours. Philip made me promise not to come to the hospital until ten. I kissed him goodnight and left as calmly as I could. We both knew that this was no simple operation, and understood without the need for words what kind of farewell this might be.

Although exhausted, I couldn't sleep. Even after taking a sedative, I awoke long before dawn. Not knowing what to do with myself, I started to clean the apartment. With New York draped in virtual darkness, I vacuumed and polished and dusted without a pause; suddenly I stopped and felt a kind of peace. I looked at the clock: it was precisely 7:30 A.M. — Philip would have been going under general anesthetic that very moment. Nothing seemed real. Not unlike the time my mother put on her best coat to meet the Germans during the war, I chose an attractive outfit, applied makeup, and carefully arranged my hair before leaving for the hospital. I knew Philip wouldn't know if I was even there, but somehow I thought it might please him that I had taken the trouble to look pretty.

Philip's brother, Sandy, arrived from Chicago, and in the waiting room we haltingly tried to reassure one another; Sandy had been through this grueling operation himself a few years before and understood the dangers entirely. At 2 P.M., Dr. Krieger, the surgeon, called us into his office and said the operation had gone extremely well; he gave us permission to visit Philip in the intensive-care unit.

The room was hypnotically dim. The only sound came from the monitors tracking the patient's heartbeat. Foolishly, I remarked to Sandy how peaceful Philip looked, how calmly he was breathing. He was on a life-support system, but Sandy was considerate enough to allow me to keep my illusions.

Suspended between life and death, Philip looked vulnerable and frail. Sandy and I spoke to him, the words one says when there is nothing adequate to say, the well-intentioned, desperately hopeful phrases one meaninglessly offers before one's greatest fears. In a manner that, under any other circumstance, I probably wouldn't have been able to do — for he would have taken it as overemotional and cloying — I said to Philip, "I love you."

Philip made a slow but triumphant recovery. As his strength picked up, it was as though he had conquered death and become immortal. For me, the specter that had haunted us so long had been, with one brilliant stroke of surgical skill, removed. I was confident our life would gradually become normal again.

One thing I feared during Philip's recovery was that a worsening in Herman's condition might cause Philip a setback. The doctor, however, assured me that he would be much better able to handle such a shock now than before.

In late November, Philip received a frantic call from Herman's nurse, Ingrid; she said Herman was choking. Philip and Sandy had already been informed by doctors that his inability to draw breath would be the final stage of the illness. Philip instructed Ingrid to call for an ambulance, telephoned Sandy in Chicago, and left alone for New Jersey.

Later that afternoon, I called the hospital. The phone was answered by Sandy's son, Jonathan; I could hear from his voice that he was crying. Herman had died after a long and painful struggle only seconds before my call. Sandy had arrived too late to say good-bye. Philip appeared to be the most in control of us all. He has written beautifully of his father's declining years in his 1990 memoir, *Patrimony*. The portrait of his father is one of warmth, honesty, and sharp observation. Herman was difficult, sentimental, rambunctious, tough, and often very funny. We got on very well despite our disagreeing on almost everything. At his funeral, I read a piece Philip had written about his father but couldn't trust himself to deliver. The last parent of his beloved early years had gone.

Despite the loss of Herman, I was so happy for Philip's new lease on life that any pain he had caused me in the past was forgotten; I was prepared to accept that the frustrated anger he exhibited was understandable dread and private suffering. My anger and hurt over *Deception* now seemed very petty indeed by comparison. I looked forward to the future in a way I hadn't allowed myself to do; up to that point, I wasn't certain how long that could be.

In early January 1990, one year after the operation, I asked him to marry me. After fifteen years together, after all we had been through in the course of our relationship, I thought it was time he made me his wife, that marriage would be of immense significance to me. I made it clear to him that, whatever he decided, I would remain with him. He said he needed some time to consider the idea. From any other man this would have been an outright rejection; but after living with Philip, I knew him well enough to understand that he never made a commitment of any kind without giving every aspect a profound consideration.

I left for London to appear at the Almeida Theatre in a revival of Ibsen's rarely performed play *When We Dead Awaken*. Three weeks later, I received a typewritten letter that read: "Dearest Actress, I love you. Will you marry me?" It was signed, "An Admirer." It was typical of Philip to answer in this fashion: a humorous — and, in this instance, charming — twist on the most serious decision a man and woman can make together; a nameless, impersonal reply to that most personal of requests. Although the time in Connecticut was 3:00 A.M., I telephoned to say, "Yes. Yes. I will."

That early morning will remain with me always as one of absolute and radiant happiness.

We were married on April 19, 1990, in the apartment of our longtime friend Barbara Epstein, where we had once spent a Christmas evening together many years before. Barbara and I filled the apartment with white flowers. Bernie made a beautiful toast hailing the union of "best friends," which was silently followed by the raising of glasses and sipping of champagne. Philip added a wry addendum of his own, in which he noted that our assembled friends, having waited expectantly so many years for this day, could finally get some sleep; it was received with cheers and applause. It was a wonderful beginning to our married life.

But something ominous had taken place during the interval between the time of my proposal and Philip's reply, which I had chosen to disregard. Had I done otherwise, it would have given me the clearest message that the marriage was no more than Philip paying lip-service to my desire to be married.

He had consulted his lawyer, Hélène Kaplan, and with her counsel a prenuptial agreement was drawn up, a document glaring in its absence of any provision for me should Philip decide, for any reason whatsoever, to seek a divorce. It did allow me a lifetime tenancy in the New York apartment, plus a generous sum of money, were Philip to predecease me. But, under its conditions, he could terminate our marriage at will, with no further responsibility toward his wife; the apartment, possessions, everything reverted back to him. With lawyerly prudence, Kaplan suggested I seek legal advice of my own choosing before signing.

I signed these papers two days prior to our wedding. So committed was I at this point to becoming Philip's wife, I accepted the insult offered, and chose to ignore it. I know that, had I objected, there would have been no marriage. We had been together for fifteen years, surely time enough for him to be certain I was scarcely out to get his money. I wanted to be his wife more than I had ever wanted anything; enough to turn my face away from this blow to my pride and my integrity.

★ ★ ★

After so many years of living together, I was Philip's wife at last. Often he would remark that, even to his own surprise, our marriage was giving him the greatest happiness; his only regret, he said, was that we hadn't married earlier, when we might have had a child.

All the strain that had grown between us seemed to vanish. The solitary months we began to enjoy again in Connecticut were balanced by the invigorating time we spent in New York. It was not to last long, however.

By the end of the second year, Philip's confidence in our relationship seemed to falter; he began to withdraw from me emotionally. Perhaps too much domestic harmony had become an obstacle to his creativity. Something unspoken was causing a rift, which came soon after in the form of another unexpected and totally unwarranted attack on my daughter.

Anna had been to visit us in Connecticut twice since our marriage — only for days. I was happy to have her, and was under the impression that Philip and Anna had reached a kind of truce. When she came to the New York City Opera to perform in the Frank Corsaro/Maurice Sendak production of *L'Heure espagnole* originally mounted at Glyndebourne, Philip was kind and affirming.

Without warning that something in her last visit had upset him, Philip handed me another letter — there had been a gap of many years since the last of these written injunctions — this time demanding that Anna was to limit her visits to Connecticut to only one week per year. He also made it clear that when Anna and I visited New York together, he would prefer that she not stay in our apartment.

I decided the only way to deal with his petty belligerence was to humor him and take no notice. As it turned out, Anna didn't enjoy Connecticut in the first place. She disliked Philip and came only because it pleased me. As for the city, I considered the apartment as much my home as his, so I had no intention of complying with this request. Back in the uncomfortable middle, I had to juggle with their emotions — another no-win situation.

I kept my relationship with Anna secret from Philip, and kept the contents of Philip's letter secret from Anna. Philip seemed to be seized by bouts of paranoia. We had argued over a small cottage I wanted to buy from our friend Gaia Servadio in Umbria, Italy, which I thought would be a small, inexpensive holiday retreat that Philip and Anna, on different occasions, might enjoy. When I called Philip to discuss this proposition, he responded with an angry outburst, making dire predictions about my financial future and covert threats regarding our future marriage. One day in Connecticut many months after our wedding, I asked Philip for a blank tape to use in my preparation for a recital. I pressed the play button by mistake, and was stunned to hear our telephone conversation in full. It had been recorded by Philip for reasons I can only guess at. As far as I know, this accidental revelation remained undiscovered by him. I certainly never mentioned it.

On the surface, our life went on as though nothing untoward had occurred. I continued to tour with my Shakespeare series, also appearing from time to time as narrator with orchestras across America. Philip was hard at work on a novel he confidently believed was to be his finest ever.

In the winter of 1992, Philip completed *Operation Shylock*. He was more optimistic about this book than about any of his previous works. He talked about it incessantly, reading passages to me that were dazzlingly incisive and entertaining. I was sure he would once again confound his critics with his superimposition of one identity upon another upon another, while delighting his admirers, who, under the spell of his masterful game, understood and appreciated his multicolored weave of fantasy and fact. The sections recounting his Halcion-induced breakdown, recording the trial of John Demjanjuk in Israel, and a scene devising a meeting between a "real" Philip Roth and a "fake" Philip Roth, were some of the best things he had ever achieved, navigating the difficult course between investigation and invention with a kind of genius. His publishers, Simon & Schuster, his friends, and his agent, Andrew Wylie, agreed that the book was, without a doubt, his masterpiece.

As with the first book that came at the beginning of our relationship, *The Professor of Desire,* he dedicated *Operation Shylock* to me.

On my sixty-second birthday in February, Philip planned a party for me in Connecticut, inviting many of our friends and accommodating them in a hotel. He arranged every detail of the evening with infinite care, and his pride in the perfect way it had all gone was touching. The openness with which he publicly expressed his love for me moved me to tears.

March 19 was Philip's birthday; he was sixty years of age.

On this occasion he was fêted and honored both in New York and his hometown of Newark for his achievements as an American writer; a documentary was also completed for British television. He was invited to go on a book tour, giving readings from his last book, *Patrimony.* Though he had developed a deep-seated fear of public readings and asked me to come with him to give him confidence, his performances were outstanding and often even inspired. It was one of the few occasions in those later years that we traveled together.

During that month, I accompanied him to San Francisco, when an unexpectedly early review of *Operation Shylock* appeared in *Time* magazine. I read it first: it called the book superb. I ran back to our hotel and showed the article to Philip. As further notices appeared, however, it gradually became obvious he wasn't going to have the critical triumph he had confidently expected.

It appeared that this great novel was not to be a favorite with the critics. Although both Alfred Kazin in the *New York Observer* and Harold Bloom in the *New York Review of Books* praised it generously, John Updike's grudging estimation in the *New Yorker* came as a great blow to Philip's morale.

In bookstores, sales, which had started promisingly, began to fizzle out. *Time* suddenly withdrew its offer of a cover story.

Despite the intensity of his disappointment, Philip remained externally self-possessed. We returned to Connecticut and tried to come to terms with our unmet expectations. By April, Philip began to experience debilitating back pain, and slowly he became physically incapacitated. The crest of the emotional wave he had been riding before the publication of the book transmuted into its polar opposite.

We were once again alone in isolation. The house that during past springtimes had offered us a haven from the outside world became again our prison. His love for me seemed to increase; his need for comfort and reassurance of my presence intensified. But the other side of this neediness was an obsessive fear of becoming overly dependent: he felt he was "groveling."

When I asked him what he feared, he replied that his terror was that I would abandon him.

CHAPTER THIRTEEN

The Journal

PHILIP BEGAN TO SUFFER from a recurrence of his previous severe depression. By the summer it had become obvious that he was extremely ill, and quickly plunging headlong into the dark territory he had inhabited five years earlier — a bleak terrain with ramifications he and I both feared, though my fears were rooted in concerns for my own welfare as well as his. In this period began the coming-apart of our long, complex, rich, rewarding, but ultimately tortured, relationship.

When the trajectory of Philip's emotional swings became so extreme that I was unable to follow them in a rational manner, I began writing a journal. Keeping these notes helped me to regain my balance in the face of his abrupt changes.

This is my account of the events that followed.

Saturday, July 17, 1993
Caramoor, New York
Performance of the narration of *A Midsummer Night's Dream* with the Orchestra of St. Luke's. Before the concert I called Philip — he was out. Then I remembered he was dining with C.H. I called the Huvelles and C.H. told me Philip had canceled their dinner. He said it was that he was too upset after a violent quarrel with me. Very strange. There was no quarrel when I left.

I called home again. When I reached Philip, he seemed surprised, and said C.H. misunderstood him. He was affectionate and normal. I gave a good performance, then came home with Werner and Maletta [our friends and neighbors in Connecticut].

Sunday, July 18
Flat Rock Farm, Connecticut

Earlier this morning I was aware of a strained atmosphere in the house. There's something more than that pall of sadness lying over everything since the return of Philip's depression.

Ross [Miller, Philip's friend, the writer] was keeping him company while I was in Caramoor. After breakfast, he left, then Philip informed me that [Philip's friend, the writer] Norman Manea would arrive in the afternoon, and could stay as long as he wanted. It was in the form of an ultimatum. Philip seems to be afraid of being alone with me, whereas I've been looking forward to two undisturbed weeks with him alone; I think a period of quiet together might calm his fears.

I objected to Norman. Yes, he is loyal and devoted, but also profoundly melancholy and depressed — and Philip knows that. He eventually agreed with me, but unexpectedly turned the screw again: he'd call Sandy and ask him to fly in from Chicago.

I found myself saying, "Yes."

Monday, July 19
Flat Rock Farm, Connecticut

Sandy arrived today, and Philip seemed calmer. He said he preferred to sleep alone for the time being, that I was keeping him awake. I'm moving to the far guest room, leaving Sandy in the room closest to his brother.

Tuesday, July 20
Flat Rock Farm, Connecticut

Sandy was woken up at 5 A.M. by Philip, crying. He was lying on the bed next to him, and Sandy told me Philip asked to be held and comforted. Sandy accompanies Philip on his walks, and goes with him to the swimming pool. Apart from cooking lunch and dinner, I'm an unwanted appendage in this house.

Wednesday, July 21
Flat Rock Farm, Connecticut

This morning Sandy and I were alone in the garden room. I have grown to love and trust Sandy over the years. He asked me how I was dealing with the recurrence of Philip's condition and I answered openly and emotionally. I admitted that I generally feel helpless and trapped, so much so that at times I almost hate Philip. Then Philip appeared in the doorway.

I think he was listening in. I suspect that Philip may have engineered this scene — through Sandy, probably against his good judgment — in order to get me to reveal my thoughts. Perhaps I'm overreacting, but I feel frightened and manipulated.

Thursday, July 22
Flat Rock Farm, Connecticut

This afternoon Sandy told me he and Philip would be leaving for Chicago for two weeks. Just like that. Cold as ice, Philip suggested I should go to London while they are away to "recuperate" from the strain of the last months. I left the table and went upstairs to the bedroom, closed the door, and when I felt a little calmer, decided to go downstairs and speak to Philip.

I bumped into Sandy by the stairs, and started to cry. I said I could never leave Philip while he's so ill. Oddly, Sandy said to me, "My God, if I were you, I would."

I ran down to the pool to speak to Philip. He didn't say a word. I realized it wasn't Sandy's idea to separate, but Philip's. I pleaded: we could go together to the same spa; he'd be seen to, and we could still be together. Again, he offered no direct reply.

Then, strangest of all, we managed somehow to have a pleasant dinner.

Friday, July 23
Flat Rock Farm, Connecticut

Early this morning Philip left the house to see Maletta for some physiotherapy. Sandy and I were alone again, and he told me that they're definitely leaving tomorrow. I went to my study and called [my brother] John to tell him what happened. He said, "You have to go along with it. There's nothing else you can do."

At noon Philip returned, looking paler and more distraught than ever. I didn't know what to say, except that Sandy had told me of their plan, and I approved. I suggested a walk outside. As we walked in the fields, I asked him to wait until Monday so we could have the weekend alone together, and then I could accompany him to Chicago, stay with [Sandy's former wife] Helen overnight, and leave. Philip said he absolutely had to leave with Sandy, and he didn't want me to come.

I agreed to everything. Nothing else I could do.

Saturday, July 24
Flat Rock Farm, Connecticut

Philip and Sandy left today. Weeks ago, Maletta and I had arranged to go to Jacob's Pillow for an afternoon recital. I decided to stick to the scheme, trying to maintain some semblance of normality.

I think I was in control until the moment when the two men stood together outside the door, waiting to say good-bye. I've said a great number of good-byes in my life, but never one like this. And never one that made me feel so humiliated.

I was holding the note Philip wrote to me only three weeks ago: "You are the most precious thing in the world to me." I thrust it into his hand, and asked him how he could have written it and still behave like this. He said he meant every word. Sandy tried to put his arms around me, and I pulled back and told him not to touch me. He shrugged and went back into the house.

Philip held me in his arms, but said nothing. Sandy returned, and as I moved toward the car and turned to leave, I told them they were two of the cruelest people in the world.

Then I lost all control: I begged Philip not to leave.

Again, he said nothing and remained still. He did something I'll never forget: he put his fingers in his mouth, like a vulnerable and lost child making a gesture of confusion and bereavement. I turned away toward the car. There was nothing left for me to do but go.

After we left, I said to Maletta I wished I hadn't said what I had said. Maletta replied, "Not one of your best moments."

That night I stayed alone in the house, and the next day I left for New York. I had a certainty that I would never return to that house again.

After a few days in New York, I flew to London. I felt completely useless. Halfway through the first week in England, I received a call from Philip. He announced that he was committing himself to Silver Hill Psychiatric Hospital in Stanford, Connecticut, and that Sandy, by now very worried about his near-suicidal condition, would accompany him there the following morning. On arrival at the hospital the next day, Philip telephoned me, and told me how miserable and lonely he was, also that his room was ugly and bare; he asked me to keep talking to him, that the sound of my voice soothed him. I said I would fly back to the United States and come to Silver Hill immediately upon my return.

Leaving a Doll's House

Friday, August 6
New York Apartment
The telephone rang as I entered the apartment from the airport. It was Philip. The sound of his voice was different; now he sounded angry, remote. I told him I'd ordered a car, and would be at the hospital tomorrow morning. Philip said he wants to see me only in the presence of his doctor, and he is not on duty until Sunday. I agreed to delay my visit until then. His voice then changed — kinder and more recognizable — when he asked me to bring along a jar of peanut butter and the Sunday *New York Times*.

He hung up, then rang again, and asked me to bring several changes of underwear. So maybe I am his wife after all.

Saturday, August 7
New York Apartment
With the help of Barbara [Epstein, friend, and editor of the *New York Review of Books*], I survived today. I've been unable to concentrate and feel very confused. I carelessly put down my handbag in the coffee shop where we stopped for lunch and it was stolen; it contained my driver's license, credit cards, money, check books — everything lost.

The perfect end to a miserable day.

Sunday, August 8
New York Apartment
I'm about to leave for Silver Hill for the first time this afternoon. Somehow I've had to get through the morning. I walked in the park from seven to nine-thirty, when I kept my appointment with Greta [Herman, my psychiatrist]. I poured out all my fear and grief, but Greta assured me Philip will never file for divorce. Nevertheless, I'm feeling extremely apprehensive. Perhaps I'll take a Valium in the car. My nerves are shot. I know that whatever lies in store, it will do neither of us any good if I get too emotional.

The Journal

Monday, August 9
New York Apartment

I will never be able to forget what happened yesterday. In some very fundamental way I shall always be scarred by what was said in that room.

Dr. Bloch, the psychiatrist at the hospital in charge of Philip's case, left a message at Reception asking me to come to his office before Philip arrived. He asked me if I understood why Philip was so agitated at the thought of seeing me and why he was so angry. I said I hadn't the faintest idea — the truth.

Philip came into the room. When I tried to put my arms around him, he turned to stone. We sat down with the doctor between us, like adversaries. He looked pale and drawn. I asked why he was trembling.

Philip stared at me with complete hatred, his jaw thrust forward, and snarled, "Because I am so angry with you."

"Why are you so angry with me?" I tried to be calm.

Philip went on to tell me, hardly pausing for breath, for two hours: My voice was so soft it made him feel alienated and I deliberately spoke to him in that way. I behaved oddly in restaurants, looking at my watch and humming to myself. I panicked in the face of his illnesses and had no idea how to deal with them. When we checked into hospital for open-heart surgery I was unable to find a nurse, and he had to run up and down the corridor looking for one. He had to take care of all the details when my mother died, waiting in the morning for the undertaker's men to come, sitting alone in the house with her dead body. When his father lost control of his bowels, I said it was a pity he couldn't control himself. I made him attend the opera, which he detested. I deliberately avoided meeting his eyes during our last weeks at home. And on, and on, and on.

He spewed out every minute mistake I had ever made. Everything that had made him angry over our seventeen years together. Nothing was omitted. Some were ridiculous; some were petty; some, unfortunately, were true, like my comment about Herman's bowels. But I laughed when he mentioned my conduct in restaurants. He said, "Friends have seen this behavior of yours."

"Philip, you're demonizing me. You're turning me into Maggie." He disregarded this.

I told him I had taken good care of him through his knee operation, heart operation, and been at his side through two major breakdowns. Philip looked at me coldly: He replied, "I am sorry to disillusion you on that point. You were no help to me whatever."

Although the expression on his face was poisonous and hateful, his voice never rose beyond its usual level. He rose and stood silently looking out of the window; he turned and said: "If Anna is coming to study in New York for three months, I wish to terminate our marriage." Then more silence.

I kept repeating to myself, "My marriage is over," but outwardly managed to keep a grip on my emotions. The Valium helped. Dr. Bloch broke the impasse: "Philip. Three months, after seventeen years?" The silence continued, and I could hear my heart racing and pounding.

I tried to explain — calmly and quietly and addressing myself to both of them — about Anna's career, about how common it is for singers to rely on certain teachers, and why she had to come to New York for a course of study with Ruth Falcon [opera singer, teacher].

Philip cut in to say that it was a plot between us — that there were plenty of teachers in Europe she could go to.

Again I tried to point out the facts: that Anna is thirty-three years old and lives in London; that she visits us only on rare occasions; that she leads an independent life and career. Nothing made any difference. Philip just went on as if I hadn't spoken.

I ran toward the door, and Philip said, "Look at her! She's always running away." Dr. Bloch asked me to come back tomorrow and see if these confrontations could prove helpful.

I ran to the car. It must have been obvious to anyone that I was in a state of near-hysteria. George [my driver] asked if there was anything he could do. Again and again, I said, "My life is over."

Tuesday, August 10
Silver Hill Hospital, Connecticut

These three days have been the most brutal of my life. In these sessions I've remained mostly silent. I am paralyzed in the face of this hatred. I also believe that Philip is seriously ill. Finally, I asked him the reason why, if he has hated me for so long, he married me three years ago. His snarled reply — "Who knows?" — said it all.

After the session, he asked me to walk with him in the gardens. It's as though he were two separate people. But I took his arm, and we walked together as companionably as any husband and wife. I desperately wanted to believe this — but in my heart I know I can't. Something irreparable has happened.

Wednesday, August 11
Silver Hill Hospital, Connecticut

Philip seems to have run out of invectives. I hoped that after venting most of his spleen he might begin to see our relationship in a different light, but he began to repeat exactly the same accusations as two days ago, like a tape that has been rewound to Side One. Dr. Bloch finally said, "Philip, nothing you hold against your wife has been more than petty annoyance." I was relieved — and surprised — that he showed such sympathy toward me.

After this session Philip and I again walked outside in the

garden together. When I left, we kissed. I hope the drugs he's taking — a high dose of Prozac, plus lithium — will help control his rage. Now if I can only get a good night's sleep.

Thursday, August 12
Silver Hill Hospital, Connecticut

Day five. Philip arrived late to the session, looking extremely ill. Dr. Bloch asked each of us how we felt after our meeting yesterday. I answered that I felt comforted walking with my husband on the grounds. I said that I have no intention of allowing what has been said during these meetings to destroy our marriage. Dr. Bloch turned to Philip, asking him if he felt the same way. Philip replied that he had never felt so alienated from anyone as when we were walking together in the garden. I was shocked and silent.

Dr. Bloch broke the silence: He said he saw little point in continuing these meetings. He asked Philip to leave us alone to talk. To my surprise Philip asked again that I meet him in the garden before leaving.

After Philip left the room, Dr. Bloch said he was as perplexed as I was at the rapid changes in Philip's behavior.

Philip said in a statement when he was admitted to the hospital that disappointment over the reception of *Shylock,* worries about his health, and John Updike's ungenerous review of the book had been major forces in inducing his deep depression. No mention of me was made until the very end when he stated, "Although Claire's extreme nervousness has alarmed me from time to time, we have enjoyed a long and happy relationship."

I began to cry. I asked Dr. Bloch what caused Philip to hate me. He said he didn't understand it.

From the doctor's office I telephoned Johnnie and Sheila in Toronto, and asked to fly over and stay with them for a couple of days. I told George I was going to the airport; then

I looked for Philip. He was sitting in the garden, looking lonely and depressed. I told him I'd be leaving for Toronto and from there would go to London. No answer.

I gave up, turned to leave. Suddenly he said, "Is that it? Will I never see you again?"

I turned to embrace and reassure him that I would be there whenever he needed me. He immediately metamorphosed into the cold and rejecting man in Dr. Bloch's office.

Friday, August 13
New York

My two days in Toronto were harrowing. I couldn't stay off the phone for more than a minute. I called Anna. I called Francine. Maletta. Barbara. Anybody I knew. Everybody says I should calm down and wait and see what happens. Poor John and Sheila. Without them, I could never have survived that weekend.

I flew back to New York in the hope that Philip might see me again before I left. I am frenzied, running from place to place and person to person. I've decided to fly to Salzburg to be with Anna. She's asked me to wait until the performances are over, but I simply can't.

I called Dr. Bloch, who said that Philip not only wishes not to see me but proposed Dr. Bloch himself ask me to remain apart from him for the next three months; i.e., Philip will stay in Connecticut while I remain in the apartment. He said he will need time alone to recover from his mental illness, that he needs absolute serenity. A half-hour later, almost as I was out of the door, Philip phoned. I tried to be calm, telling him that I was going to stay with friends in Ireland who had no telephone — a lie. I thought it would calm him if I said that I accepted to live separately for the next three months.

"No, that is not what I told the doctor," he said. "I never want to live under the same roof with you again."

Sunday, August 15
Salzburg, Austria

I think I've had some kind of physical and mental breakdown.
I have been staying with Anna for a few days. I am unable to
breathe properly, and while she is at the Festspielhaus, I've
been lying on the sofa, crying uncontrollably. Anna was right:
I shouldn't have come. I am appalled to bring such despair
into her life, but I can't seem to help myself. She, John, and
Sheila have given me back the modicum of self-respect I
have left.

Monday, August 16
Salzburg, Austria

While Anna was at the theater, Sheila rang. She said Philip
had called her, asking how he could get in touch with me.
My lie about Ireland had to catch up with me. But I knew
his response to any mention of Anna well in advance. I told
Sheila I would call him.

Half an hour later I called him, and kept up the pretense
about Ireland. He wanted to know where I would be staying
in Dublin — I told him. It was a brief conversation. And, let's
hope, not a tactical error.

Before Philip and Sandy made their exit together to Chicago,
Philip had suggested I take a television role that had been offered to me a while before. I had turned it down on the grounds
that my husband was ill. It was offered again and I accepted.
The film would provide some much-needed income if I was to
be on my own. Anna agreed to accompany me, as it was obvious to her I couldn't manage alone, and together we flew to
Dublin to begin the film.

Thursday, August 19
Dublin, Ireland

Only minutes after we checked into the hotel, Dr. Bloch telephoned from Silver Hill to say Philip has asked if I'll let him have the apartment for six months. Apparently he can't face living alone in the country. Now he wants to be in the city, near his friends, near his psychotherapist, and will give me $5,000 a month to cover my expenses and accommodation in a hotel or furnished apartment. Translation: I must find somewhere else to live while he recovers alone. I asked for time to consider.

Anna said that Philip wants a divorce and told me to call a lawyer. He's trying to get me out of the apartment by making me feel guilty, she said. Maybe she's right.

Then I received a call from Maletta, who told me she visited Philip at Silver Hill; she said he's afraid of being alone in the country. She said she's certain he will commit suicide in that house, and begged me to give him the apartment. I think Philip is using Maletta to manipulate me, but I have to take what she says on good faith — maybe Philip is in danger. It feels like a premeditated plan to evict me. I want to say no.

Then Francine comes on the phone. She tells me that Maletta and Judith [Thurman, close friend of Philip's] have been to see her, and pleaded with her to use her influence to secure Philip the apartment. They stressed the fact, said Francine, that he was definitely suicidal. Francine emphasized that I would never forgive myself if Philip committed suicide.

I asked Anna what my best option was. About asking for the studio Anna was adamant: she said if I move into the studio, I'll never get back into the apartment.

[Later that night, I continued.]

I've just called Dr. Bloch, and informed him that I am prepared to move out.

Dublin was a disaster. The following morning I began filming and was shaking so much that everyone on the set saw the state I was in; I was suffering from shock as much as anything else. The trembling in my hands would continue for the next months, together with the crying fits, which, embarrassing as they might be, were absolutely beyond my control.

To add mishap to misery, Anna was involved in an armed robbery at the bank while trying to change money. I was clinging to Anna for dear life. I finished filming on August 27. At the airport Anna and I said good-bye, and I returned to New York for a week.

Upon my arrival I received a fax from Philip. He addressed me as his dearest friend of seventeen years, and expressed his gratitude to me for giving him the time he needed alone before he felt strong enough to resume our domestic life together. He repeated once more his understanding of the sacrifice he knew I had made in moving into a hotel for the next six months. He sent me his love.

He also made two calls to me in those days. In one he wept, telling me how much he missed me; in the other he said he wanted to continue our marriage, but that we must resume our relationship slowly. I took him at his word — that the separation was intended for him to regain his health, that he valued me and wanted to continue our life together. He didn't want to see me until he felt emotionally stronger. I would have preferred not to return to London, but I had no choice. My house was sold, and I had to put everything in storage as the new owners planned to take possession on September 21. I stayed with Sheila so as not to be alone in my house. I must have been a difficult guest. The mornings were always the worst. Sheila would let me speak and listen patiently to my unhappiness and anxiety. She has always been able to calm me, to talk sense. She helped me survive those dreadful weeks.

The Journal

Sunday, September 5
London

At three in the morning I got a desperate call from Philip in Connecticut. He said he was incapable of coping by himself, and had asked to be accepted again into Silver Hill. He couldn't stay alone and said he would sleep at the Pfeiffers'.

When I called him there earlier this afternoon, Maletta told me he had been hallucinating all night and didn't sleep. When I spoke to him, his voice sounded lifeless. Maletta said she would drive him back to the hospital.

Sheila came round to help close up the house.

Monday, September 20
London

My nephew James came over to help me with the final packing, electricity board, gas board, telephone company, and so on. Although greatly relieved that this turmoil is finally over so I can return to Philip, it's a great wrench to leave this house, my home for the last twenty years.

Wednesday, September 22
New York

I've just arrived at the apartment. Francine rang to check up on me. I called Dr. Jacob's [psychiatrist] office to confirm my appointment for tomorrow; Greta is away. Janet [Malcolm, writer and friend] called to speak on Philip's behalf. I don't know why he didn't ask me himself: I've been asked to move out by the 27th, instead of October 1st as agreed, to allow Philip a full week's start on his therapy. I called the Cosmo and the answer was, yes, they can take me a few days early.

Thursday, September 23
New York

I asked George to drive me to Silver Hill. Philip and I met. I was disappointed to find him still so withdrawn; he is far from well, and appears heavily sedated. Once again we walked in the gardens, round and round the same path. I tried to make normal conversation, to tell him news from home. Philip was only interested in hearing about my psychotherapy; he asked me whether I had been, or was now, suicidal. Is this a projection?

We had dinner. Philip said he would spend the weekend alone in Connecticut. I knew better than to suggest otherwise. I simply nodded in agreement.

I'm in a state of suspension: I move out of the apartment and into the Cosmo on Monday.

I waited for him to say something affectionate; his phone calls to London had led me to hope for that. He's completely noncommittal.

Friday, September 24
New York

This morning, in terrible emotional shape, I went to see Greta, who suggested that my passivity in the face of chaos is the problem. She asked me to outline what I want. I told her that the Cosmo can only keep me for eight weeks, and after that I want to return to the apartment. She said I should address that to Philip, and I think she's right. I'm just about to leave for Silver Hill.

Saturday, September 25
New York Apartment

I spent last night at Silver Hill.

As a patient.

I arrived at the hospital at 5 P.M., and tried to keep my

wits about me. I waited for Philip in the lounge. When he
arrived, he suggested we go to his room. We went upstairs to
talk, and he lay on the bed. This was to be his last night at the
hospital. I began the conversation.

"You have said what you want, now give me the chance to
say what I want. We have been apart over two months. Take
another two months to complete your recovery and then,
please, let me come home."

There was a long silence. For at least fifteen minutes he
just sat there, staring at me with absolute hatred. I went over
and sat on the edge of his bed. I asked him to please say
something.

"There is nothing to say. I will not have my equilibrium
destroyed. Let's go down to dinner." We went down to the
dining room, and I tried to make conversation. Philip was
shaking with fury by now. Halfway through the meal, he
asked if I had finished, and made a move to go back to his
room.

In the room, he accused me of trying to poison him. He
accused me of breaking a contract that had been meticulously
worked out. He attacked Francine and accused her of
spreading lies about him. Then he said that no one had ever
come to a hospital on the night before a patient was
discharged and done what I had done. I had completely
destroyed any step forward he had made in returning to
normal.

This final outburst took me over the edge, and I ran out of
the room into the doctor's office, crying out for someone to
come and help Philip. The nurse on duty asked me what
happened. I told her I wanted to die.

She gave me a sedative, and went into Philip's room. She
assured me that he appeared calm. She called Dr. Bloch, who
said I must not be allowed to go home alone. I was taken to
the crisis ward, given pajamas, and another nurse came in to
interview me. She asked if I was suicidal, or had ever

contemplated killing someone else: "Only myself," I replied.
I kept repeating I could never get through the night. "I won't
leave you," she said. "You are getting through the night. A
half hour has gone. And now another half hour . . ." She gave
me a second, stronger sedative.

Before I fell asleep, I gave them John's number in Toronto,
and he was contacted. Although extremely busy editing his
film, he agreed to come to collect me, which he did this
morning.

Before I left, Dr. Bloch came to visit me, as always,
extremely kind and concerned. I asked him why he still
showed sympathy for me after all the things Philip has said,
and he replied that the things Philip has been saying about me
don't ring true.

I asked if Philip would ever come back to me; he neither
confirmed nor denied that. I asked if there was another
woman; he neither confirmed nor denied that. He merely
said that I could gather whatever I wished from his silence.

John brought me home from the hospital, and is spending
the night with me.

Sunday, September 26
New York Apartment

As a prelude to an orchestral concert, I read a Shakespeare
narration this afternoon at Avery Fisher Hall. God knows
how I did it. Completely exhausted, I was shown into the
dressing room an hour before the performance, and
immediately fell asleep. I was woken about five minutes
before I was due to go on. John came to the concert but has
to leave again for Toronto tonight.

Monday, September 27
New York Apartment

This is the day I have promised to leave the apartment; I'm
buying some good things to eat, and I'll set the table for

lunch, turn on all the lights, and leave the radio playing so the apartment will seem more welcoming. I've just written a note:

"Farewell old life; welcome new life. You will come through!"

[Later that day, I continued.]

I've moved into the Cosmo. Philip just called to thank me. He says he knows what a sacrifice I've made and he'd like to join me for dinner tomorrow. He says he'll leave early — he becomes tired easily. Perhaps the sedatives are taking their toll.

The day preceding any meeting is full of tension for me. I never know which Philip I am going to meet; the removed, brutal antagonist; the concerned, caring patient/doctor, who talks about his treatment and medical progress, and usually ends by asking me if I am contemplating suicide; or the impersonal colleague, the one concerned with my work and professional life, but with no interest in the woman he's lived with for almost eighteen years.

The following evening, Philip arrived in the dining room of the Cosmopolitan Club wearing a tie he had knotted poorly, which touched me somehow, bringing me a bunch of my favorite yellow roses. He also brought a compact disc player for my room. Neither at dinner, nor at any other time, did he discuss our having a future together. At 7:30 he left; I accompanied him to a taxi. A cursory parting kiss, and he was gone. I knew that, after making my request to him in the hospital, and with such predictable results, if there was ever to be any chance of a rapprochement, I had to be patient, say nothing, and simply wait. The most passive — and, therefore, least favorable — position for anyone to be in.

Several days later there was another message from Philip. Would I meet him for dinner the next night? I called his answering machine and accepted.

Monday, October 4
The Cosmopolitan Club, New York

Dinner was strained and miserable. Philip and I were not alone; he had invited Joel [Conarroe, friend] to keep a distance. When I arrived he gave me an unfriendly greeting, turning away to talk to Joel as though I wasn't there. When the bill arrived, Philip asked for Joel's credit card to divide the bill, as is their custom. I said: "Well, you're not going to get mine. I assume you're taking me to dinner."

"Am I?" Philip asked. Then he paid for my third of the bill.

After dinner, Joel and I walked around the city. "That was some evening," I said. "Why the hell did he invite me?" It turns out that Joel was no less surprised to see me than I was to see him; we both thought we were there to have a tête à tête with Philip. I am beginning to realize that I have no grasp on anything he does. The whys, the hows, the wherefores, are impossible to predict. I just go along with everything that happens.

One weekend morning at the Cosmopolitan Club, Philip telephoned. He asked me a strange, leading question. "How do you feel about the last five months?" I hesitated, sensing that this might be a trap, and, hyperaware that I must be very careful now, I answered.

"That is a large question, Philip," I said, playing for time.

"Nevertheless," he replied, "tell me."

So I did. I told him I was devastated by what had happened, that I still loved him, that at this moment my life held no promise and very little pleasure.

"And now," I said, "tell me how you feel."

After a long pause, he replied, "I have nothing to say."

"Surely, Philip, after I have told you so much, can't you say something in return?"

"I have amnesia about these last months," he answered.

"I wish I had," I thought. By his inquisitiveness about me and reticence about himself, I wondered whether he might be recording the conversation for some mysterious use of his own; I wasn't sure. At this point, we were so unable to communicate properly that it wasn't clear what either of us wanted to hear.

The more I told him that I loved him, the more cold and rejecting he became. The more cold and rejecting he became, the more I felt motivated to tell him that I loved him.

Wednesday, October 20
The Wyndham Hotel, New York

I have moved to the Wyndham, where I have a small suite for almost the same amount of money I was paying at the club. Rachael [Hallawell, singer and close friend of Anna's who had become almost a daughter to me] has flown in from London to stay with me. Anna will follow soon.

Thursday, October 21
The Wyndham Hotel, New York

Tonight I'm performing my third Shakespeare program, the one that I worked out and rehearsed with Philip last summer. It is called, ironically enough, *Women in Love*. Philip says he's coming to this performance with Joel and has offered to take me to dinner afterward.

[Later that night, I continued.]

We had a reasonably pleasant dinner. I'm happy Philip was pleased with my performance. He can be a stern and harsh critic. At dinner, he was silent while I jabbered. He asked if I'd drop him off on my way home.

In the cab I asked him how he felt: "Never better," he said aggressively. He got out of the cab, and slammed the door after him. He looked very much alone crossing the street.

But this is the life he wants. And it's the life of a bitter, lonely, aging ascetic with no human ties; like Kafka, he's chosen a cold, solitary journey. For the first time I'm beginning to see how being out of the marriage might be best for both of us. A future with Philip — even if he should choose to have one with me — would be very hard.

Friday, October 22
The Wyndham Hotel, New York

This morning a large and beautiful bunch of tulips arrived, with a note from Philip that read, "You have never given a more intelligent or beautiful performance." I've just called the apartment, and left a message telling him how much the flowers and note mean to me. Rachael and I are going out to have a celebration dinner. As Rachael has never been to New York, we're doing some sightseeing. I feel such relief, I'm almost hopeful.

Saturday, October 23
The Wyndham Hotel, New York

I should have guessed. There's always a disarming gesture before the body blow. When we got back to the hotel today there was a special-delivery letter waiting for me at the desk. The envelope contained papers of "legal separation." Philip is asking for a six-month separation. There's a clause stating that I have to ask my husband's permission before I enter the apartment — which is still legally our marital home.

Now I understand why Philip wanted our separation to remain a personal arrangement between us with no lawyer involved. More maneuvering space, and he could strike first.

What I don't understand is why there is no letterhead or official stamp of any kind on these documents. I was stupid to put off seeking legal advice.

I called him and shouted, "Why the hell have you done this?" into the machine.

Within the hour, Philip called back. "Why are you so angry?" he asked, cool as a cucumber. I told him he was insulting and making a fool of me. He said he's afraid that I will break my word, and try to move back in with him. I told him he was wrong: I wouldn't want to live with him as he is now. He then loudly began ranting, first against me, then the Grays, claiming that he'd received a poison pen letter and could prove Francine had written it. He accused us all of conspiring against him. He was shouting so loudly that Rachael, who was sitting next to me on the end of the bed, could hear him.

Then I said: "Philip, you are insane. I am not." There was a click.

All this happened just moments ago. This is exactly what he wanted — I would lash out, and he'd have his ammunition.

Monday, October 25
The Wyndham Hotel, New York

Anna is due to arrive today. And again she's going to find me in despair. I had hoped that somehow I could manage this situation during her stay. Now she's walking right back into the center of the whirlwind. Anna predicted that.

I've been to see Sidney Liebowitz [lawyer]. He read the document, and said he sees nothing wrong in my signing; at least it legally guarantees the $5,000 monthly maintenance Philip had offered. At this point I asked if I should just divorce him. Sidney replied that this is precisely what he wants; further, that I would have no chance of a settlement under the terms of the prenuptial agreement. I would receive virtually nothing.

So, I have to simply wait for him to divorce me.

Wednesday, October 27
The Wyndham Hotel, New York

Last year I agreed to give three performances of my
Shakespeare program in Litchfield [Connecticut]. It seemed at
the time a pleasant and convenient engagement — so near our
house, after all.

I asked the two girls if they wanted to come along;
understandably they said no. They are going to Florida for the
weekend.

On October 28, Rachael and Anna flew to Florida to stay with
a friend and I went on to Ann Arbor, Michigan, to narrate
Stravinsky's *A Soldier's Tale* with Boston Musica Viva. I stayed
in a depressingly drab inn and was taken out to lunch by friends
of the conductor whom I didn't know. To relieve my ever-
growing anxiety, I covertly took a sedative with my large glass
of white wine. This had a disastrous effect:

The phone fever returned. I tried to call my sister-in-law in
London. No answer. Then my therapist in New York. No
answer. Then I called my husband. I told him how sorry I was.
Philip replied that I had been cruel and insulting, and that he
would never speak to me again. He hung up. Somehow I got
through the performance, although I missed my first, critical
cue from the conductor.

Friday, October 29
Litchfield, Connecticut

I performed the first of my three scheduled Shakespeare
programs earlier tonight. I'm staying with C.H. and Bab; as
always, they welcomed me as a family member. Philip was
supposed to attend, but didn't on account of Francine, or so
he wrote. C.H. took a call, leaving the room first — was it
Philip? — and when he returned he said it was, preferring not
to speak to me, asking if I was all right.

I made a call to Greta, asking her for an appointment next week. She seemed evasive at first, and I felt perhaps she didn't want to continue our sessions. I asked her if this was the case, and she said she had preferred not to tell me, but she had just found out she was suffering from a terminal disease, and would gradually have to start letting go of her patients. She said she didn't want me to be stranded. I could hear that she was holding back tears.

Two more performances to get through this weekend, and now, such terrible news.

Vita Muir [director of the Litchfield Arts] also showed great concern for me. Before the performance, I told her about wanting to cancel the two shows I am scheduled to give in Georgia and Kentucky; I can't face the isolation. Vita, whom I have dealt with only in a professional capacity, offered to come with me. An incredibly generous offer. Like Blanche, I'm relying on the kindness of strangers.

Saturday, October 30
Litchfield, Connecticut

Maletta came over today to deliver a large black suitcase I had asked Philip for, containing clothes I need for the winter. Earlier, C.H. had come into my room and asked to have a few words in private. Uncompromisingly honest as always, he said: "Much as my heart goes out to you, I want you to know that my primary allegiance is to Philip."

When I flew back to New York, Anna and Rachael were waiting for me, back from their trip to Miami. We went out to dinner. I was relieved that Philip had sent over my mail without enclosing a vituperative letter. He did, however, somewhat to my surprise, send over a number of health-insurance forms that required my signature; he seemed to be on closer terms with my insurance plan than with me. I knew that his medical expenses were high, and that he might need to make a claim.

Anna, Rachael, and I arranged to have dinner on the West Side, so that I could drop off the forms at the apartment.

Early the following morning I received a strange message from the hotel operator. Someone called "Frederick" wanted to speak to me. Would I accept the call? I didn't know who "Frederick" was. When I accepted, I heard the receiver quickly replaced. I told Rachael — Anna was asleep in the next room — that I didn't like this: either it was a reporter angling for a story, or someone delivering legal papers. The phone rang yet again; this time it was the front desk. A man was waiting downstairs, the concierge said, with a message he could deliver only in person.

I was paralyzed. I asked Rachael what I should do. She said we might as well get it over with; I allowed him to come up. He rang the bell, and handed me a folder from a satchel. Then, unbelievably, he asked me for my autograph, which I declined.

I opened the folder and found divorce papers, summoning me to appear in court within twenty days, and accusing me of "the cruel and inhuman treatment" of my husband, Philip Roth.

CHAPTER FOURTEEN

The Fun Begins

My journal ended abruptly. There was nothing left to say.

The girls and I crossed the Avenue of the Americas for coffee at Wolf's Delicatessen. It was a drizzly, miserable New York day. Shaking and wearing sunglasses despite the gray light, I couldn't stop crying; my life had crumbled to bits. Anna's face was bone-white and vacant; in her mind, she was torn between commiseration for a mother suffering another emotional catastrophe and uneasiness at the prospect of shouldering the full responsibility of her welfare alone. Rachael was quietly reassuring.

We silently entered the coffee shop. The waitress, a blustery, platinum blond, powerfully built southerner, came over, pad open and pencil poised, to take our order.

"Howya doin'?" she bellowed indomitably, flashing a smile wider than the state of Texas, quickly proceeding with the force of a stampede to the particulars of the menu: "Our special today is tuna salad! That's pure albacore white tuna!" As she left the table, came an invitation: "Let the fun begin!"

For the next forty-five minutes, it was her *cri de guerre*. Whether it was menus, sandwiches, bowls of soup, or tuna salads she delivered to neighboring tables, her "Let the fun begin!" followed as brightly and unflaggingly as a radio jingle. One look at us, she might have considered that the fun ended there; but there was no putting a halt to her particular brand of oblivious optimism. Anna began to cry; Rachael looked to the ceiling. The waitress came over again to set down our coffees. After another, less exultant but resolute "Let the fun begin!" she tapped Anna's arm, and cooed: "Honey, I sure hope that, whatever it is, you feel better soon."

Anna and Rachael were due to leave for London the following day. Feeling totally alone now, I begged them to stay a few days longer, but they had lives of their own to lead, and of course had to go home as planned. The day they left was the saddest one of all.

Alone in the hotel, I was forced to accept that Philip never had any intention of living with me again; worse, I had been coerced by him and his women friends into leaving the two homes we had lived in as man and wife. On top of everything else, I felt such a fool. With so much hanging in the balance and so many unanswered questions preying on my mind, the nights in my room were sleepless and the mornings desolate and miserable. Francine, Janet, and Linda Asher called me every morning to give me courage.

I immediately consulted my lawyer, Sidney Liebowitz. I wanted to know whether it was possible that I would have to defend myself against Philip's bizarre charges of "cruel and inhuman treatment."

In his office, he told me he was appalled by my predicament. His bargaining powers were severely limited as a result of the prenuptial agreement, which he described to me as "unconscionable," the most brutal document of its kind he had ever encountered. Although Philip had filed for divorce, Sidney reckoned that, once in court, pursuing his original case against me would be troublesome and substantiating those claims next to impossible. In order to obtain his coveted speedy divorce, Philip would be required to make some financial gesture toward me before I signed the papers.

Taking me completely by surprise when I got back to the hotel, Philip rang me to inquire about my well-being. I had in mind a bill of particulars I wanted to acquaint him with when we next spoke. As shameful as this seems, I forgot everything upon hearing his voice.

Once again, my role was to be the reassuring, placating partner. I told him that once I was no longer his legal wife, he might come to view me differently; he would see me again as the woman with whom he had happily lived for so long. He replied that his affection for me had never diminished; he counted on my support during the coming months; and he would always be there to give me his. Once again I was caught inside the eternal conundrum: which was the real Philip Roth? The chasm between his words and deeds was immense.

My vacillation during this adjustment period made my lawyer's job impossible. Whenever he suggested an aggressive strategy, I vetoed it on the grounds that if I fought Philip, I would lose any hope for us to restore the valued friendship that he had promised, and that I was feverishly counting on. I placed a higher premium on his promise than on my own judgment. In the end, any chance I might have had to negotiate a decent settlement was squandered.

There was a nagging pebble across our legal path. As Philip was a resident of Connecticut, there seemed no obvious reason why he shouldn't sue me in that state for "no fault divorce," which was not an option in New York. Under those circumstances, my assent wouldn't even have been necessary, nor would I have had anything to barter in exchange for my signature. The only rationale seemed to be that his lawyers advised him against it, on the grounds that prenuptial agreements, rarely broken in New York, had occasionally been overturned in Connecticut. But the devil in all this, Sidney insisted, was the agreement itself, which, in his opinion, "was unfair at the time of the marriage and unfair at the time of the breakup."

My own position was precarious. Assuming I had been disposed to bring a case against Philip in Connecticut to overturn the agreement, one of the few alternatives available to me, it would have been a colossal gamble. Among other things, it meant engaging an entirely new firm of Connecticut lawyers; the cost of bringing such a suit would have been prohibitive. And Philip, who had more funds at his disposal and was hardly profligate in his financial affairs, warned me he would sooner lose $200,000 in legal fees than be forced to hand over a penny to me. My resources were inadequate; but more to the point, I lacked the courage to take him on.

A story came to light around this time that neither Anna nor Rachael had previously felt at liberty to disclose. Sheila first revealed it to me back in London, when I was in such despair I was willing to do anything — even accept a financial pittance — in order to remain connected to Philip. Sheila thought it would wake me up to some hard truths. Now, in light of the divorce papers, Rachael and Anna were finally prepared to confirm it.

Allegedly, when she was staying with us in 1981, then again, more explicitly, in 1988, while I was away making a television film in Kenya and the two of them were alone in the house, Rachael had been subjected to sexual advances from Philip.

She rejected both of them, the second time telling him it was hardly the way for her to repay my hospitality. Rachael told me she hadn't let the cat out of the bag because she knew Philip would have defended himself by discrediting her in any number of ways — and that I would consequently accept his version. (The assumption was probably correct.) Seeing that he was getting nowhere, Philip introduced a game of cat-and-mouse: he casually asked her which way she "would like to play it"; if she spoke out, he could "play it that way." Then he left a question hanging in the air: "Who do you think will win?" There were two choices: either Rachael was prepared to accept the role of unwilling participant to a secret, or take the alternative, an even less pleasant role — scapegoat.

It was yet another no-win situation.

Was he trying to break up the close relationship the three of us had enjoyed these years? At first, that seemed to me the only motivation for such an act.

Closer scrutiny and recent events have uncovered intricate, subtle layers of intent, shining examples of the masterful manner in which Philip contrived, in life even more than in art, within the dark corridors of sexuality. Breaking a friendship was small potatoes. What was irresistible to a game-playing, Machiavellian strategist like Philip was the opportunity to divide and conquer in order to kill three birds with one stone.

First, he would take revenge on me for his perceived exclusion from my "symbiotic relationship with Anna." He had once stated angrily that my real marriage was to my daughter, and claimed he was incensed by my "neurotic and obsessive attempts to run after her and seek her approval." By choosing Rachael he was not only striking the heart of any wife's worst fear — that of being overlooked for a younger woman — but also perpetrating a virtually incestuous betrayal.

Second, he would also take revenge on Anna for being the cuckoo in the nest and encroaching on his position. He resented her continuing presence in our lives at twenty-eight and found her spoiled, greedy, grandiose, and intrusive — his exact words. Philip had lately been interested in Anna's personal life and inquired about her romantic prospects to Rachael. By making a pass at her, he hoped to strike at the heart of what he imagined to be Anna's Achilles heel.

Third, having identified Rachael as an underconfident young woman, he set about trying to win her trust by providing a fatherly interest and concern in her welfare. If he could flatter her into believing they had some "special understanding," perhaps she could be manipulated into being a pawn on his emotional chessboard.

It was an ambitious and virtually foolproof plan. If he succeeded, Rachael would have served her purpose, at the price of her own integrity and two important friendships. If he failed, he would still enjoy the satisfaction of having compromised her and injured Anna as well; and, whatever the outcome, I would still believe him. In other words, each woman was to be punished in some way.

Following the second occasion, Rachael left the house in the early morning and went to stay with her grandmother. The next evening she called Philip and left an angry message on the answering machine — calling his bluff, she left it up to him to explain to me why she had moved out, adding that she wouldn't be seeing him for a long time.

Rachael retained in her possession a handwritten letter in which Philip replied that her "performance of virtue defiled" had amused him greatly; he had played the tape for his American friends, who had also been amused by it; that it was a "priceless piece of sexual hysteria"; and finished by claiming that if I didn't find it equally entertaining upon my return from Africa, he would eat his hat.

The letter was dated and signed, "Kisses, Philip."

Needless to say, Philip never played me Rachael's message, nor made any mention of these events. The revelations came as a great shock to me, and went a long way to explain Rachael's steering clear of our home in the ensuing years and Anna's absolute and irreparable hatred of Philip.

After a relatively brief period of negotiation and much against my lawyer's strong advice, I settled with Philip for the sum of $100,000. This sum could not buy even a one-bedroom apartment in New York; it was scarcely enough to pay for a studio in an average neighborhood. But it came down to this: anything was preferable to continuing a war of nerves between us; better to get the whole ugly business over with. Sidney's parting words were: "You negotiated a settlement because you could not afford, emotionally or financially, a long, costly, and uncertain litigation."

I was in my sixties — a time of life when the struggles of youth are distant, when security is the attainable priority. But I was to be alone, and to rely solely on my own emotional and economic resources. I became obsessively concerned about money: I obsessively counted how much might get me by, presuming I were to live another fifteen years, another twenty.

My profession had never offered any guarantee that the security of regular work would come my way.

I was implacable on the issue of where I would live: I was not going to leave the city that had become my home and professional base, nor would I return to another hotel room. If I couldn't afford to buy an apartment, I would rent one. No sooner determined than done: I read an advertisement for a moderately priced East Side apartment, and went to see it that day. It was sunny, overlooked a pleasant communal garden, was clean and well-protected. I agreed to take it immediately.

On my lawyer's advice, I wrote out a list of furniture, china, and linens from my former home, items I considered to be my personal property. I was scrupulously careful not to include anything I hadn't paid for myself.

In December, I left for Cambridge, Massachusetts, to begin rehearsals at the American Repertory Theatre for *The Cherry Orchard,* Chekhov's great play of loss and regeneration.

An actress rarely receives the opportunity to play a demanding role twice in her life. I had had that with Juliet and Ophelia, then with Nora. Now, a little later in life, I tackled Mme. Ranevskaya again. The first time came along with Philip's formal collaboration in his adaptation of the play at the Chichester Festival in 1981. Despite the advantage of Philip's interpretative insight and the satisfaction of acting with the late Emrys James as the landowning businessman, Lopakhin, and Joss Ackland as Lyuba's gentle brother, Gayev, it was an approximate achievement. I was not entirely satisfied with my performance.

Mme. Ranevskaya's bitter grief over the sale of her beloved orchard, symbol of her lost dreams, youth, and happiness, her belated farewell to the past, and her wry acceptance of a doubtful future: the chance had come for me to reinterpret these aspects with the added light of my own feelings of failure and regret. It is not without irony that for this deeper insight I presume to be grateful to Philip Roth.

There was another reward in the form of Ranevskaya's cathartic, restorative effect on the actress playing her; through putting some of my private anguish into her, she gave me some of her winning optimism. By the end of the run I found myself facing the future with an easier heart. Despite the almost Russian cold of Cambridge in the winter of 1994, the new environment provided a good, clean break with the recent past. The kindness of my colleagues, the familiar feeling of being part of a company again, supplied the atmosphere I needed to heal and replenish much of my confidence. Even the reviews were fine.

Just before I returned to New York, I received another surprise from Philip. He telephoned to thank me for agreeing to accept the settlement; he also expressed his relief that we could now once more be friends. As I still believed mental illness had been the cause of Philip's cruel and erratic behavior, that seemed to go some way toward lessening any resentment I felt toward him. Again, the sound of his voice, familiar and now even affectionate, threw me completely off balance.

Excited at the prospect of taking possession of my new apartment and believing I could now talk to him freely, as a friend, I asked him when I could expect to receive my personal effects. Philip answered reservedly that he knew nothing about this and hadn't received my list. I assured him that, some weeks before, my lawyer had been in contact with his; I offered to fax it over to him right away. I was in better spirits, I assured him, and was only waiting to set up my new apartment and get on with my life. Music to his ears, I would have thought.

After the wretchedness of our last time together, I was looking forward to a visit from Anna that same afternoon. She arrived before I returned from the theater; as I entered the door, she wordlessly handed me a fistful of faxes that had come through, one after another.

In rapid, staccato succession, Philip demanded the return of everything he had provided for me during our years together. His list included the gold snake ring with the emerald head from Bulgari; $28,500 per annum he had given me over twelve years; $100,000 of his money used to buy bonds in my name; $10,000 for a "special travel fund" of my own; $150 per hour for the "five or six hundred hours" he had spent going over scripts with me; a mirror he had bought to sit over the fireplace in my London house; a portable heater for the kitchen there; numerous books and records he had purchased; forty percent of the sale from my car, to which he had contributed forty percent of the original cost; the stereo equipment from the house in London; half of the costs incurred on our holiday to Marrakesh in 1978, for which I could expect the original receipts in due course; and "a little something" for adapting *The Cherry Orchard* and writing a play about the writer Jean Rhys; and last, for refusing to honor my prenuptial agreement, he levied a fine of sixty-two billion dollars — a billion dollars for every year of my life. Those items I wished to retain or was otherwise unable to return were to be compensated by way of his choruslike directive: "Cash equivalent."

There was more yet: he required me to insure the ring to the tune of $7,500 and return it to him, along with his original notes for *The Cherry Orchard,* immediately by overnight mail. He reiterated that he wanted his belongings back, but most of all he wanted the money: "Just send a check."

And last: He graciously offered to give me $104 per week that had gone to the maid in New York, which he claimed was my "sole contribution to living costs that averaged between $80,000 and $100,000 per year."

At first, the element of mockery I was doubtless intended to read into these messages was entirely lost on me. Anna and I sat there, both stunned into silence, as another fax began to grind its way out. Could it have been the ninth or the tenth that evening? The ludicrousness of this scenario started to dawn on us, and we began to laugh like children.

It took four months before he saw fit to release some, though not all, of the items on my list. The machine-gun fusillade of faxes that night in Massachusetts had concluded with a final blast ordering me never to disturb him again — either by fax, telephone, or in person. By now I was only too happy to oblige, but Philip appeared to have overlooked the fact that he was the one initiating contact. Then, suddenly, communication between us ceased.

Unfortunately, remuneration from *The Cherry Orchard* was minimal, and my worries about money were real. Soon after, I was offered a role in *As the World Turns,* a CBS soap opera that had been running for the last thirty-odd years. I weighed the advantages of a regular salary and the opportunity of remaining in New York to develop my own projects against shutting myself up for several months in a job that was far from the kind of work I had ever wanted to do. The idea of steady employment, a contradiction in terms where actors are concerned, seemed a safer alternative than the speculation of the open marketplace. The bargain was well worth taking: I took it.

On March 12, 1994, my husband went to his lawyer's office to sign the separation papers. That date I narrated an orchestral piece at the Brooklyn Academy of Music.

The role I played was Medea.

Outcast and abandoned, Medea curses her unfaithful husband, Jason, and swears vengeance upon him. The role of this demonic sorceress was a great release for me; a strange and wonderful conduit, in the guise of someone else, to release the grief and anger I had been holding back over the last few months.

Before the performance I looked straight at myself in the dressing-room mirror: "Get on with it," I said to my reflection. "Get on with the future. Let go of the past."

I walked onto the stage. The moment the orchestra began to play I immediately felt calm, alert, confident. This was where I was most at one with myself.

Later that year, in May, at 7:00 A.M. precisely, my possessions arrived in my new apartment. There, neatly contained in bound cardboard boxes, were all that remained of my married life. A book inscribed "Look, we have come through, for my darling girl"; a photograph of myself taken as a child in dancing class, with my frilled panties slipped down one side, which had stood on Philip's desk because he found it amusing; my summer wardrobe that had always been kept in Connecticut; all the contents of the small studio inside the house that had been my work space; some, not all, of my china, all my cosmetics, each individually wrapped in bubble paper; my typewriter, fax machine, plus the plastic figure that had stood on top of our wedding cake; the few hidden, playful mementos of a deep and consuming love.

My friend Vita Muir once said to me that every divorce ends with a fight over who gets the side table. Mine was no different: I didn't get it.

Later that month came the anniversary of my mother's death. It coincided with an unreasonably cheerful, fragile happiness that descended upon me suddenly for no particular reason. Eleven years had passed since my mother died. I never had the opportunity to show her I had more resilience than either of us could have suspected.

In an attempt to lay old ghosts to rest, I went to stay over the Independence Day weekend with Francine and Cleve Gray. They have become a second family for me. I had held up through the first year — thus, the holiday was aptly named. The Grays' house is located one and a half miles from my former home, but the man living there was no longer a man I knew. The only nod Francine and I made toward his neighboring presence, a very slight one, was to change our pattern to avoid walking past the house. On one occasion, and to my own surprise, I asked her to drive me past the clapboard house down the dirt road. It was as I remembered it: still, beautiful, and austere. I looked out the car window and said to Francine, quite objectively, "Well, it existed."

I hadn't heard from Philip, except for a few cursory notes about his health coverage, since Cambridge.

During our final months together in Connecticut, Philip

asked me many times if I was as resilient as he suspected. With a certain amount of naïveté, I answered that I was as resilient as old bed springs. Perhaps this eased his conscience — and opened the door toward his unyielding path away from me.

I survived 1994 with the help, support, and solidarity of my daughter and my own friends, plus some old friends of Philip's who nonetheless stood by me; also, without apology, with the aid of Prozac and the assistance of Valium.

Some friendly voices stirring amidst the rubble of our breakup had offered one explanation: that there had to have been a woman involved in Philip's decision to leave me. Based on my history with Philip, I thought it was, at best, highly unlikely. In due course, as often happens, the unmistakable evidence materialized, making two things irrefutable: Philip had been as spectacularly manipulative as I had been astonishingly blind.

Dr. Bloch had given me an enigmatic clue at Silver Hill Hospital the morning after my voluntary stay there. What he had said was this: "You will find out the truth, little by little. And then you will understand."

CHAPTER FIFTEEN

The Truth

I LEARNED THE TRUTH sometime after I had ceased to be a factor in Philip's life. He left me for "Erda": a beautiful woman who had been a close friend to both of us for years. As the saying goes, the wife is the last to know.

Erda's father had committed suicide when she was a young girl, afflicting her with a lifelong burden of guilt and remorse. I had always known Erda to be possessed of a warm, gentle, and maternal nature. It was inevitable that she would have wished to save Philip during his illness, when he was at his most emotionally stricken. Philip was drawn to her calm, undemanding presence, Erda was consummating her destiny in the rescue of a desperate man.

Trusting and somewhat naïve, she also found herself reluctantly playing a role in removing me from Philip's life. Her ambiguous position as friend to me and lover to him must have confused and disturbed her greatly. But once started, there was no way to halt the sequence of events: I moved out and Erda moved in.

Totally committed to this new relationship, Erda abruptly asked her husband of twenty-five years to give her a divorce; on Philip's strict injunction, she gave no hint that her decision was anything save arbitrary. Confused, bitter, and distraught, Erda's husband couldn't understand what had happened between them. It was only after the end of her relationship with Philip that she was able to confront him with the truth.

So far as I can gather, Philip and Erda's life together was, in the beginning, fulfilling to both. But soon some familiar patterns began to reassert themselves. With their increasing intimacy Philip's anxieties over being emotionally engulfed by a woman were galvanized, and he began to withdraw from her. Erda learned that he had been involved with a young woman when they were both patients of Silver Hill Hospital. Shattered by his manipulation of her and his ultimate betrayal, she suffered a collapse. During this time, on the advice of her doctors, she found the strength to break off the relationship. She has embarked upon a new life with new surroundings — but the anger, hurt, and humiliation remain.

I spoke to Erda about her affair with Philip, setting aside my own ambivalent feelings toward a friend who had been so cruelly coerced by my husband. Our meeting took place after the dust had settled on our misfortunes. She seems to echo my own experience: throughout the relationship, his pitilessly furious face terrified her; she was paralyzed by his invective; and there wasn't anything she wouldn't do to avoid a confrontation with him. Everything that had passed between my former husband and myself during the eighteen years we lived together seemed to reoccur in the space of a few months between them. The process had simply accelerated.

As I listened to Erda tell her terrible story — a story that revealed layer upon layer of subterfuge, treachery, and darkness — the feelings of need and disappointment she expressed could easily have been my own. Except that I was a survivor; he was right about that.

The Disappearing Shadow

But there remained unresolved questions about the relationships in my life and the patterns governing my responses through the years. Was I predestined to repeat these patterns over and over again, like a spider meticulously weaving the same web? Was there a way to unravel the reasons why, having been cast in the role of the dutiful daughter so early in life, I never had the courage to seek a healthy alternative? Had my role been so rigidly predetermined that I unquestioningly followed its path?

Across my path there had passed good, affectionate men whose overtures I had ignored; they were not exciting enough, I said to myself. One was a politician, the other a gifted architect. With either of these men I had the possibility of a good and productive life. But I chose instead difficult, if talented, men who could never bring me contentment. I seemed to need to meet a challenge, to re-create the lack of certainty of my early childhood.

For a long period after my parting with Philip I remained lonely and full of regrets, trying to comprehend what had gone wrong. I became aware that some of the ways I responded to Philip's silent cries for help and understanding must have appeared to him lacking in compassion, but were in reality only my own panic in the face of his fears. There were occasions when my lack of emotional control threatened his fragile equilibrium. Above all else — both for him and for me — the subject of my relationship with Anna became an eternal battlefield. My vulnerability became a burden he no longer wanted to carry; his emotional withdrawal became a permanent source of pain and frustration to me.

As a consequence of the symbiotic relationship I had shared with my mother, I clung to Anna in ways that were extremely unsuitable, especially as she grew older; this made Philip feel as though he was an intruder in our closed circle, something he was well within his rights to resent. I had unwittingly used Anna as emotional insurance against my fear of desertion; for, whatever our problems as mother and daughter, I knew neither she nor I could ever untie our bond of blood.

Ever since the episode concerning the purchase of the house in Italy, I believed my only option was to be secretive with Philip about my finances. I was beset by two fears: first, that should my daughter ever find herself in financial difficulty, I would need to assist her. And second, that in rushing to her assistance, I would incur the wrath of my husband. Therefore, I squirreled away as much money as I could. This secrecy did none of us any good. Anna came to resist my incursions into her life; and Philip began to doubt my priorities.

In a marriage such as ours, it was inevitable that we began to experience an increasing sense of misery and bewilderment, I to feel more and more deserted and Philip to feel more and more swamped by my neediness. Neither of us truly understood our confusion.

Philip once observed that it was a strange coincidence that his most consequential and far-reaching relationships had always been with fatherless women. Strange, possibly, but hardly a coincidence: fatherless women gravitate toward emotionally unavailable men. And Philip played that elusive role — one moment an understanding, thoughtful, compassionate surrogate parent, the next a remote, unyielding, punishing adversary. What is ultimately stranger is that any of the women who shared even a morsel of his life — and here I must include myself — could have hoped to find a paternal figure in Philip Roth, so austere, so conditional, so far removed from the warm and protective father of our childhood imagination. Instead, he was the fleeting shadow of the one who disappeared.

That was Eddie's legacy to me.

What I reaped from the process of self-examination was this: I had looked for answers in the wrong places and counted on the men in my life and my daughter to provide me with missing portions of myself. Not surprisingly, there were to be no easy answers, only more difficult questions.

Despite the tragic end of my marriage, I was immensely enriched by my years with Philip, but I recognize now that there were essential components missing in me — and, I believe, in him as well. Notwithstanding our own professional achievements, there were undeveloped dark regions in us both that proved to be insurmountable obstacles.

The loss of the most important relationship of my life was the price I paid for coming to know myself.

Two years had passed since the divorce papers were served in New York; by mutual consent, our divorce became final in June of 1995. These years had been difficult, lonely, and disorienting. I filled every moment with as much activity as I could, accepted every engagement, both social and professional; the less time I had to dwell on this last period of my life, the better.

In early November 1995, I worked for four months in Rome, that most beautiful of cities. I had come to feature in a "disaster" film starring Sylvester Stallone.

The film, entitled *Daylight,* was filmmaking at its harshest and least glamorous. The star of the film, aside from Stallone, was New York's Holland Tunnel.

I accepted the challenge as the most unexpected adventure — and I wasn't disappointed.

My closest bond in the film was to my screen pet, Cooper. The affection I was meant to feel for the dog swiftly changed on both our parts into feelings of mutual dislike. The second the cameras began to roll, Cooper, an extremely powerful wei-maraner, made a beeline for his trainer, to whose comforting presence he appeared to be umbilically attached, dragging me along as I pulled and tugged fruitlessly in his wake. My screen husband kindly took over his care; I was certain he would understand better than I how to deal with a temperamental artiste like Cooper.

The tunnel, one third as long as the Holland, had been faithfully recreated at Cinecittà.

The director, Rob Cohen, warned us that *Daylight* would be a grueling shoot. The tunnel would alternately be puffed full of smoke and flooded with water. The water, of which there were to be umpteen thousand gallons at their disposal, would be comfortable and warm — he added that he would happily drink it.

Over the years — and with considerable dismay — I've read

accounts by intrepid actors claiming to perform their own stunts as a means of injecting a little more excitement into the protracted business of filmmaking. My own disposition points more toward the attitude of Victor Mature, who, decades ago, speaking seriously about his craft, declared: "I wouldn't walk up a wet step."

Suffice to say that there wasn't a single physically rigorous moment that I didn't balk at. For the record, I was bold beyond my previous expectation. I took on a thousand live rats without blinking an eye, and after a great deal of encouragement from my patient director, submerged myself in his tepid potable water and swam through a series of underwater obstacles. To be sure, I was no Esther Williams, but I was not a total embarrassment.

I swore to myself that nothing, absolutely nothing, was going to spoil the months in Rome I had so opportunely been given. Unlike London and New York — or even Paris, where Philip and I had spent many happy times — Rome held no memories whatsoever of our past together. My only recollections were of the years I had spent there during the sixties, when Anna was a little girl and my marriage to Rod was still imbued with the affectionate regard we felt for each other. Also, in Rome, I had worked successfully on two fine Italian films, opposite great stars of the cinema, Alberto Sordi and Charles Aznavour.

My apartment was located in the center of the ancient city. The view from my terrace overlooked honey-gold houses and domes and spires of neighboring churches which — with the exception of a forest of television aerials — appeared to have changed very little since the Renaissance.

Some of the happiest memories of my time in Rome came as a result of my long friendship with Gore Vidal. We had explored exhaustively all the historical landmarks of the city, with Gore the most knowledgeable guide to Ancient Rome.

Gore no longer keeps his beautiful Rome apartment overlooking the Teatro Argentina, the site of the disastrous first performance of Rossini's masterpiece, *The Barber of Seville*. He now lives in Ravello.

On All-Saint's Day, 1995, production closed at Cinecittá for the weekend, and I took the train to Naples, then hired a car to Ravello. It must have been twenty years before, when Gore and I walked along his villa high above the Tyrrhenian Sea, that I asked him if he thought it was a good idea for me to pursue a relationship with a fellow writer of his, by the name of Philip Roth. His response was an unequivocal "No."

"You have already had Portnoy's complaint," proclaimed Gore firmly, referring, of course, to my marriage to Elkins. "Do not involve yourself with Portnoy."

As one who wished to protect me from yet another misadventure, Gore turned out to be utterly correct in his advice. Philip's novels provided all one needed to know about his relationships with women, most of which had been just short of catastrophic. I was certain that with me it would be different — that I could have a positive effect on whatever compulsion had led him to discard one woman after another. In spite of everything, our relationship lasted eighteen years.

But perhaps I should have listened to my old friend.

Back in Rome, on my free days from shooting, I visited again all the places I remembered with such pleasure: the Borromini church of St. Ivo in Sapienza, with its curled and convoluted white-and-gold baroque spire; St. Clement's basilica, old enough itself, covering layer upon layer of the city's history. The Bernini baby elephant, which carries a small, exquisite obelisk on its back; the *foro romano;* the Palatine Hill; the tomb of Keats resting beside the pyramid-shaped funerary monument of Caius Sestius at the Protestant Cemetery. Steeping myself in the distant past allowed me to come to terms with my difficult present. I decided to go to London, see my family and friends, and then return to the realities of New York. By the time I left the Eternal City, I knew I was better equipped to face whatever challenge lay ahead.

London is different from anywhere else: London is where I belong. I love this city above all others, and could find my way around it in my sleep; every street has some memory, every theater I visit some connection.

In New York, apart from one or two pieces of furniture rescued from my former homes with Philip, everything I own is a trifle lacking in character. In Anna's small house in Fulham I am surrounded by all that remains of my mother's house; unmarketable objects from her shop I recognize immediately through the large chunks of china that are always missing, knocked off by the constant shaking of her hands. These fractured heirlooms have passed from her, through me, to Anna.

Walking around the most evocative parts of the old city, I often make my way toward the memory-laden district of Covent Garden. Although radically altered, this is still the place I walked all those years ago with Chaplin.

Not long ago, I visited St. Paul's — not to be confused with St. Paul's Cathedral — otherwise known as the actor's church. It is the burial place of Charles Macklin, the eighteenth-century comedian; and there a small, silver urn contains the ashes of Ellen Terry, all that remains of that glowing, golden-haired, nineteenth-century actress who was the greatest Beatrice and Rosalind of her era.

There is a connection here with something very vital to me — a link to my own guild. I have no religious affiliations, but I am an actress. The London theater is what made me.

Plaques surrounding the interior carry the names and identities of men and women whose lives touched my own. I noticed, to my surprise, that several people with whom I had worked were born in the late nineteenth century. Then it dawned on me that I began my career so young; I had been privileged to cross paths with over a hundred years of theatrical tradition.

As I walked round the church, I realized that I had known and worked with nearly all the artists whose names were engraved on the wall of the nave. Apart from their reflections on the screen or echoes in the memories of people who experienced their contributions firsthand, here was all that was left:

Edith Evans, D.B.E., Actor, 1889–1976
Margaret Rutherford, Actress, 1892–1972
Vivien Leigh, Actress, 1913–1967
Sir Robert Helpmann, C.B.E., Dancer, Choreographer,
    Actor, Director, 1909–1986
Hugh Beaumont, Theatrical Manager, 1908–1973
Michael Benthall, C.B.E., Director, 1919–1974
Sir Charles Chaplin, K.B.E., Actor, 1889–1977

I can always count when I return to my Upper East Side apartment that the phone will be ringing, my diary will be full, and my friends and colleagues will add to my pleasure of being back. There are always many things to look forward to, professionally and otherwise. After the gray light of London, the brightness of the New York sky — particularly in winter — makes me feel vibrant and alive.

This is my official home. This is my base of operations.

I received an unexpected letter one day. It was from Philip, and contained the following message: "Dear Claire, can we be friends?"

I had awaited these words since our separation; regardless of the past, I knew I only needed to be patient and, eventually, the illness that had been the true cause of our parting would pass. In the interim, I had attempted to remain quiet, undemanding, productive. And most important, probably, for Philip: I had given him his own freedom to make a recovery in peace as he had requested. I called Sheila and John. "Everything is going to be fine." Their reaction was cautious, their voices reserved.

Replying to his letter, I wrote that there was nothing I desired more than to resume our friendship — it was up to him to state the terms, and name the place where we should meet. Philip suggested a local restaurant not far from my new home, in one week's time. I spent the next seven days counting each hour, in a state of anxious anticipation.

The day before we met, I treated myself to a facial, a manicure; I picked out a pretty outfit I had been saving for a special occasion. And now, here it was.

I caught sight of Philip before he saw me. His expression was grave and serious; he was wearing the same raincoat we had bought together in London many years before. He looked, I thought, somewhat apprehensive — but then, so was I. After a careful greeting, we sat down at our table, surveying one another.

Philip was considering me from behind his glasses, sizing me up. After our coffees were ordered, there was a long silence. After they were delivered, I tried to conceal the tremor in my hand as I lifted the cup toward my mouth. He also appeared tense.

I was determined to be at my most charming and witty. I began the conversation by saying that it was good to see him — and so it was, despite all that had passed between us. Speaking calmly, Philip replied that he had expected me to be full of resentment. I assured him that a meeting would have been pointless if resentment was all I could feel. Good-naturedly, we shook hands in agreement.

I noticed he was a trifle grayer than before, but otherwise looked much healthier than when I had last seen him. I wondered if there was a new woman in his life. There was another long pause. "You begin," I said.

For the next twenty minutes, nonstop, he performed for me a string of wisecracks and anecdotes, sharply funny as ever, completely impersonal, and unrelated to the friendship we were supposedly there to address and reestablish. Immobilized once again by another surprise tactic, I sat and listened, wondering how long this coffee-table tour de force could endure without something warm — or, actually, something relevant — being said.

I interrupted the flow and looked at him directly.

"Philip, why do you want to be friends with me?"

He looked back, and the suspicion of a smile crept across his lips.

"Oh, perversion . . ."

Let down and deeply disappointed, I left the restaurant; I swore I would never again go through such an ordeal. But then, a few days later, Philip wrote back, asking to meet once more — same reason, same restaurant, same time. Still clinging to my improbable illusion, I warily accepted.

The careful greeting, the coffee, mirrored our last encounter. There was the same atmosphere on my part of unspoken expectation. This time the string of comic stories lasted longer, half an hour by my count. Just as I was considering whether or not to risk another interruption — and what that might unleash — Philip paused, looked away, then said quietly: "I want our old life back."

I took his hand and said nothing — there was nothing to say.

We left Manhattan in daylight and arrived in Connecticut when it was nearly dark. Our beautiful eighteenth-century farmhouse basked in the warm, fading light as never before, its elegant lines and smoking chimney the image of a children's storybook. The colonial brass ornaments I had bought for the entrance gleamed as though newly polished. My cozy old kitchen was warm and comforting — unchanged, really. The overflowing bookcases in the drawing room, the chestnut floors and scatter rugs, took me back to our beginning. I looked over at the log fire, flickering and crackling gently, and then Philip took my hand. I smiled openly for the first time in two years. I knew I had finally come home.

One meeting is truth. The other is fiction.

It is difficult to escape the power of dreams. I had spent over a quarter of my life in that house; I knew some part of me would always remain there, part of a long-cherished but largely imaginary past. The man who lived inside was no longer the custodian of my heart and mind. All my friends, aspirations, fortunes, and fulfillments were through the door, outside in the real world.

Now begins the rest of my life.

Index

Index

Bloom, Claire (*continued*)
Spy Who Came in from the Cold, 118;
Three into Two Won't Go, 123
STAGE PERFORMANCES: amateur and
early professional, 28–29, 32, 41–43;
The Cherry Orchard, 60, 227–228,
230; *A Doll's House,* 60, 129–130;
Duel of Angels, 99, 102, 105; *Hamlet,*
46–47, 83; *Hedda Gabler,* 129; *The
Innocents,* 149, 151, 152; *Ivanov,* 117;
King Lear, 117; *The Lady's Not for
Burning,* 48–50, 53, 54, 117; *The
Merchant of Venice,* 79; narrations/
monodramas, 182, 191, 195, 212,
218, 230; one-woman performances,
181, 182, 215, 219; *Rashomon,* 109;
The Red Devil Battery Sign, 136–141;
Richard II, 93; *Ring Round the Moon,*
51, 53, 54; *Romeo and Juliet,* 68–73,
75, 78, 93; *Rosmersholm,* 156; *A
Streetcar Named Desire,* 60, 130–133;
When We Dead Awaken, 188
TELEVISION: *As the World Turns,*
230; *Brideshead Revisited,* 159–162;
Cyrano de Bergerac, 94; *The Ghost
Writer,* 168; *Queenie,* 175–176; *Romeo
and Juliet,* 94; *Shadowlands,* 174–175
Bloom, David, 18, 19, 22, 25
Bloom, Dolly, 15, 16
Bloom, Edward (Eddie; father; né
Blumenthal, later Blume), 3, 15, 17,
124, 236; marriage to Elizabeth
Bloom, 8; during World War II, 17,
18, 19, 20, 27, 35, 36; divorce from
Elizabeth Bloom, 43–44; returns
with second wife, 78; death of, 79
Bloom, Elizabeth (Alice; née Grew;
mother), 150, 151, 152, 153;
birth and birthplace of, 3, 4; antique
shop business run by, 4; early career
of, 7; marries Edward Bloom, 8;
during World War II, 13–37; divorce
from Edward Bloom, 43–44; trips to
America for *Limelight,* 55–59, 62–65;
purchases house in Chelsea, 77; death
of Edward Bloom, 79; visits
Hollywood, 99; granddaughter born,
111; death of, 171–173
Bloom, Erica, 15, 16
Bloom, Estelle, 18, 19, 22, 23, 25

Bloom, Freida, 43
Bloom, Harold, 192
Bloom, Isadore, 15, 16
Bloom, John, 112, 172, 204, 206, 241;
birth of, 11; childhood years of, 12–
14, 43; during World War II, 14, 17,
22, 25, 28, 29, 31, 32, 36, 44; career
of, 62
Bloom, Michael, 15
Bloom, Richard, 22, 23
Bloom, Sheila, 62, 171, 172, 204, 206,
208, 224, 241
Bloom, Shirley, 22
Blumenthal, Caroline, 3
Bondarchuk, Sergei, 124
Borowski, Tadeusz, 166
Boston Musica Viva, 218
Boxer, Betty, 23
Boyer, Charles, 99
Brando, Marlon, 110
Brenner, Bobbie, 7
Brideshead Revisited (television
production), 159–162
British Film and Television Awards, 175
British War Relief Organization, 23, 28
Britten, Benjamin, 172
Broken Heart, The (Ford), 115
Brontë, Charlotte, 166, 182
Brontë family, 26
Brook, Peter, 51
Brooklyn Academy of Music, 230
Brooks (costumier), 58
Brothers Karamazov, The (film), 95, 99
Brown, Pamela, 48
Brynner, Yul, 95, 97–100, 136
Buccaneer, The (film), 99, 100, 136, 137
Burns and Allen radio show, 27
Burton, Richard, 50, 51, 79; first
meeting with CB, 48; relationship
with CB, 80–87, 93–94, 105–106,
108, 111; marriage to Sybil, 49, 50,
81, 82, 83, 84, 93, 105, 109; marriage
to Elizabeth Taylor, 118, 119, 120;
death of, 121–122
Burton, Sybil, 49, 50, 81, 82, 83, 84, 93,
105, 109

Cardiff, Jack, 86
Carné, Marcel, 102
Casson, Sir Lewis, 69

246

Index

Index

Index

Index

Index

Spy Who Came in from the Cold, The (le Carré), 118; film version, 107, 118, 120

Stallone, Sylvester, 237

Steiger, Anna Justine, 111, 155, 162–163, 171–173, 202, 205; impact of parents' divorce on, 127–128; difficulties with Philip Roth, 157–159, 190–191, 225–226, 235–236; performances and awards, 163, 190, 205

Steiger, Rodney Stephen (Rod), 84, 111, 144, 159, 238; marriage to CB, 110–126; performances and awards, 110, 112, 113, 114

Strasberg, Susan, 105, 106

Stratford Theater, 46, 47

Stravinsky, Igor, 218

Streetcar Named Desire, A (Williams), 60, 130, 131, 132, 135

Styron, William, 180

Styron, Rose, 180

Taylor, Elizabeth, 95, 118, 119, 120

Ten Commandments, The (film), 100

Terry, Ellen, 240

Theater Royal Copenhagen, 129

Then Let Men Know (one-woman show), 181

Theodorakis, Mikis, 138

Three into Two Won't Go (film), 123

Three Sisters, The (Chekhov), 29, 30, 116

Thucydides, 117

Thurman, Judith, 207

Time magazine, 77, 192, 193

Time Remembered (Anouilh), 105

Tolstoy, Leo, 166, 182

Tornado (film), 27

Treadwell, Sophie, 6

Tsvetaeva, Marina, 182

Turn of the Screw, The (James), 182

Tutin, Dorothy, 68, 103

Tynan, Kenneth, 73

U-boats, 21

Uncle Vanya (Chekhov), 115

United States: pre-Pearl Harbor, 18; CB's World War II stay in, 22–32

United States Immigration Office, 73

Updike, John, 192, 204

Ure, Mary, 107, 108

V-E Day, 18

Vidal, Gore, 117–118, 130–131, 238–239

Vogue, 77

Voight, Jon, 164

Volcano (film), 27

Volkova, Vera, 42

Warhol, Andy, 185

Watergate scandal, 137

Waterloo (film), 124

Waugh, Evelyn, 160, 161

Weil, Jiri, 166

We Moderns (Zangwill), 5

When We Dead Awaken (Ibsen), 188

White Devil, The (Webster), 42

Who's Afraid of Virginia Woolf? (film), 107

Williams, Tennessee, 60, 130, 131, 135, 136, 137, 141

Winger, Debra, 175

Women in Love (one-woman show), 182, 215

Woolf, Virginia, 166

World War II, 13, 17, 18, 26, 39; CB in England, 13–18, 35–37; CB in America, 22–32

Worth, Irene, 68

Writers from the Other Europe (book series), 166

Wuthering Heights (film), 161

Wylie, Andrew, 192

Zangwill, Israel, 5

Zuckerman Trilogy (Roth), 168, 180